The Japanese House
Architecture and Life after 1945

Forewords 5

Essays
   Hiroyasu Fujioka
   A History of the Individual House in Modern Japan 13

   Pippo Ciorra
   'I Love Japanese Culture' 25

   Florence Ostende
   Architecture and Life: Human Agency and Forms of Living in the Japanese House 37

   Kenjiro Hosaka
   Why Houses? 57

Houses
   Japaneseness 67
   Mass Production 85
   Earth and Concrete 103
   A House is a Work of Art 119
   Closed to Open 139
   Inhabiting the Experimental 165
   Sensorial 187
   Beyond Family 207
   The Machiya 231
   Redefining the Gap 243
   Lightness 255
   The Vernacular 277
   Unmarketable 293

Appendix
   Architects' biographies 307
   Endmatter 316

Forewords

The Japanese House: Architecture and Life after 1945 marks the first collaboration and joint venture of MAXXI, National Museum of the 21st Century Arts, in Rome and Barbican Centre in London – two European institutions known for their iconic buildings and remarkable history of staging architecture exhibitions. MAXXI in Rome – designed by Zaha Hadid and a beacon for all that is bright and progressive in the world of culture – gives architecture and architects a permanent platform. Similarly, the Barbican Centre at the heart of the Barbican Estate, an architectural landmark and utopian project, has a history of staging architecture exhibitions within an enlightened programme that celebrates the exchange between art and design, art and life. Although there are subtle nuances of difference in our respective programmes, we share the belief that architecture matters. MAXXI started its young life with landmark exhibitions on Pier Luigi Nervi, Le Corbusier, Gerrit Rietveld, and Superstudio, as well as interdisciplinary projects on *Recycle, Energy, Food*. The Barbican has staged major shows on the work of Daniel Libeskind, Alvar Aalto as seen by Shigeru Ban, Le Corbusier, and OMA. But it is perhaps *The Surreal House* in 2010, an exhibition that was the first to look at the importance of the house within surrealism and surrealism within architecture, that feels like the closest forerunner to this new exhibition, which similarly puts the domestic space centre stage. Like *The Surreal House*, *The Japanese House* weaves architecture with film to illuminate the life within and the socio-historic context of domestic architecture in Japan.

When the Japan Foundation in Tokyo approached both institutions to stage a major exhibition celebrating Japanese culture, we saw it as a timely and unmissable opportunity to bring the best of Japanese post-war architecture to audiences in Rome and then London who have had little exposure to it. Equally, it was an opportunity to invite Japanese scholars to take part in the project, thus ensuring the exhibition included an exemplary selection of houses from 1945 to the present day. As such, this book and the exhibition open the door to a world that, tantalizingly seductive and profoundly influential as it is, has been under-represented on the international stage. Our task has been to do justice to the material represented and to the comprehensive selection of architects or their respective families or estates who have been willing to co-operate on this internationally significant project.

This project poses fundamental questions. Why the house? Why the Japanese house? Why now? We start from a position of seeing the house as a unit for dwelling. It is this human aspect that is intriguing and, in many respects, touching, for we relate to the intimacy and particularities of the house in a way that we cannot do with corporate or public buildings. Take, for instance, the utterly charming photographs of Kenzo Tange relaxing with his family in his breathtakingly beautiful home of 1953. Visionary patrons of architecture or very often architects themselves, such as Tange, live in the houses included here, houses that are especially present, in both senses of the word. Tadao Ando's monumental Row House in Sumiyoshi (1976) and Kazuyo Sejima's ethereal House in a Plum Grove (2003) are alive to materials and to their place within the city. Others, such as Antonin Raymond's own house and studio (1951), speak to the world of nature or draw on the vernacular tradition. The post-war condition in Japan created a window for the languages of tradition and modernity to variously fuse and for the house to become a special unit of experiment. Seiichi Shirai's House in Kureha (1965) and Kazuo Shinohara's House in White (1966) are among those that exemplify this synthesis. Today, we see it again in the work of Terunobu Fujimori, Atelier Bow-Wow, Kumiko Inui, and Chie Konno's reinterpretation of vernacular architecture. In extreme synthesis, this is what makes the Japanese house in post-war Japan so special and so worthy of our consideration.

Photography, film, models, and drawings are crucial bedfellows in a project such as this as they alone must capture the essence of space, both interior and exterior, when the actual architecture exists elsewhere. We have sought the best examples in order to expand our understanding. Kazuo Shinohara's conceptual houses are illuminated by Koji Taki's stark, abstract photographs, while Terunobu Fujimori's own roughly carved wooden model for Leek House (1997) reveals the building's unique engagement with materials, craft, and the natural world. Hideyuki Nakayama's childlike concept sketches illustrate his emotive, intuitive approach to creating spaces, while tracings taken of Takamitsu Azuma's Tower House bear witness to that building's incredible material presence.

In Rome and in London – and also in Tokyo when this project takes shape at The National Museum of Modern Art, Tokyo (MOMAT) – the 1:1 reconstruction is a key component in the staging of *The Japanese House*. In Rome, a re-creation of part of Toyo Ito's White U (1976), the section of a facade of one of Itsuko Hasegawa's houses, and Shigeru Ban's UNHCR emergency unit (1994) form the centrepiece of the exhibition, while in London there is a complete reconstruction of Ryue Nishizawa's Moriyama House (2005) and a newly commissioned tea house and garden by Terunobu Fujimori. The intention is to make the architecture – as far as this is humanly possible – a real experience rather than an absence.

An internationally ambitious project such as this could not have been possible without the at times seemingly superhuman efforts of individuals, more often than not working in different parts of the world in different time zones. It has been extraordinarily demanding, but in the process something essential has been achieved: a genuinely cross-cultural collaboration that brings the work of already well-known architects to a broader audience, and the work of unsung heroes of Japanese architecture to eager cognoscenti as well as a wider public.

We would like to extend our deepest thanks first of all to the Japan Foundation for embarking on this long-awaited exhibition and so consummately dealing with the organizational complexities in Tokyo. Special thanks go to Masanobu Ito, Managing Director, Arts and Culture Department for making all this possible, to Atsuko Sato, Director, who has facilitated this collaboration, to Keiko Tasaki, who has superintended the organizational effort and been our chief point of contact, and to Ayako Nagata and Akiko Tokuyama, who have adroitly liaised with architects, advisors, and archives to bring the exhibits together for both this book and the exhibition itself. The project was commendably developed in its formative stages by MOMAT curator Kenjiro Hosaka, along with the chief advisor to the exhibition Yoshiharu Tsukamoto of the internationally acclaimed architectural practice Atelier Bow-Wow, as well as the architectural historian, Hiroyasu Fujioka, Professor Emeritus, Tokyo Institute of Technology. Much of the groundwork was laid thanks to their insights into the field. We are eternally indebted to them for sharing that knowledge.

Pippo Ciorra and Florence Ostende, curators at MAXXI and Barbican respectively, joined the curatorial team at the beginning of 2016. Each has brought extensive curatorial expertise to this project – Ciorra from an exquisitely architectural background, and Ostende from her specialization in modern and contemporary art. Both have personally met many of the architects, undertaken in-depth research, and worked in harmony and with great tenacity and commitment to ensure the success of their exhibitions at their respective institutions, as well as taken on the formidable task of editing this jointly published book. They have been aided by equally talented teams of individuals. In Rome, the realization of the exhibition has entirely been made possible by the passionate and expert dedication of the curatorial team led by Elena Motisi, including Alessandra Spagnoli, who has spent long days on the texts. Silvia La Pergola has collaborated with Atelier Bow-Wow to produce an impressive exhibition design, for which we are especially grateful to Yoshiharu

Tsukamoto and his main collaborator for this project Simona Ferrari, who spent never-ending nights on Skype to tune up with our team. We also acknowledge Etaoin Shrdlu Studio, responsible for the show's graphic design. In London, Luke Naessens has been responsible for researching and writing the majority of the extended captions in this book, as well as lending his support to every aspect of the exhibition's development. Sonoko Nakanishi joined the project in June 2016, and has greatly assisted the team's research on Japanese art and architecture, liaised with Japanese architects and institutions, and contributed to the realization of the catalogue. The exhibition at the Barbican has been designed by the immensely talented architect Lucy Styles, who has also contributed ideas from the outset of the project. As a longstanding SANAA collaborator and employee, her knowledge of Japanese architecture has been invaluable and deeply appreciated. We would like to thank the architects Ryue Nishizawa and Terunobu Fujimori for their commitment and the inspiring re-creation of their work in the Barbican Art Gallery. We are indebted to the architect Takeshi Hayatsu for his support and to his students at Kingston University London, who have accompanied the staging of the creative world of Terunobu Fujimori in the gallery. We would like to thank Yasuo Moriyama for his support and filmmakers Ila Bêka and Louise Lemoine for capturing the vibrant essence of Mr Moriyama's life in their new film. The graphic design for this book and for the exhibition in London has been handled with flair and sensitivity by Eva Kellenberger and Sebastian White of Kellenberger–White. We would like to thank Martina Mian of Marsilio Editori for her professionalism, good humour, and tremendous commitment to this project. We would like to thank MOMAT – our partner institution in Tokyo – as well as all the lenders, estates, archives, and photographers who have allowed us to represent their work in this exhibition and book.

At MAXXI, we have to thank Gagliardini srl, a loyal friend to architecture, and SAD, the school of architecture of UNICAM, for the support in the production of new models. In London, we are grateful to Simon Wright, the Director of Programming at Japan House, to Junko Takekawa at The Japan Foundation in London, to Ellis Woodman of the Architecture Foundation, to Tom Emerson of 6A for his immediate enthusiasm and his introductions, to Giulia Guaitoli for her research on Japanese cinema, to Coralie Malissard for her research on Japanese collections in the United Kingdom, and to Daniela Puga for her collaboration on the public programme. Finally, we would like to express our deepest thanks to Japan Centre and the Great Britain Sasakawa Foundation for their generosity in supporting this project. Their help has meant we can do so much more.

    Jane Alison Head of Visual Arts, Barbican Centre
    Giovanna Melandri President, Fondazione MAXXI

Our Home is the Entire City – Notes on Japanese 'House Design'

Sitting in the office–home of Atelier Bow-Wow, I became immediately charmed by the ingenious spatial organization of the design that fluidly links – dividing but also connecting – working and living spaces, or public and private spaces in a highly limited footprint and volume. And it is so agreeable to swing through the office, the kitchen, and the living room and be able to glance at the sleeping room. Downstairs, a crowd of assistants are intently typing away on their computers. Upstairs, one can enjoy a moment of solitude in a wide open, even empty, private room. What is even more fascinating is that, across the little terrace and the transparent walls surrounding the living room where we had our working session around the dining table accompanied with freshly brewed tea, we found ourselves in the middle of the city, with the walls of the neighbours' houses, covered by plants and water stains, standing only a few centimetres away. One can peep into the neighbour's kitchen through the little windows hanging on the walls like dressing mirrors. Next to us on the other side are electricity and phone lines flying over our heads like a semi-transparent curtain floating between the skyline of the dynamic but peaceful city and our sights...

It is here that discussions and debates, filled with curiosity, passion, and love, take place on the questions of density and invention of the most creative houses and urban structures 'designed' by the normal people living here – a topic central to the research of Atelier Bow-Wow (and many of their colleagues).

This is where Japanese architects live, imagine, and design. Around them is an amazingly dense, dynamic, yet poetic environment full of stories or histories of everyday life, in which utopian visions and practical solutions have to be combined to produce 'interesting' dwelling structures. They are human, not only functional but also providing sensuality of living – comfortable and peaceful but always brimming with fantasy, tension, and a passion for weird forms. They always therefore tend to be playful, sensual, and even erotic, tinged with a bit of melancholy, just like the ambience of everyday life in Japan. You are immersed in a mixture incorporating extremities of beauty: absolutely innovative and stubbornly ancient, radically speedy and profoundly serene...

Once the photographer Kyoichi Tsuzuki, who famously documented hundreds of Japanese houses from family interiors to love hotels in his books (including *Tokyo: A Certain Style*[1]) told me that when you live in Tokyo your home is the entire city – you go to work in the office, eat in restaurants, and sleep at home. You don't even need a refrigerator because there are convenient stores and vending machines on every street corner... How do you build a 'single family house' in a city like this when the whole city can be your house? For generations, Japanese architects – from pre-war modernists to today's global stars via Metabolism – have come up with the most inventive and insightful designs that at once preserve moments of 'sleeping at home' and prolong the liveliness of 'living in the city', with resolutely avant-garde languages and technologies. Their houses are uniquely outstanding with their originally intelligent and often 'extravagant' forms, provoking moments of 'insurgency' by adding a totally novel layer of difference to the harmonious urban environment formed by patchworks of architectural styles of various periods of history. The urban textile of Japanese cities has been famously rich and complex, forming an astonishing harmony constantly negotiating between the unplanned and the ordered, the inherited and the speculated, the traditional and the 'high tech'. Contemporary designs, especially smaller scales of constructive interventions like family houses, add pungent touches to 'spice up' the movement of the eternal negotiation for the coexistence between the new and the old. At the same time, with the dazzling audacity of playing around with interactions between opening and enclosure, between local materials and new technology, between built structure and unbuilt occupation, Japanese architects often manage to conceive effective strategies to produce ever-renewing friendships among neighbours, extending the longevity of urban communities. Radical cases in point are Toyo Ito's White U, which turns entirely in to the private, and Sou Fujimoto's House NA, which opens up to the street as a naked body... These are at once utopian and dystopian. They are also firmly realistic, yet delightedly aloof. They exemplify a singular but universally significant form of contemporaneity, and inspire us to understand the future of the everyday dwelling in the age of global communication and overexposure of everything – our age of urban spectacle. What is really social in the time of social media and reproduction of image that increasingly deprive us of physical human contacts? And how can privacy survive, and be revitalized in the midst of an excessive exposure to the other?

To introduce Japanese domestic architecture to the European public is first to share this singular contemporaneity. And with these Japanese architects – as well as those who inhabit these creatively designed houses – we are encouraged to raise fundamental questions regarding the essence of today's home, and life in general...

Hou Hanru Artistic Director, Fondazione MAXXI

1   Kyoichi Tsuzuki, *Tokyo: A Certain Style* (San Francisco: Chronicle Books, 1999).

The Japan Foundation is pleased to have co-organized the exhibition *The Japanese House: Architecture and Life after 1945* – a survey of the history of residential architecture in Japan since World War II – along with MAXXI, Rome, the Barbican Centre, London and MOMAT, the National Museum of Modern Art, Tokyo.

Every year, Japan sees the construction of myriad new houses, a significant number of which are designed by internationally active Japanese architects. The work of these architects, however, has only fragmentarily been introduced to the broader public. There have been virtually no large-scale exhibitions overseas devoted to introducing Japanese residential architecture – this exhibition boldly attempts to fill that gap with hundreds of hitherto unseen models, plans, photographs, and films, illustrating the great variety of domestic residences designed by Japanese architects from the post-war period to the present day.

Its broad approach is this exhibition's most distinctive feature. MOMAT curator Kenjiro Hosaka and architect Yoshiharu Tsukamoto, who provided invaluable curatorial guidance from the outset, have drawn on Michel Foucault's concept of 'genealogy' and divided the residences into several distinct genealogies. Their expertise, along with that of curators Pippo Ciorra of MAXXI and Florence Ostende of Barbican, has successfully teased out and revealed connections between residences that were built many years apart or whose connections might otherwise have remained obscure or seemed merely tenuous. This exhibition is therefore an experiment that probes more profoundly, to greater depths, and from a broader perspective than the customary exhibition, which is most often centred on superficial design and novelty.

Recovery from defeat in World War II, rapid economic growth, the maturity and stagnation of a consumerist society, accelerating and ever more massive urbanization, falling birth rates and an increasingly aged society, disasters such as the Great East Japan Earthquake – through all these changes spanning the seven decades since the end of the war, architects have thought long and hard about residential architecture and have asked themselves what the role of architecture should be in shaping the most fundamental of human behaviours. We will be very pleased, indeed, if visitors to the exhibition come away with a sense of the organic connections between these architects' experiments and the residences that resulted from them.

We are profoundly grateful to MAXXI in Rome and the Barbican Centre in London, who sustained and supported our goals for this exhibition and have co-organized it with us. Fully respecting their efforts and taking into account the distinctive features and approaches of our partner institutions, we have granted the curators autonomy and allowed the exhibition at each site to take on its own life. We are confident that visitors, in referring to the exhibition concept described in this catalogue, will enjoy the world of Japanese residential architecture it presents and appreciate their contact with Japanese society and culture.

In closing, I would like to thank the architects and architectural offices and collectors who provided the materials displayed in this exhibition. We are also grateful to Japan Airlines and Alitalia for their support, to the National Museum of Modern Art, Tokyo, for providing the Tokyo venue for this exhibition, and to the many others without whose co-operation this exhibition would not have been possible. Our special thanks must also go to Jane Alison and Hou Hanru for believing in this project, to Pippo Ciorra and Florence Ostende along with their institutions' staff, to Kenjiro Hosaka, Hiroyasu Fujioka, and Yoshiharu Tsukamoto for their indefatigable efforts, and to the staff of Atelier Bow-Wow.

Hiroyasu Ando President, The Japan Foundation

Essays

A History of the Individual House in Modern Japan
Hiroyasu Fujioka

It may sound strange to focus on the history of the individual house to talk about architecture in post-war Japan, but it actually helps us to understand the thoughts and designs of Japanese architects. Since many individual houses in Japan are privately owned and rather often rebuilt, with frequent changes in ownership and new owners wishing to make their house suitable for their own needs and dreams, these houses can be seen as an effective medium with which to showcase architects' ideas and aesthetics as well as clients' tastes and status. Studying these houses affords insight into what has happened to the architecture and society of post-war Japan.

Though it is true that Japanese houses are different from their Western counterparts, understanding how different they are and how they were formed offers a new perspective, relativizing and reshaping our ideas about housing and living in Japan.

1. From Rental to Home Ownership

Before World War II, ordinary citizens in Japan often rented their accommodation. A survey reveals that nearly 80% of Tokyo's population lived in rented housing in 1932, even though this figure had gradually been diminishing since the rise of the middle class – whose social status was based on academic background and specialization – in the late 1910s. This new middle class tended to form nuclear family units, which were new to Japan at that time, and many hoped to own their own house and have it reflect their social and cultural rank. To do so, they bought plots of land in suburban areas where they could build houses surrounded by gardens and greenery.

Right after Japan's defeat in World War II there was a severe accommodation shortage brought about by two important facts: the wholesale destruction inflicted by wartime air raids, and the 1939 Housing Rent Restricting Law. This law, which imposed low fixed rents despite the skyrocketing inflation, meant that landlords, whose income was decimated by the sharp rise in commodity prices, eventually gave up the rental business. It is said that in the immediate post-war period a quarter of the Japanese population found it hard to put a roof over their head.

The Japanese government tried to supply public housing to help alleviate the housing crisis, but was thwarted by the difficulty of finding sufficient lots for large apartment buildings in convenient places, even though the Japan Housing Corporation, which was established in 1955, supplied many apartments – mostly in rather remote suburban areas – with shopping centres and schools. In 1950, the government also set up the Housing Loan Corporation to help landowners build detached homes on their own lots by providing low-interest loans for construction. This meant that the government, in dealing with the housing shortage, virtually backed individual efforts to purchase land and build houses on it.

As the confusion after the war gradually subsided, rapid economic growth started in the late 1950s in Japan. With more and more people migrating to big cities to find jobs, urban sprawl began to define cities' suburban areas, where farmland and forests were turned into housing areas without any planning. With inflation showing no signs of slowing down, many believed that land was the only reliable asset whose value would never be compromised, thus leading to a rush on even tiny lots to build small houses on. However minuscule, a house with its own garden was a dream that many Japanese shared, a downsized version of the pre-war middle class ideal.

Some say the Japanese have traditionally clung to the land, but this does not mean there has always been ownership of the land in any modern sense. Land for the warrior class, who had long ruled Japan up to the Meiji Restoration in 1868, could not be sold or purchased, for instance, and could only be apportioned following consent from a superior, such as the *shogunate* or *daimyo* (warrior class leaders who governed areas known as *han*). A minority of people, in other words, were granted the right to *use* this land, but not to *own* it.

The land tax reform of 1873, which was part of a drive to modernize and bring capitalism to Japan, triggered an important shift in long entrenched ideas regarding land. The law identified an individual owner and determined the value of each plot, which was then taxed at a rate of 3% (shortly thereafter reduced to 2.5%) of the land's value. From this moment on, land became a commodity like any other and could be exchanged in the open market. Considering there were no other stable sources of income for the economically challenged government of Japan at that time, this new land tax provided a stable and lucrative revenue. The new government therefore inevitably relied on these landowners, and it would be safe to say that this system promoted an 'ownership comes first' policy among Japanese people. Without consent from landowners, after all, city planning could not be brought to realization, and a notion that has defined Japan in the modern era was born: private ownership takes precedence over public interest.

Land for housing, however, was in limited supply, and people who longed for their own home did not necessarily have their needs met. The government therefore tailored an act in 1963 to help build condominiums, which have since become so popular that they now account for more than 40% of Japanese housing. As most people own the condominium they live in, the Japanese housing market is still mainly an ownership, as opposed to a rental, market.

Japan's economy has been struggling with a prolonged recession since the 1990s. With low birth rates and an aging population, suburban areas have begun to decline: once residents are too old to drive, basic activities including shopping and going to the doctor's become problematic. On the other hand, however, the number of single-person households is increasing, their share in the Tokyo housing market now standing at roughly 50%. Even though the standard government definition of the family unit is still two parents with two children, only 8.5% of Tokyo households now correspond to this definition. Further radical change to the Japanese lifestyle has also been brought about by the disastrous 2011 earthquake, making many Japanese more conscious of eco-friendly choices.

2. Japanese Architects and the Individual House

Japanese architects have often used the theme of the individual house as a vehicle for their architectural ideas and aesthetics. In the late 1910s, members of the emerging middle class sometimes commissioned architects to design their houses. Those houses were occasionally modern in style, reflecting the client's tastes or the architect's own perceptions and notions. With the advent of modernism in Japan in the mid 1920s, some architects – including Antonin Raymond, Kameki Tsuchiura, and Yoshiro Taniguchi – designed houses in the newest style not only for the middle class but also themselves (images 1, 2, 3). In Taniguchi's house (1935; image 1), the architect determined the depth of the eaves along the house's southern elevation according to the angle of the sun at the summer solstice and arranged the partitioning of the windows to control airflow, his modernist attitude to design providing the *raison d'être* for his motifs.

The most notable of modern architects at that time was Sutemi Horiguchi, who regarded the individual house as a vehicle for the manifestation of his architectural ideas and aesthetics. Whenever he presented his latest project as a monograph or in a magazine, he proposed ideas that could be shared by other architects.

1 Yoshiro Taniguchi, Taniguchi House, 1935, exterior
2 Kameki Tsuchiura, Tsuchiura House, 1935, exterior
3 Antonin Raymond, Reinanzaka House, 1924, exterior
4 Sutemi Horiguchi, Baron Kikkawa House, 1930, exterior

In one of his monographs – *Ichi-Konkurito-Jutaku-Zushu* (A Reinforced-Concrete House, Koyo-sha, 1930), introducing his Baron Kikkawa House (1930; image 4) – Horiguchi says that the elevation was the 'result' of trying to fit together the given conditions, including the site, function, structure, and materials. The monograph, however, did not quite give a fully accurate account in that it failed to mention that the planning of the house was similar to a former proposal for a different site with a different shape and size, and that the elevation of the executed building was different from the former. It might nonetheless be better, here, to highlight what Horiguchi tried to present rather than to point out the contradictions between his words and actions. Though designing an individual house might be seen as a trivial event, Horiguchi tried to find some architectural meanings in it that other architects could share and develop. Of course, performance is commonplace among leading contemporary architects, but Horiguchi was the first to do this in Japan.

The concept of 'fitting the purpose', which echoed the term *Zweckbau* used by the German architectural critic Adolf Behne, was popular among Japanese modernists at the time. In many cases, however, architectural requirements cannot easily coexist together, and it is essential that these should be organized according to a certain methodology and aesthetics when designing a building. As no Japanese architects had attempted to delve into these, however, this functionalist slogan had yet to be developed and turned into a viable methodology.

In Horiguchi's case, it is more important to note the aesthetics displayed in the elevation, where the architectural expression is a composition of abstract lines and planes. He was, in fact, the first Japanese architect to acknowledge the new abstract art defined by Theodor Lipps.

Horiguchi also led the discussion on Japan's architectural tradition. This was a period when nationalistic expression was an important question in both fascist and democratic nations. In Japan, several monumental buildings displayed an angled, tiled roof atop a building in the neoclassical style. The roof motif was derived from temples, whose origin was Chinese. Rejecting this 'affiliation', Japan's modernists presented their own interpretation of the architectural tradition by focusing on shrines, houses, and tea-ceremony houses as indigenous to Japan. The characteristics they derived from those building types were simplicity in plan and structure, respect for the beauty of materials, a lack of ornamentation, asymmetrical composition, harmony with the natural environment, and the use of modular units – all of which, in fact, were the same as the norms for modern architecture. This was the inevitable consequence of looking at old shrines and houses through the filter of modernism – they simply found what they wanted to find.

Horiguchi looked closely at new buildings when he visited Europe in 1923. As modernist architecture was just emerging there, he thought he could rival European modernists in the area. He discovered similar characteristics to modernist architecture in traditional houses, asserting they were functional and asymmetrical. As such, the traditional house and tea-ceremony house became valuable to Japanese architects as a source of new ideas and a medium of self-esteem. For Japanese modernists, the 'traditional Japanese house' was virtually synonymous with the *sukiya* style developed in the late sixteenth century. The *sukiya* style is the most influential type among traditional Japanese house styles, and is based on the earlier *shoin* style, which is characterized by the *toko* (decorated alcove), *chigai-dana* (staggered shelves), *tsuke-shoin* (desk with an opening), and *chodai-gamae* (set of four sliding doors), all specifically arranged to represent authority. The *sukiya* style introduced motifs and design elements culled from tea-ceremony rooms, which emphasized the asymmetrical and informal setting of the above-mentioned motifs and rustic materials including mud walls and bamboo. This style is freer in design elements and was felt to be more appropriate for men of culture, who could thus display their ideas and their ingenuity through their buildings. The design aimed to find meaningful ways to distance oneself from a shared standard, in this case the *shoin* style.

Japanese architects as well as various modernists abroad found much of interest in the traditional Japanese house (as opposed to large temples and castle buildings) because they also believed it shared important characteristics with modern architecture. After World War II, as modernist architecture became common the world over, some architects in the West began to wonder if metropolitan cityscapes had not in fact become one with the modernist perspective, communicating a disdain for tradition, local conditions, and materials. The large glazed steel-structured buildings seemed too inorganic and impersonal to them. They expected traditional houses in Japan to offer clues that would help them imagine a better architectural model, making use of organic materials and respecting human scale in keeping with disciplines similar to modern architecture. These notions were shared with Japanese modernists.

3. Ideas and Designs of the House as Developed by Japanese Architects in the Post-war Era

Considering the severe housing shortage in the immediate post-war period, some architects proposed a so-called 'minimum house' of less than $50\,m^2$. Makoto Masuzawa designed his own house in wood in 1952 (images pp. 92–95). The house had a square plan of 5.5 m by 5.5 m, a double-height living–dining space, and large traditional glass *shoji* sliding doors. In Residence for Mr H (1953; image 7), he proposed a plan combining a utility core surrounded by free space.

As conventional planning was clearly impossible in such small houses, architects had to come up with different ideas to create a habitable dwelling. They therefore used free space and furniture that was appropriate for small spaces. Their attitude should have been very functional, but what exactly does the term 'functional' mean and how is it realized? The architecture critic Ryuichi Hamaguchi commented on this very issue in his book *Hyumanizumu-no-kenchiku* (Architecture Based on Humanism, Ondori-sha, 1947), saying that sticking to the notion of fulfilling functions could lead to a virtuous – and sometimes beautiful – building, which was actually similar to the slogan the Japanese modernists had advocated before the war. In criticizing Hamaguchi's opportunistic stance, Tange Laboratory, a group of architects led by Kenzo Tange, asserted that function should be considered in relation to space. The idea of 'space' began to attract the attention of several Japanese architects in the early 1940s, but it was Tange Laboratory who first fully extended this idea to architectural thinking not only in relation to modernism but also to traditional architecture. The individual house was not a major theme as far as they were concerned, but it was through them that a new way of thinking about how to make the best use of the idea of 'space' began to circulate among Japanese architects. This abstract idea could be deployed to realize the relationship between the building and its surroundings as a wholly spatial composition, thus creating a house from an innovative viewpoint, as if it were a conformation of public and private spaces, unlike the traditional understanding of a combination of 'rooms'.

Several architects used this idea to plan houses featuring free space. Kiyoshi Seike, for example, designed the House for Prof. K Saito (1953; images pp. 72–73). With large openings fitted with sliding doors, this house had an open plan that extended free space out on to its gardens on both sides but that nonetheless allowed for privacy when the sliding doors are closed. In applying the notion of freely arranging furniture as evinced in the ancient

5   Kazuo Shinohara, Umbrella House, 1962, interior
6   Kazuo Shinohara, Umbrella House, 1962, plan of ceiling
7   Makoto Masuzawa, Residence for Mr H, 1953, exterior

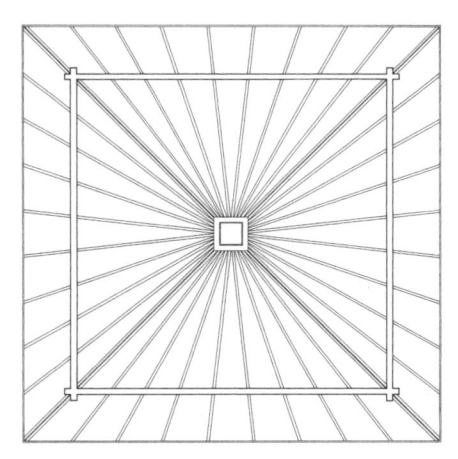

eleventh- and twelfth-century *shinden-dukuri* house style, Seike devised a square, *tatami*-mat pedestal with four castors that could be placed anywhere in the living area as a mobile *tatami*-mat 'floor'.

In the 1950s and 1960s, many Japanese architects were expected to design small yet comfortable houses, and one of the most renowned of these was Junzo Yoshimura. He designed his Mountain Lodge A (images pp. 108–111) in a mountain resort in 1963. Its living space in wood is elevated by a reinforced concrete structure, which enhances the feeling of being close to nature.

Subsequently, a number of architects found that reinforced concrete offered possibilities for creating unique shapes and austere expressions, to say nothing of its fire- and earthquake-resistant qualities. Sky House (1958; images pp. 258–261), designed by Kiyonori Kikutake, is a master class in the use of reinforced concrete. Its small living space (7.2 m by 7.2 m) surrounded by open corridors is supported by four flat reinforced-concrete pillars standing along each side of the square plan. The bathroom and kitchen are placed along the periphery of the living space as independently replaced gadgets which he called 'movenettes'. This idea of articulating the living and service spaces is defined by Metabolism, an architectural movement that started in Japan in that very period.

Tower House (1966; images pp. 112–117), designed by the architect Takamitsu Azuma for himself, is a notable example of how indebted to concrete Japanese architects were as an architectural material. The house stands on a tiny site of only 20 m^2 in a busy Tokyo district. Azuma vertically allocated each function to a different level along the stairs. The interior space was open-plan (or, rather, 'open-section') without any doors. The exposed concrete walls are roughly finished, which expresses his resolution to live in the heart of the city.

Row House in Sumiyoshi (1976; images pp. 233–235), designed by Tadao Ando, is noteworthy for its austere, exquisite use of reinforced concrete. As it was built in a row of townhouses, each with a narrow facade, Ando inserted a court dividing the house block into two sections to enhance sunlight and the breeze. The walls and ceilings are finished with fine exposed concrete. The concrete facade, whose only opening is the entrance, looks simple, but the plugged holes in which the spacers were inserted are meticulously arranged to 'tidy up' the wall. This austere yet meticulous treatment confers a solemn air to this tiny building.

In the 1960s, the architect Kazuo Shinohara defined a new horizon for house design. In an age when almost all architects were designing houses with an eye to efficient planning and reasonable structure, he challenged them by advocating that 'the larger the house the better' and 'the house is a work of art'. In Umbrella House (1962; images 5, 6), he proposed a square plan whose sides were divided by two orthogonal lines by a proportion of 4:3 to allocate spaces for different functions with a column at the intersection to support the beams along the two lines. For the roof structure, he exposed thin beams radially on the pyramid-shaped ceiling. He demonstrated that even this geometrical setting could make for a liveable dwelling, and the inner space itself was equally impressive. In House in Uehara (1976; images pp. 130–133) in reinforced concrete, Shinohara iconically exposed the large roof-supporting structures in its living space. Even a brutal setting such as this allows residents to enjoy living here, discovering new roles for those artistic objects.

Shinohara also influenced members of the younger generations, including Toyo Ito, who created a closed, introspective U-shaped space for White U (1976; images pp. 192–195).

For Villa in the Forest (1994; images 8, 9, 10), Kazuyo Sejima used a simple, geometrical procedure to form the overall plan: a combination of two circles, the smaller of which was included in the larger circle, with both centres slightly staggered. The walls were all painted white. In this case, the building was not made to 'perform', but was instead organized as a backdrop for the play of sunlight and tree shadows constantly moving along the round white walls. Sejima wanted this building to be ephemeral, different from Shinohara's.

Kazunari Sakamoto, another of Shinohara's disciples, designed Machiya in Minase (1970; images pp. 141–145), a symbolic yet serene space with a top-light inside, and House F (1988; images pp. 162, 163), where he dismantled building elements into individual pieces and rearranged them, eschewing symmetry or regular geometrical design. He purposefully made this building less conspicuous and articulated so that it could freely and loosely relate with the constantly changing townscape it was a part of. He was not a devotee of modernism and his House SA (1999; image 11) demonstrates a similar attitude to construction, its planning, structural system, and materials all carefully sidestepping orthodox methods. There is no trace here of any *de rigueur* disciplines, once used by architects to determine what to do in design. He is no postmodernist, either, but it was through the years of postmodernism that flourished in the 1970s and 1980s and then soon waned that the architectural scene changed once more.

4. From 'Have-To Architecture' to 'Can-Be Architecture'

As modernism gradually relaxed its hold, the idea of architecture began to dissolve in the 1990s, and solid and reliable principles and design methods were no longer automatically to be found. Many ideas that had been regarded as effective and a given were brought into doubt. Ideas such as the efficiency of building types, the relationship between buildings and their surroundings, the use of technology and materials, and what design is in the first place began to be revisited and re-evaluated. Extending Robert Venturi's famous axiom regarding modernism and postmodernism – from 'either–or architecture' to 'both–and architecture' – I see the shift as being from 'have-to architecture' (in modernism, being functional, reasonable, and ensuring a close relationship between the elevation and the composition of the inner space were a must) to 'can-be architecture' (the ability to embrace different definitions and designs such as the ones shown later in referring the new generations' house designs). 'Can-be architecture' may look great because it allows architects to propose anything they like thanks to cutting-edge digital technology, but the truth is that, as there are no definite or shared principles with which to evaluate what is good or bad, any design could quite simply be consumed and given away.

In this new context, attempts have been made by members of the younger generations to reshape the 'individual house' from different perspectives. One such case in point is Yoshiharu Tsukamoto and Momoyo Kaijima, who reflect on the historical and social contexts that have led to a stratification of different customs and behaviours. In their House and Atelier Bow-Wow (2005; images pp. 222, 223), an office and house combination, they manage to create a new lifestyle where office and living spaces are intertwined in a busy Tokyo neighbourhood. The house was unique in terms of the spatial composition of this building type. In Nora House (2006), which is situated in a suburban area with individual houses using the traditional subdivision of space into a specific room for each family member and where each house is surrounded by conventional gardens, Tsukamoto and Kaijima proposed a new house type with natural ventilation and agricultural work within the self-same structural unit.

Sou Fujimoto designed House N (2008; image p. 181), with its flat, layered walls and roofs with randomly arranged square openings. In this house, which has no clear borders demarcating the limits between the inside and the outside, residents are invited to enjoy the constantly changing sunlight and airflow.

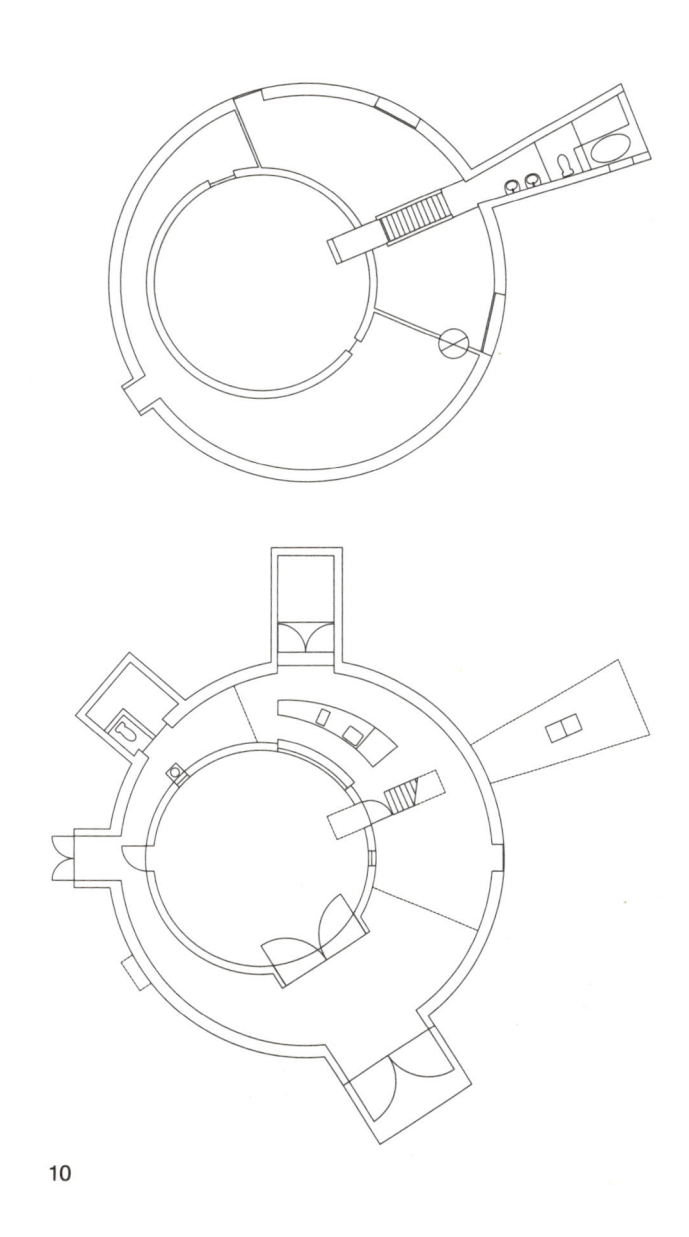

8   Kazuyo Sejima, Villa in the Forest, 1994, exterior
9   Kazuyo Sejima, Villa in the Forest, 1994, interior
10 Kazuyo Sejima, Villa in the Forest, 1994, floor plan

11 Kazunari Sakamoto,
    House SA, 1999, interior
12 Akihisa Hirata, Kotoriku,
    2014, exterior

Kotoriku (2014, image 12), a small apartment in a housing district, was designed by Akihisa Hirata. He believes that houses, although small, should be more than simply a building, and Kotoriku includes natural objects such as the ground, greenery, and even birds within the same housing unit.

The history of the individual house in Japan as briefly outlined here reflects how Japanese architects designed houses, at first relying on and then questioning modernism. They have brought various architectural ciphers to the fore, including function, planning, structure, and 'space'. In the 1990s, following important shifts in Japanese society, architectural thinking itself, and their attitude toward design, new generations of architects began to pursue different ideas and approaches. Thanks to these, we may want to rethink our own housing from now on.

'I Love Japanese Culture'
Pippo Ciorra

Bruno Taut's enthusiastic declaration, carved by Japanese friends onto a stone monument erected in memory of the architect,[1] is an excellent point from which to start elucidating the reasons for staging an exhibition on the architecture of the single-family house in contemporary Japan. In fact it is undeniable that the main reason for an exhibition of this kind in a Western museum lies in the fascination and undisputed interest aroused as much by the historic imagery of Japan's art and architecture as the global success of its most recent designers. Quite apart from the legacy of a couple of centuries of Japanophilia, we should not forget that some of today's most highly regarded architects are Japanese, and that three of the last six Pritzker laureates have come from Japan.[2] (This exhibition, in fact, includes five Pritzker winners.)

A good reason, then, but not the only one. The theme of the architecture of the single-family home in post-war Japan[3] branches out, in fact, into a series of other connected themes which are today at the centre of the worldwide debate over the relations between architecture, society, ecology, and the city. The first and most obvious is the fact that the best way to approach the work of these architects and the exchange that takes place between them and the society they operate in is through their home design. The second theme we intend to explore is the relationship between the spaces people inhabit and the form / organization of the cities they live in, which is a pressing question in every context and at every latitude. The third theme comprises all those variables – which are so remarkably specific in Japan – that have to do with time: the relationship with memory and with individual and collective traditions; the long-term effects of modernity (what Koolhaas has defined as 'absorbed modernity'); and the preservation and transformability of older buildings. One last theme is central to this exhibition and to contemporary debates over architecture – the conflict between utopia and realism, between general order and local solutions, and between the desire for permanent construction and spatiality in the making. (*Sakui* versus *jinen*, if we want to take advantage of an established historical categorization.)[4]

In conclusion, our aim is to present examples that will demonstrate how, throughout the twentieth century, and especially in the period following World War II right up to the present day, there have been architects who have grasped the sense of 'natural modernity' in Japanese domestic architecture and who have deftly applied this awareness to their own way of conceiving space and tackling problems posed by modes of living and the contemporary city.

An Architecture of Houses

In 2006, Arata Isozaki published an illuminating collection of essays on the subject of 'Japan-ness', that is the specific identity of Japanese architecture, viewed above all in relation to the gaze of those who observe it 'from the outside'.[5] For Isozaki the discourse on Japan-ness has a beginning and an end. The precise beginning of Japan-ness (rather than an earlier *japonisme*), in fact, is considered the second day of Bruno Taut's stay in Japan (1933), when his friend Isaburo Ueno took him on a visit to the Katsura Imperial Villa.[6] The end of Japan-ness, though less clear-cut, is equally easy to identify as it corresponds to the early 1990s, the most frantic and expansive phase of globalization, when the world of nations and blocs as well as culture morphed into an archipelago with an infinite number of centres. Japan was now no longer a remote, faraway place located beyond the clearly defined bounds of exoticism, but simply another of these centres, conceptually equidistant and part of the worldwide artistic and political scene just like all the others. 'That is to say,' writes Isozaki, 'that the very border that once gave substance to Japan-ness has been decomposing.'[7] This new context has made the work of architects

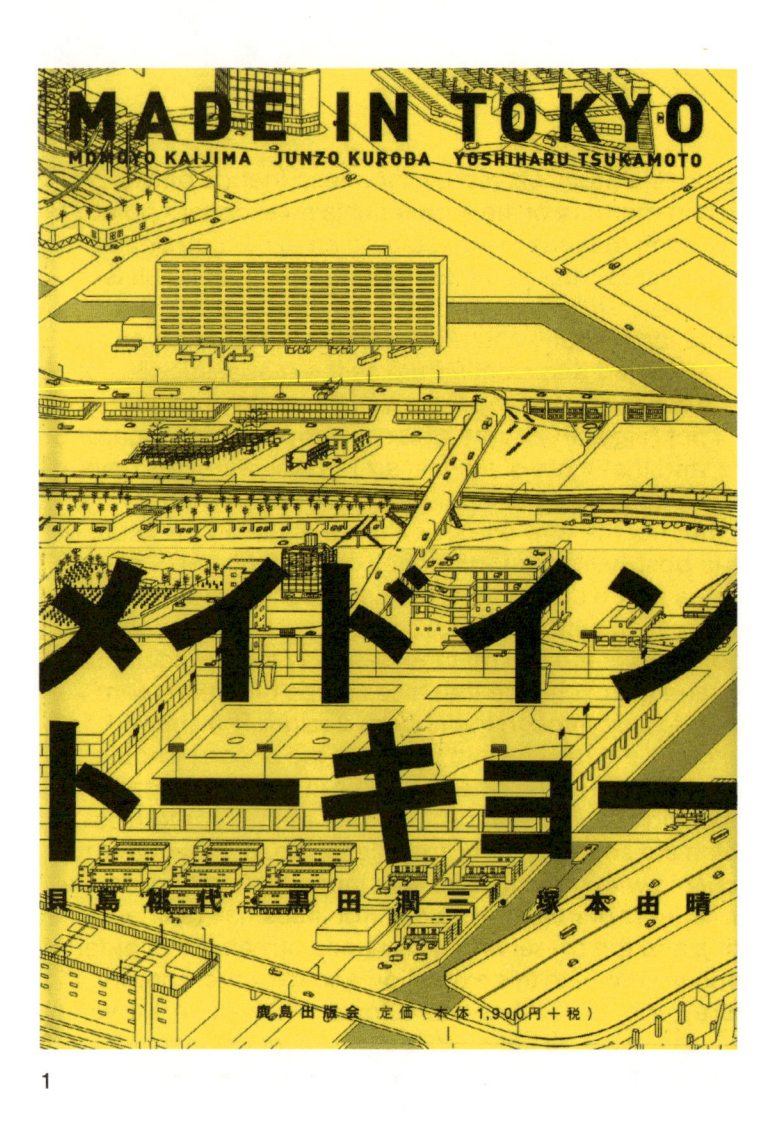

1 Cover of *Made in Tokyo*, 2001, by Momoyo Kajima, Junzo Kuroda and Yoshiharu Tsukamoto
2 Partial mock-up of White U (1966) by Toyo Ito, MAXXI, Gallery 2, 2016

active in Japan more accessible, and they have made the most of it by laying siege to the global market for architecture with their sophisticated simplicity, winning important, prestigious prizes and competitions. Although engaged in the construction of important museums and institutions the world over, even the best-known of Japanese architects have never turned down the chance to build small single-family houses in their own country. And it is precisely with regard to the continuity of this commitment to the design of homes, from the end of World War II until the present day, that this exhibition takes a slightly different position from Isozaki's and suggests the possible survival of a particular aspect of Japan-ness in the design of the individual house. The proposition in this sense is clear. Ever since the Japanese government decided to base the country's post-war reconstruction on the owner-occupied 'detached house',[8] architects working in Japan have accepted the idea of the home as the primary, privileged place in which to carry out their most authentic experimentation. This is true from the viewpoint of 'design research', but also from that of the social role of the architect. The home is the conceptual *locus* where Japanese designers test their ability to reconcile the immutable concepts of an extremely 'durable' spatial tradition with the requirements and qualities of contemporary daily life. Architects also therefore reassert their place in society, taking on the task of dealing in spatial terms with the conflicts inevitably generated by technological and anthropological evolution, by the hybridizing of taste and the intrusive nature of economic, management, and communicational priorities. All this finds expression in a form of collective identity (Japan-ness again) of the country's architecture, which allows us to interpret a theme – the relationship between design and dwelling – that is once again of paramount importance in the contemporary world.

A City of Houses
In their introduction to *Made in Tokyo* (image 1), the authors accurately describe the sense of uneasiness, vaguely reminiscent of *Blade Runner* (1982), that strikes the Japanese when they return to Tokyo from Europe: 'Roads and trainlines run over buildings, expressways wind themselves over rivers, cars can drive up ramps to the rooftop of a six-storey building. . .'[9] How could all this have happened? What has gone wrong in Tokyo? After a few days, however, the question quietly subsides, along with the sensation that anything is wrong. Gradually they start to feel at home again, as if there were something, a secret architectural device, that allows the feeling of urban disorientation to be gently absorbed and compensated in the life of individuals. It seems evident that for Atelier Bow-Wow, some of whose research is contained in *Made in Tokyo*, this device is the single-family house, whose efficacy clearly encompasses the plane of both urban and human relations. In a social space that is highly organized in a modern and productivist sense, often very remote from the 'human scale', and where collective modes of behaviour are meticulously regulated, the house is ultimately a place of compensation where the Japanese can more freely express their individuality. Houses often take the form of the 'free behavior'[10] of those who live in them and have an average lifespan of twenty-six years (that is, one generation) – the city has no choice but to derive much of its own unstable form directly from the sum of these single units. Perfectly expressed in the Japanese Pavilion of the 2010 Venice Architecture Biennale,[11] this seems to be the true nature of Tokyo's urban metabolism. This biennale – directed by Kazuyo Sejima, as it happens – was held when the 'urban question' still dominated the debate over planning. Not yet diverted by the economic crisis, the debate centred on how to put a stop to the boundless housing sprawl brought about by what Aldo Bonomi calls 'molecular capitalism' and extending swiftly and more or less consistently all over the world, from the suburbs of South America to the coastal areas of Asia, from the metropolitan zones of sub-Saharan Africa

3   Yashuiro Ishimoto, *Main Room, Left, the Hearth Room, Right, of the Old Shoin, Viewed from the North-east. Second Room in the Foreground*, from the series *Katsura*, 1953-1954

to the shores of the Mediterranean. The authors of *Tokyo Metabolizing*,[12] drawing on the Japanese experience, proposed an unprecedented and provocative solution to the problem: as there was no point in restoring a lost (and Eurocentric) urbanistic order, would it not be better to try to understand the rules and rhythms of the metabolism of contemporary urban space and learn how to work within them? For this to be possible, it was necessary to realize that traditional distinctions of scale were no longer applicable and that, once a sound infrastructural network has been established, the basic unit of construction, that is the single-family house, is just as important – if not more so – than a public building, a shopping mall, or an office tower.

The Space of the House and the Space of Time
In order to understand just how intimately the many legacies of tradition and modernity, aristocratic and rural life, and ancient and recent technologies are intertwined in the Japanese home, we must go back to those first few days that Bruno Taut spent in Japan after fleeing from Nazi Germany in 1933. His diary entry on day one is all about his encounter with the humbler, poorer aspects of the Japanese home: the cold, the absence of 'European-style' furniture, the communal bathroom, the basic simplicity of the utensils, the low beams (which he occasionally bumped his head on), the pain of having to sit on his haunches. On day two, the Taut family left the home of his host Mamada-san and were taken to Katsura, where Taut discovered the other, far more aristocratic aspect of Japanese spatial culture, with its severe, simple spaces, its regular arrangement and right angles, and its discreet compositions that spoke to a subtle equilibrium between artifice and nature. He was profoundly impressed. 'What would you call this architecture in modern terms?' Taut asked his friends.[13] The response was unanimous and rousing: 'an architecture of function or [...] motive'. In one fell swoop Taut laid the foundations for a global perception of Japanese architecture as 'naturally modern', a perception that, when all is said and done, still holds. Many years later, in fact, when Katsura was being described by Walter Gropius and photographed by Yasuhiro Ishimoto,[14] (image 3) the 'detached villa' was again presented as a sort of backdated archetype of neoplastic architecture,[15] where the elements of Japanese life (*tokonoma*, *engawa*, *tatami*) were directly connected with a space defined by areas, layout, and geometries typical of northern European modernism. Like Taut's diary, Ishimoto's photographs gloss over pitched roofs, structural details, and decorative elements, even though at Katsura there was an abundance of these features, many of which connected the buildings to the more vernacular aspects of the local tradition.

During the period after the end of World War II when Japanese architects fell in love with single-family houses, designers approached the theme without any particular qualms or restrictions and without feeling the need to fall in line with an 'international' norm. The young Kenzo Tange, Seiichi Shirai (who had just returned from studying philosophy in Germany), and Antonin Raymond (who came to Japan with Frank Lloyd Wright) tackled the question of Japan-ness freely and gracefully, utilizing the traditional elements of space and construction to design incontestably modern buildings. There are two basic factors that entrenched this approach, making it still relevant today: on the one hand, the absence of our Western obsession with 'origins' and the consequent desire for a paradigm against which architects can measure themselves, its place taken by a circular and recurrent 'space of time' founded on generations and genealogies; on the other, the increasing importance of the client, seen as the bearer of tastes, habits, and 'modes of behaviour' that directly condition the form of the house and function as an 'enzyme' capable of harmonizing the coexistence of what derives from tradition with everything that comes to us from contemporary life. 'Each building,' we read in Atelier Bow-Wow's *Behaviorology*, 'can be viewed as a sentient creature',[16] and like every sentient creature each building has a lifespan, which we have already identified as twenty-six years, not coincidentally the length of a generation. This is how Tokyo has operated over the last seventy years, and is thus how the city has developed a form of void metabolism[17] (as opposed to the core metabolism described in *Project Japan*[18]) that has allowed Japanese city planning to function well, contrary to all of the architectural profession's common sense. However, there now also seems to be something new in the circular, 'genealogical' time of Japan, visible for example in the works on show in the Japanese Pavilion at the 2016 Architecture Biennale. It is a series of house designs assembled by the curator Yoshiyuki Yamana,[19] whose common denominator is the idea of extending the concept of the household to communities beyond the limits of the traditional family and – something truly unprecedented in a country in which the most important temple, the Ise Grand Shrine, is moved and reconstructed every twenty years – of recycling existing buildings to realize or improve housing projects. In short, preservation and recycling are making headway even in 'metabolizing' Tokyo and raising new and stimulating problems for the practice and theory of architectural behaviourism.

Utopia and Realism

Mentioning Japan to a Western architect inevitably evokes visions of bold technocratic structures spanning Tokyo Bay, immense tentacular towers around which building blocks are tethered like spaceships taking on fuel, and massive Fun Palaces[20] transformed into huge roofs for the Osaka Expo. However, the present context (a period of crisis and depression) is particularly ripe for the cultivation of utopias and thus makes the architectural public highly sensitive to the allure of any radical visionary alternative. Although it cannot be said that the Japanese house is devoid of the Metabolism of the 1960s – suffice it to cite the radicalism of Kurokawa's Capsule Tower (1972; images pp. 98–99) or the trenchant force of Kikutake's Sky House (1958; images pp. 258–261), for example – it is nonetheless true that the research underpinning this exhibition presents an essentially 'realistic' vision to the observer. Once again, the Japanese single-family home obliquely introduces an architectural debate that is as topical as it is broad in its scope, as the 2016 Biennale referred to above clearly evinces. The Biennale's pavilions and the Arsenale are teeming with installations inspired by a nostalgia for 'public' intervention as an engine for the construction of collective housing (preferably around ten storeys high and several kilometres long) and for the architect as a demiurge graciously disseminating knowledge, cities, and democracy throughout the land. This exhibition (and the Japanese Pavilion) offers a different response: keep well away from all those cases in which the client is not the person who is actually going to live in the building, and start out instead from a promiscuous relationship between the designer and the inhabitant, between the planner and the city, between the architect and the physical and spatial materials of the house. Construct an alternative based on the multitude of 'modes of behaviour' and not on a revival of metanarratives. Clearly, this is a form of realism that is not immune from a certain measure of utopia, but a utopia that does not stake everything on 'all or nothing' but permits an endless series of partial victories or defeats, with gaps between them in which the figure of the architect can survive. Apparently chaotic, as Atelier Bow-Wow once again explains,[21] the 'city of houses' represents a highly sustainable alternative that is able to seamlessly regenerate itself, founded on the initiative of individuals rather than the accumulation of central capital and the resources and power this implies. This is still an open question, but we would like to take this opportunity to stress the potential of research into the single-family house in Japan as a key to the current political debate on architecture and the forms of the city.

4   Carlo Scarpa, Brion Tomb,
    1969–1978, doorway

5   Carlo Scarpa, Brion Tomb,
    1969–1978, external view
    of small temple
6   Carlo Scarpa, Brion Tomb,
    1969–1978, study of plan, facade,
    and section of entrance *propylaea*

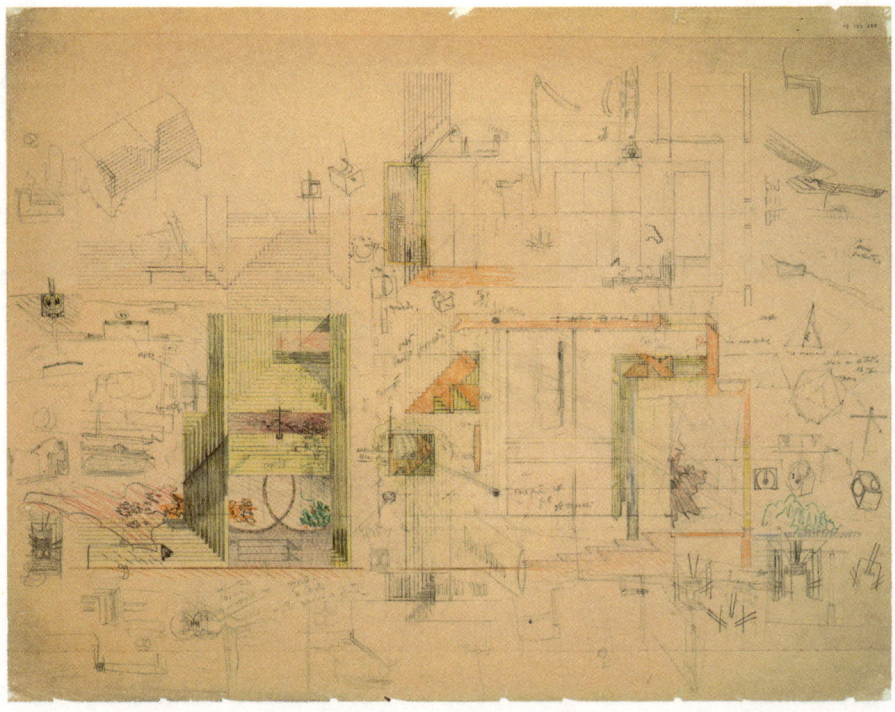

Learning from Japan

In most Western architectural scenarios, the theme of the single-family house for the middle classes is nonexistent or still somewhat taboo. Extraneous to the 'collective' nature of European modernism and generally finding expression in the regressive and exclusive theme of the detached villa, the single-family house is seen as an indulgence for which the masters (Mies van der Rohe, Le Corbusier) are forgiven in the early stages of their careers. It is considered a training ground, an inevitable initiation to the profession for young architects who have yet to earn the kind of reputation that will allow them to obtain commissions for well-subsidized public institutions or poorly subsidized public housing. For this reason the modern form of *japonisme* encountered in the early decades of the twentieth century is Frank Lloyd Wright's and Taut's own orthodox and much-admired take on the theme. Wright is perhaps the only acclaimed architect in the West to have consistently worked on the theme of the single-family home for the contemporary middle class, in the Prairie School houses and in his designs for 'kit homes'. Taut, as we have seen, was for a long time the official arbitrator between modernist aesthetics and Japan. After these two architects, it was the Eameses who fastened on the most interesting typological characteristic of the Japanese house, and that is its emptiness[22] and flexibility, with no fixed walls or rooms used for a single function. The horizontality, rationality, and multifunctionality of the spaces shaped a modernity that was foreign to Europe's Bauhaus-inspired typological obsessions, and this allowed the Japanese architects of the second half of the twentieth century to design houses more freely and creatively than their Western counterparts. Japanese house design moves from the ground up, from family to society; in the West it almost always moves top–down, from society to the family, with different degrees of negotiation and imposition. For Dimitris Pikionis,[23] the architect who landscaped the area around the Acropolis, Japan was the typical source of inspiration for anyone looking for an unstable – albeit convincing – equilibrium between tradition and modernity. His wooden porticos and carefully arranged stones to guide people as they climb up toward the Parthenon are reminiscent of another recurrent claim in Japanese writings: Western architecture 'takes' space from nature, while nature 'bestows' it on Japanese architecture. Carlo Scarpa died in Japan in 1978, about a year after the Japanese magazine *Space Design* devoted a special issue of almost two hundred pages to him[24] and ten years after his first visit on the occasion of an exhibition of Cassina furniture organized by his son Tobia. Officially, Scarpa's passion for Japan was an offshoot of his devotion to Wright, but he actually got much closer to the Japanese sensibility than Wright ever did. He is often quite rightly compared with his contemporary Seiichi Shirai, whose artistic career he somewhat paralleled – neither had received regular professional training, and both operated in opposition to modernist orthodoxy and were extraneous to the mainstream of their own country. To see how Scarpa brought about a perfect synthesis between the structural and material nature of Western architecture and the 'spatial and dynamic' character of Japanese architecture,[25] you need look no further than his Brion Tomb (1969–1978), which Japanese architects quite fittingly often visit (images 4, 5, 6).

As far as more recent history is concerned, we see how the passion for the features of Japanese architecture tends to go beyond the aesthetic sphere and expand into the realm of the theme to which this exhibition is dedicated. The single-family home, in fact, is regarded as a social mechanism capable of connecting the middle class and architecture, two entities that in Western countries, despite the fact that 'detached' houses are built in their millions, seem to have ignored one another almost completely up to now. In some countries the socioeconomic landscape tends to favour this process. BLAF Architecten and AND'ROL Architecture in Belgium, Bevk Perović Arhitekti and Dekleva Gregorič Arhitekti in Slovenia, and Clavien Rossier and GOA in

Switzerland seem to be working on a European version of the architectural behaviourism that we are tackling in *The Japanese House*.
Maria Giuseppina Grasso Cannizzo, a decidedly 'unaligned' Italian architect who displays an almost 'Scarpian' persistence, is even closer to the Japanese vibe. Her houses in Sicily, which display rigorous devotion to space, a commitment to the involvement of clients and their modes of 'behaviour', and a capacity to modulate density and rarefaction, would not at all look out of place in an exhibition dedicated to Japanese works, and they are also a precious indication of a possible future for Italian architecture.

7

7   Maria Giuseppina Grasso Cannizzo,
    FCN Noto 2009, Summer House,
    exterior

Endnotes

1. See Manfred Speidel, 'Japanese Traditional Architecture in the Face of Its Modernisation: Bruno Taut in Japan', in *Questioning Oriental Aesthetics and Thinking Conflicting Visions of 'Asia' under the Colonial Empires*, ed. Inaga Shigemi (Kyoto: International Research Center for Japanese Studies, 2011), 93–111. See also Winfried Nerdinger and Manfred Speidel, eds, *Bruno Taut 1880–1938. Architektur zwischen Tradition und Avantgarde* (Stuttgart: Deutsche Verlags-Anstalt, 2001).
2. Kazuyo Sejima and Ryue Nishizawa (2010), Toyo Ito (2013), and Shigeru Ban (2014). See www.pritzkerprize.com.
3. For the historical background to the questions tackled in this exhibition, readers are referred to the essay written for this catalogue by Hiroyasu Fujioka, 'A History of Individual Houses in Modern Japan'.
4. See Arata Isozaki, 'Western Structure vs Japanese Space', in Arata Isozaki, *Japan-ness in Architecture* (Cambridge Mass.: MIT Press, 2006), 23.
5. *Ibidem*.
6. Bruno Taut, *Houses and People of Japan* (Tokyo: Sanseido, 1958; first ed. 1937), 279–307.
7. Isozaki, 'Western Structure vs Japanese Space', 57.
8. See note 3.
9. Momoyo Kajima, Junzo Kuroda, and Yoshiharu Tsukamoto, *Made in Tokyo* (Tokyo: Kaijima Institute Publishing, 2014), 8.
10. See Atelier Bow-Wow, *Behaviorology* (New York: Rizzoli International Publications, 2010).
11. La Biennale di Venezia, 12th International Architecture Exhibition, *People Meet in Architecture* (August 29–November 22, 2010), directed by Kazuyo Sejima. For the Japanese Pavilion, see Ryue Nishizawa, *Tokyo Metabolizing*, ed. Koh Kitayama (Tokyo: TOTO Publishing, 2010).
12. See note 11.
13. Taut, *Houses and People of Japan*, 293.
14. After some time spent in the United States, Yasuhiro Ishimoto returned to Japan in 1953 and the same year was commissioned by the MoMA to photograph the imperial villa of Katsura.
15. Ishimoto's photographs were published in Yasuhiro Ishimoto and Kenzo Tange, *Katsura: Tradition and Creation in Japanese Architecture* (New Haven: Yale University Press, 1960), with texts by Walter Gropius and Kenzo Tange.
16. Atelier Bow-Wow, *Behaviorology*, 9.
17. Atelier Bow-Wow, *Behaviorology*, 13.
18. Rem Koolhaas and Hans Ulrich-Obrist, *Project Japan. Metabolism Talks* (Berlin: Taschen, 2011).
19. Yoshiyuki Yamana, Seiichi Hishikawa, Masaki Uchino, Masatake Shinohara, eds, *En: art of nexus* (Tokyo: TOTO Publishing, 2016).
20. Isozaki, 'Western Structure vs Japanese Space', 56.
21. Atelier Bow-Wow, *Behaviorology*, 13.
22. 'The simplicity of the completely empty spaces in Japan surprises [Bruno Taut] even more [. . .]', in Speidel, 'Japanese Traditional Architecture', 100.
23. The love Pikionis felt for Japan, a country he never visited, was also platonic and literary. His sources were Taut's report on the one hand and the books of his friend the writer Nikos Kazantzakis on the other, in particular *Le Jardin des rochers* [The rock garden], a volume Kazantzakis published in French in 1936.
24. *Space Design*, 153 (1977).
25. Isozaki, 'Western Structure vs Japanese Space', 24.

Architecture and Life: Human Agency and Forms of Living
in the Japanese House
Florence Ostende

> A house and its master
> are like the dew that gathers
> on the morning glory.
> Which will be the first to pass?
> Kamo-no-Chomei, *Hojoki*, 1212[1]

The representation of the house in art, literature, and cinema is mostly used as a stage for human drama, the composition of the space becoming a mere backdrop to the characters' lives. By contrast, in architecture as a discipline, the house is often presented devoid of human presence. In models, plans, and elevations, the human figure is generally absent, or at best a pretext to give a sense of scale. The considerable number of publications on the history of the Japanese house are no exception.[2] A canonical case study in Japanese architectural history, the seventeenth-century Katsura Imperial Villa in Kyoto, is exemplary in this regard. The countless volumes on this widely represented and frequently debated residence mainly offer a modernist interpretation of its geometrical proportions through measured drawings, abstract photography, and diagrams of the rising moon.[3] The exhibition *The Japanese House: Architecture and Life after 1945* investigates the role of the single family house as the foremost site for architectural experimentation and debate from the end of World War II to the present. Its subtitle 'Architecture and Life' reflects our emphasis on innovative solutions to changing lifestyles in the light of important shifts occurring in the Japanese economy, urban landscape, and family structure. In this essay, I will investigate the multifaceted representation of the Japanese house and examine how, after 1945, the oscillating presence and absence of human agency within its built environment reflects rising debates on subjectivity, leading to a redefinition of subject-centred perceptions and a new understanding of forms of living.

In the early eleventh-century romantic fiction *The Tale of Genji*,[4] illustrations of the interior space serve as a *topos* of traditional Japanese architecture with sliding doors and large surrounding verandas open to the outside. Written by a woman known as Murasaki Shikibu, the novel unravels the romantic exploits of the Prince of Genji and his search for love in Heian period court life (image 21). The preponderance of indoor settings in the illustrated handscrolls and manuscripts are well-known for using the geometric forces of the architectural elements to convey the psychological tensions of the characters. The famous compositional device known as the *fukinuki yatai* (literally meaning blown-off roof) has been the subject of many studies revolving around the 'psycho-perspective' of the pictorial space – the removal of roofs, walls, and beams allowing two existing narrative spaces to reveal the emotions of characters.[5]

However, the blown-off roof also lies at the heart of a renewed interest in the gendered voyeurism inherent in the romantic fiction, as the intimacy of the palace is exposed to the spectator's gaze. The use of the open roof, commonly attributed to a female perspective and a codification of feminine voyeurism, has been reinterpreted by Doris Croissant as a male appropriation of the female aesthetics assigned to Genji.[6] In mainstream art history and Japanese architecture, the palace life illustrated in the *Tale of Genji* from the twelfth century onward became a symbol of the imperial power in the old capital of Kyoto, which was soon to be disrupted by the turbulence of the late Heian period in medieval Japan. At that time, poet Kamo-no-Chomei retired from the world in a tiny hut he built in the mountains surrounding Kyoto. Running away from a city ravaged by natural disaster, civil unrest, and political turmoil, Chomei chronicled his retreat as a hermit in the *Hojoki* ('Record of the ten-foot-square hut'), a short first-person chronicle written in 1212.[7]

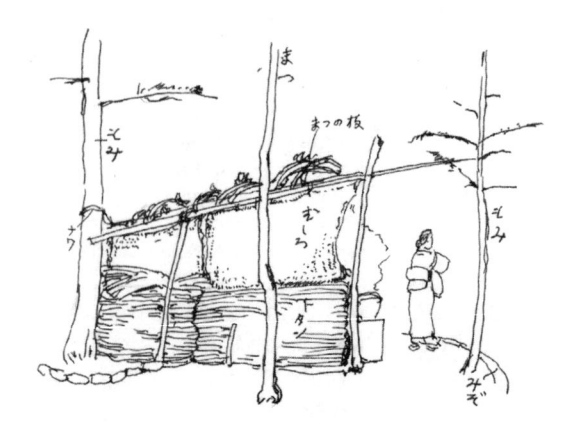

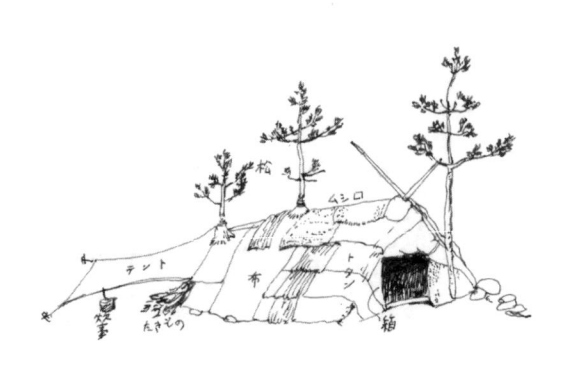

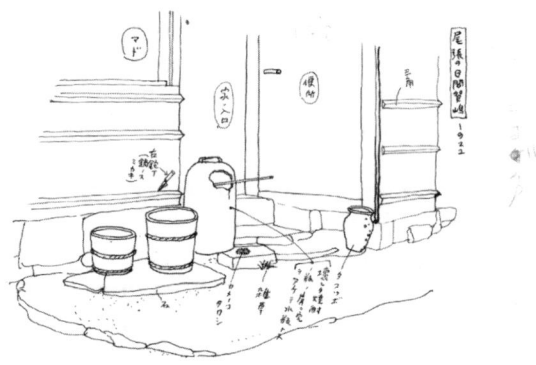

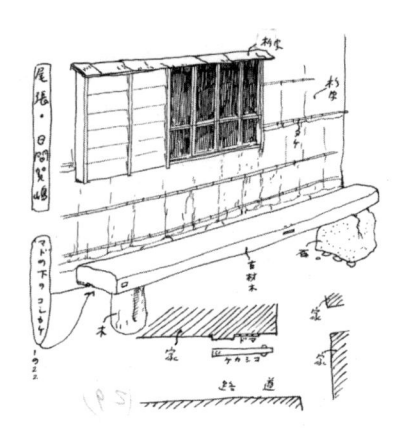

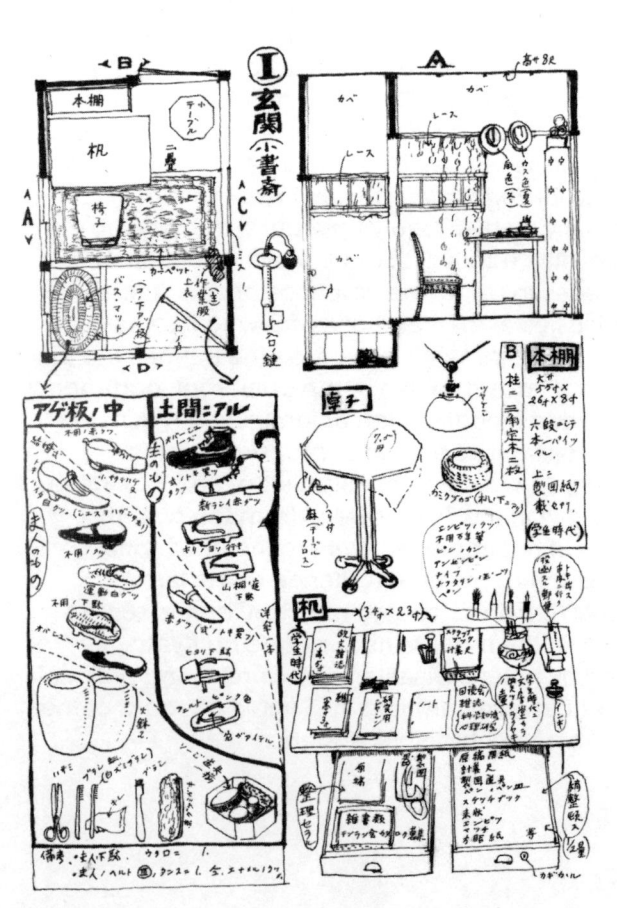

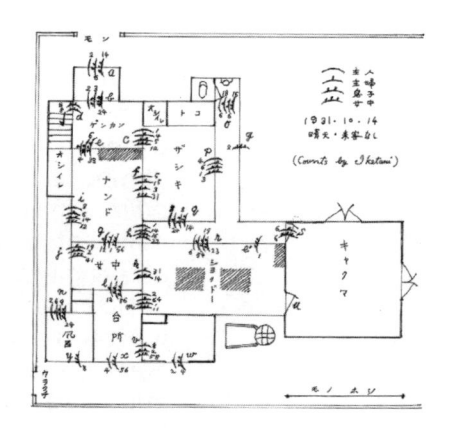

1 Wajiro Kon, *Shack with wood branches on its roof*, sketch drawn as part of survey after the Great Kanto Earthquake, 1923
2 Wajiro Kon, *Cave-like shack*, sketch drawn as part of survey after the Great Kanto Earthquake, 1923
3 Wajiro Kon, *Fisherman's kitchen*, 1927
4 Wajiro Kon, *Window and bench*, 1927
5 Wajiro Kon, *Room I*, from *A Comprehensive Illustration of the Household of a Newly-married Couple*, 1925
6 Wajiro Kon, *Diagram of the Traffic in a House*, 1931

Standing on the margin of the axonometric space system of the imperial palace and its voyeuristic exposure of male–female erotic communication, the isolated hut of a solitary man could be seen as the inversion of the court, the repressed niche in the literary imagination of Japanese culture.[8]

The recurring destruction of houses caused by fire, famine, disease, earthquake, and whirlwind (irrespective of social status) is an obsessive motif for Chomei. The razed house, raised again, is associated with the impermanence of human life and nature, like the flowing river or the morning dew. The staccato and accelerated pace of his prose, along with a strong visual vocabulary, demonstrate the merging of the house with the poet's mind and the natural elements. The hut nestled in the mountain becomes an outpost for capturing the voices of the cicadas, the cuckoos, the crying monkeys, and the hooting owls. Describing himself as 'an old silk worm spinning one last cocoon', Chomei exposes his inner spiritual life in the form of a hermit crab in his tiny shell.[9] Leaving behind the social life of the court and poetic circles, Chomei made his hut with planks of timber and joints with metal hasps so it could easily be transformed, dismantled, and moved elsewhere: 'With no commitment / to any one place / I laid no claim to the land'.[10]

* * *

The ingenuity of vernacular architecture encapsulated in Chomei's writing resurfaced centuries later in the rising field of early twentieth-century Japanese ethnography, but this time in a radically transformed Japanese society facing rapid modernization and industrialization. While Chomei's lonely dwelling served as a personal metaphor for the poet's inner solitary spirit, the houses depicted in ethnographic travelogues hoped to produce an objective examination of social change. Initially based on the preservation of craftsmanship in rural areas, the tradition of house-oriented surveys slowly evolved toward urban domestic life seen as an emblem of the emerging material culture. Architect, designer, and educator Wajiro Kon participated in field trips to record traditional folk houses and artefacts in rural villages. Looking at a fisherman's house on Himaka island, Kon's drawings depict a homemade bench of recycled timber ingeniously supported by a stone and a piece of wood (image 4), or a broken *shochu* pot transformed into a water jar (image 3).

After the devastating Great Kanto Earthquake of 1923, Kon pioneered the use of survey methods in the metropolis. Following his study of makeshift shelters built by survivors in the ruins of Tokyo (images 1, 2), his 1930 book *Modernologio*[11] charted the reconstruction and modernization of the city from 1924 onward. Kon's techniques relied on visual observation, statistics, and first-person commentary. Alongside a drawing of a student's messy closet, including a detailed list of the young man's possessions, Kon wrote: 'I witnessed a pair of serge *hakama* [loose trousers] hanging themselves or old socks stuffed between other belongings'.[12] Over plan and section views of the wardrobe of a newly-wed couple, Kon dissected their hidden material expression using bubbles and pointing arrows like the storyboard of a manga (image 5).

Although Kon was sometimes criticized for his amateurish approach – embracing lifestyles, body postures, social manners, and storage behaviours – his integration of graphic design, architecture, fashion, and interior design makes him a pioneer of cultural studies. His interior surveys were also prescient in raising issues such as class and gender. Based on the idea of crossing the threshold, Kon's 1931 diagram of a middle-class family's 'traffic' in their suburban Tokyo house (image 6) is a detailed record of the number of times each person went from one room to another: 'This investigation will serve as a basic survey which can be used as the foundation for planning an ideal residential floor plan. It will also reveal the behavior of the occupants of a contemporary Japanese house [. . .]. In the case of this type of family, you will sympathise most with the maid, and then the wife. It comes as no surprise to learn the maid crossed the kitchen thresholds 181 times from the moment she woke up to the time she went to bed.'[13]

Kon's anthropology of material culture in a newly-born consumer society sought to understand the desire for individuation – a need for distinction from the masses: 'I have been recording and describing every object in people's living spaces in detail, trying to discover the differences between each individual'.[14]

In the context of the 1930s, Kon's sketches of precarious shelters and messy closets were in sharp contrast with the idealized refinement, harmonious simplicity, and geometric proportions of the Japanese house promoted by European modernists. The stereotyping of the traditional Japanese house by modernists took a decisive turn after World War II when the notion of tradition was instrumentalized to face the loss of identity after the defeat. Partly a reaction to the occupation by the Allied Forces, which ended in 1952, the politicized return to tradition revealed a need to reconnect with – and redefine – the national identity. In 1953, architect Junzo Yoshimura travelled with curator Arthur Drexler, architectural historian Masaru Sekino, and photographer Yasuhiro Ishimoto to Kyoto, Shiga, and Nara in search of an iconic representation of a traditional Japanese house intended for the series of exhibitions *House in the Garden* to be staged at the Museum of Modern Art Sculpture Garden in New York.[15] Following Marcel Breuer's Museum Garden House and Gregory Ain's prefabricated house, Yoshimura conceived a paradigmatic Japanese dwelling which was modelled on the seventeenth-century Kojo-in guest house in Onjo-ji temple. Yoshimura therefore considered his *shoin-zukuri*-style villa, named the Pine Breeze Villa (Shofu-so), an archetype of the Japanese house.[16] Photographs of the exhibition (1954–1955) illustrate how different the house is to its surroundings, an alien presence amongst the New York skyscrapers. Built as a post-war gift of peace from Japan to the United States, the house also stood as a gentle reminder that traditional Japanese architecture already contained many of the characteristics of modernism.

During the same research trip, American-Japanese photographer Ishimoto was deeply impressed by the Katsura Villa. Trained in the philosophy of Bauhaus at the Institute of Design in Chicago (1948–1952), Ishimoto famously exclaimed that 'Katsura is Mondrianesque!'[17] He later collaborated with architect Kenzo Tange, resulting in the release of the 1960 blockbuster book *Katsura: Tradition and Creation in Japanese Architecture*.[18] Although Bruno Taut had already introduced the Katsura to the modernist discourse in the 1930s,[19] Tange, who made his career on the reconstruction of war-devastated cities, promoted a new vision of Japanese architecture that would combine traditional architecture with modernist design. Tange selected, cropped, and sequenced Ishimoto's photographs to emphasize the grid-like composition and geometric abstraction of the villa.

* * *

The photogenic composition of traditional Japanese houses offered great possibilities to the modernist lens. The *tatami* flooring and *shoji* screens create a pattern of vertical and horizontal lines that meet on multiple points, establishing a dominant grid pattern and creating the impression of an infinite space. These homogeneous modules offer a pre-existing compositional grid for the camera. Similarly, the film camera could capture the succession of rooms sequenced by the planar surface of semi-mobile partitions. The axial movement of characters is facilitated by the fluidity of circulation, which means actors can enter from any side. Rooms are modular units that can be merged or separated. We could even say that the camera dramatizes

7

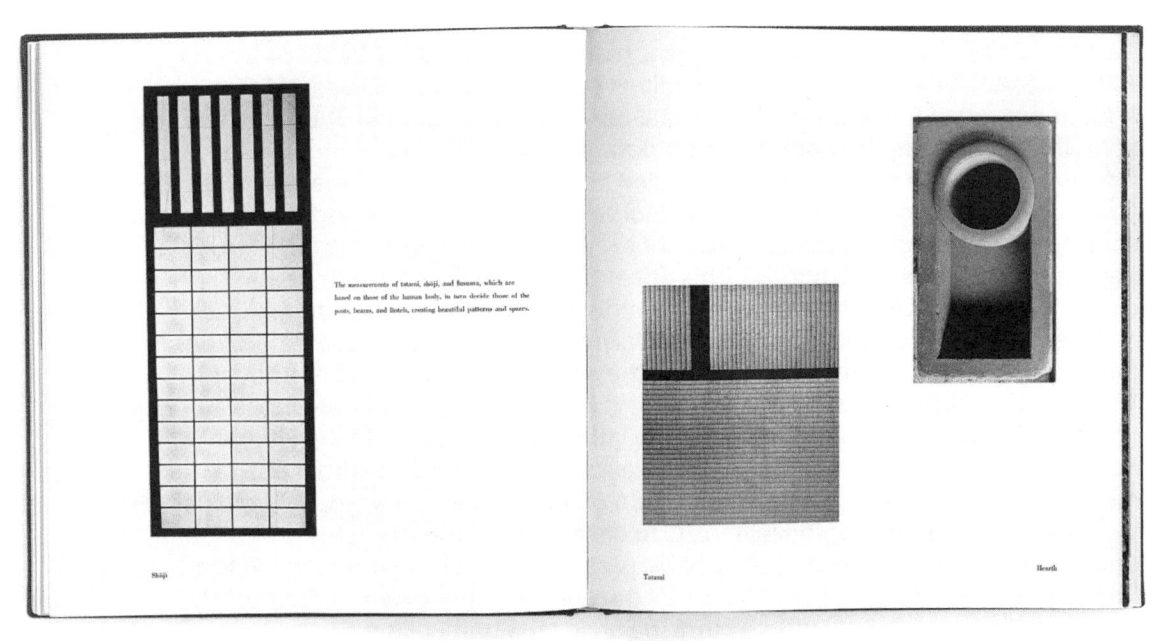

8

7 Junzo Yoshimura, 'Japanese Exhibition House' (Pine Breeze Villa), The Museum of Modern Art, New York, 1956, aerial view
8 Spread from *Katsura: Tradition and Creation in Japanese Architecture*, 1960, with photographs by Yasuhiro Ishimoto and edited by Kenzo Tange

the standardization of the traditional interior. With no clear doors or windows, vistas are produced as 'cellular sub-divisions of the screen-surface'.[20]

The single-family dwelling became a seductive motif for Japanese filmmakers grouped under the banner of the 'home drama genre', in which the family played a central role.[21] Yasujiro Ozu's famously static shots emphasized the geometric proportions and extreme simplicity of Japanese middle-class homes (images 9, 10, 11, 12). The architectural structure of the house and the careful composition of the interior contributed to the signature style of his late-career films in the 1950s. Ozu's artistic sensibility was perceived as quintessentially Japanese. He often fixed his camera at a very low angle to reflect the sitter's point of view; the static *tatami* shot positioned on the floor emphasized the passivity of the viewer, encouraging comparison to traditional arts such as the staging of the tea ceremony. Keeping the outside world at a distance, the viewer becomes a recorder of impression and an idealized embodiment of Buddhist precepts.[22] The 1960s activist avant-garde regarded Ozu's films as conservative and reactionary, an example of the kind of nostalgic attachment to traditional Japanese arts of the generation before them.[23]

However, the 'empty narratives' of Ozu's films carefully avoid moral judgement and dogmatic closure. With minimal plots and no dramatic climax, his films reveal an obsession with cyclicality – of life events and seasons – rather than causality. The repetition of morning scenes and the invariable similarity of domestic interiors reveal his interest in the immutable impermanence of all phenomena. Ozu's art of the empty shot was praised by radical filmmaker Yoshishige Yoshida as the ultimate form of 'anti-cinema'.[24] Ozu's carefully framed interiors are spaces of absolute ambiguity. The opening scene of *Good Morning* (1959), for example, is a montage of sliding doors opening and closing in houses located in extreme proximity to each other. This confusion of thresholds creates an anonymous labyrinth in which neighbours seem to live in interchangeable homes. Reflecting on the uniformity of post-war life, *Good Morning* charts the quest for a television set by two children living in the standardized, mass-produced houses that spread rapidly across Japan in the period.

Despite the aesthetic unity of the domestic space and recurring patterns in the plot, Ozu's houses reveal a spatial anomaly described by Shigehiko Hasumi as the 'absent staircase'.[25] In Ozu's late films such as *Equinox Flower* (1958) and *An Autumn Afternoon* (1962), the staircase is never exposed. Although it is sometimes visible at the back of the corridor, it is deprived of any architectural function, giving the impression that the first floor is suspended in the air. Ozu's late films revolve around the psychology of ageing fathers and their soon-to-be-married daughters, whose bedrooms on the upper floor are deprived of any staircase access. This absent staircase is an 'invisible wall' dissociating characters in two distinct territories. Women vanish instantaneously in the empty corridor and reappear upstairs in a dissident space protected from the male gaze – a floating room in which they can remain twenty-five forever. The final, post-wedding scene in *An Autumn Afternoon* reveals a rare close-up of an empty staircase juxtaposed with the father drinking alone in the kitchen. Hasumi insists that the absent or empty staircase is neither a symbol nor a metaphor but the anti-lyrical materialization of an architectural void. By exposing the irrational ambiguity of the interior, Ozu distances himself from the so-called formalist purity and static detachment he is associated with. If the father in the home long formed a feudal metaphor for the emperor of the nation, Ozu subtly questions the patriarchal authority that maintains the unity of the house.[26]

* * *

The collapse of personal and national identity after the war led to a loss of faith in humanism. The recurring motif of disfigured corpses in a genre art critic

9

10

9 Still from *An Autumn Afternoon*, directed by Yasujiro Ozu, 1962
10 Still from *Equinox Flower*, directed by Yasujiro Ozu, 1958

11

12

11 Still from *Late Autumn*, directed by Yasujiro Ozu, 1960
12 Still from *An Autumn Afternoon*, directed by Yasujiro Ozu, 1962

Yusuke Nakahara has called 'locked-room paintings' reflects the on-going debate regarding realism. Deformed, dismembered human bodies stage an internal world cut off from social mechanisms.

Kiichi Sasaki commented that On Kawara's Bathroom series (1953–1954) present 'the abyss of loneliness, [where] humans are cut up mercilessly and dumped in a closet like junked machines, and in this way are turned completely into things. But then they come back to life by becoming homogeneous inorganic matter.'[27] In the aftermath of the human devastation of war, interrogations were necessary into the ontology of the self and its materiality. The emergence of a phenomenological discourse was embraced by Lee Ufan of the Mono-ha group (The School of Things), who believed that the human needed to transcend the controlling reality of industrial society. The illusion of identity called for a need to use materials as a vector of relationships between the interiority of the self and the externality of the world. Criticized by activist groups as an expression of apolitical mysticism, the need to find alternative forms of subjectivities was torn between the expression of human agency through the social protest of the political body and the liberation of the self through an introspective withdrawal.

The rapid growth of the country in the post-war era was characterized by the transformation of the economic and political structure of the country. As a result of the housing shortage after the war, collective housing rapidly developed in the suburbs of sprawling cities. In contrast, the individual house embodied the last surviving dream of ownership of the land – a conquest of the individual over the government and companies. In his text-manifesto 'A House is a Work of Art' (1962), architect Kazuo Shinohara distances himself from the mega-structures of urban planning produced by the Metabolists and presents the house as a weapon against the pragmatism of mainstream industry.[28] Against the increasing construction of functionalist buildings, Shinohara pioneered a vision of residential design as a form of art, a 'commentary' on the over-mechanization of society. Shinohara posits the home as being in opposition to the factory. As he explained: 'I believe that it will further become possible for the homes we create to offer a total view of what it is to be human'.[29]

The same year Shinohara published his manifesto (1962), Kobo Abe published *The Woman in the Dunes*,[30] a novel in which a traditional wooden house crumbles under the heavy weight of sand dunes while the imprisoned protagonist slowly disintegrates. The static wooden dwelling collapses under the mutable threat of the sand, illustrating the loss of humanity in the multitude. In the film adaptation by Hiroshi Teshigahara, the grainy texture of the sand sinking in the house is closely captured by the camera (image 13). Kobo Abe was exploring a new realism based on concrete matter which he defined as an existence 'outside of consciousness': matter is 'singular, unique, unstable, a spatial experience that defies or completely resists a common-sense understanding of space, and is fragmentary, never capable of totality'.[31]

The volatile, free-floating particles of sand stood for what Abe called the 'depths of the matter', a reaction to the atomic structure and the squeezing cells of the molecular urban landscape. In *The Embryo Hunts in Secret* (1966), filmmaker Koji Wakamatsu depicts Japan's apartment buildings (the *danchi*) as a claustrophobic agglomerate of endlessly multiplying carceral cells. The *danchi* is filmed as a panoptic machine of voyeurism monitored by a surveillance society.[32] The capitalist homogenization of space conveyed through the biological metaphor points to a growing loss of subjectivity.

The radical transformation of urban spaces in the late 1960s was stimulated by the unprecedented economic boom galvanized by the 1964 Summer Olympics and Expo '70 in Osaka. Under the reign of information terminals and a corporate mechanical world, in 1971 Toyo Ito created URBOT-001, his very first house. A combination of vernacular and industrial architecture,

13

14

13 Still from *Woman in the Dunes*, directed by Hiroshi Teshigahara, 1964
14 Toyo Ito, White U, 1976, interior, photograph by Koji Taki

the walls were clad with aluminium sheets and the interior made of timber. Aluminium House advocated incoherence and uselessness rather than rationality and functionalism. Ito considered the house the child of a persona he called Urban Robot. In his essay 'The Logic of Uselessness' (1971),[33] he anthropomorphizes his architecture as the birth of a malformed bastard, a useless member of society. In this way, the house personifies for Ito the irrational emotions that run counter to the illusionary fate of the alienated business man.

In his writing on White U (1976), a house built for Ito's sister and her two daughters following the tragic loss of her husband, the architect describes how its shape was informed by the corporeality and the warmth of human breath.[34] With no windows facing the street, the interiority of the house results from the contrast between the U-shape of the house, based on the fluid flow of air, light, and bodies, and the static courtyard of black soil. Looking for 'unanticipated outcomes', Ito saw the house as a musical score, a notation of 'morphemes' to compose changing shapes of light: 'Rather than transmitting the gloomy history of family life, what I want from a white wall is no more than a notation of the shapes of people casually leaping about'.[35] Photographs by philosopher and critic Koji Taki emphasize the white curved walls on which overlapping shadows of the young daughters play under spotlights resting on the floor (image 14).

The shadows do not convey an impression of theatrical immateriality but rather the opposite, reinforcing the corporeal materiality of the inhabitants. A founding member of influential photography group Provoke, Taki saw photography as an expression of materiality rather than subjectivity.[36] The only way to access the real existence is to let the 'body penetrate the elusive membrane of the phenomenal world'. As a hybrid of human and machine, the camera shows objects *outside* of the consciousness of the subject. Photography represents a naked world beyond the self: 'The world is woven out of the totality of anti-human and trans-human structure and the raw concreteness of individuals'.[37]

Ito was influenced by Taki's *Ikirareta ie* (The House as Living Experience, 1976)[38] in which he argues there is a wide gap between space as it is formed by lived experience and the abstract or 'lyrical' space of architecture. Ito claimed the twentieth-century individual has two bodies: 'The body as living experience is insufficient to satisfy us, so we always carry within us another body which is trying to break out of the former'.[39] In an information-driven world, Ito wanted to create an architecture for the extended body. In 1985, he created an installation for an exhibition in a department store in Tokyo that revolved around a nomadic girl drifting in hyper-consumerized society. His Pao: A Dwelling for Tokyo Nomad Women (1985) is inspired by the shape of huts in Mongolia. The flexible mobile furniture for dressing up, acquiring knowledge, and eating alone reflect Ito's vision of a de-centred architecture: 'Consider a person's house which forms a centre from where all communication or information is transmitted; it is something absolute. Being a nomad doesn't necessarily mean that the living space disappears or shifts, but it does mean that everything works in a decentralised way and in a mutual relationship.'[40]

Ito admitted retrospectively that he was initially cynical about the nomad girl and the way she immersed herself in fashionable urban life. However, he endeavoured to allow her to regain sensitivity, to give her a new reality in a futuristic urban life, to make her 'swim through the sea of consumption' to reach the far shore.[41] In his 1988 essay 'Dismantling and Reconstituting the "House" in a Disordered City',[42] Ito introduces the Pao as a space that fractures the traditional house and in which the protagonist is a liberated woman living alone. The Pao is a reaction against the stage-set television dramas and their fictional houses for fictional families. In the 1980s, the disassembling of the household was also the preoccupation of filmmakers Sogo Ishii and Yoshimitsu Morita, who released personal satires of the Japanese nuclear family. In Morita's *The Family Game* (1983), a stranger disrupts the family unit, revealing the failure of communication among its members who sit side by side on a large dinner table without facing each other. Liberating the pathologies resulting from social pressure, Ishii's *The Crazy Family* (1984) depicts the maddening absurdity of the middle-class ideal of the suburban home. As the family moves into their new house, the risk of a termite attack coming from the building foundations unleashes the paranoia of a family out of control (image 15).[43]

* * *

In his writing on Japanese art and architecture, philosopher Félix Guattari defines 1980s post-Metabolist architecture as involving a process of 'resingularization' against postmodernist imitations.[44] According to Guattari, the subject can only re-emerge through an expanded definition of the human hypersensitive to the environment. In architecture, the decentred perception of the anthropological gaze has emerged through what he called 'creative becomings', which are: the becoming-child, the becoming-vegetal, the becoming-animal, the becoming-non-object, and the becoming-machine.[45] At the time, the biological metaphor 'owned' by the Metabolists was being heavily criticized as promoting a hierarchical structure fuelled by capitalist needs: 'While metabolism intended to radicalize function, its structural model was the organic whole, based on hierarchy – stem (or spinal chord), branch, leaf, organ, cell', Isozaki and Asada write.[46] Similarly, as Thomas Daniell explains, Terunobu Fujimori was in opposition with Kisho Kurokawa's philosophy of symbiosis, suggesting the concept of 'parasitism' in which man-made things behave as parasitic to the natural world – an idea he would later materialize in his architecture through the wrapping of natural textures to cover a technological core.[47]

In the late 1990s, the formation of Atelier Bow-Wow led to the emergence of their theory on behaviour, reflecting their interest in the making of individual houses in the overcrowded city of Tokyo. The twenty-six-year life expectancy of a house in Japan meant that the dwelling had to adapt to accumulated layers of gaps and leftovers: 'The regeneration of houses would revolve not around a core, but a void – the gap space between buildings – and would be propelled by the initiatives of individual families, rather than the accumulation of central capital. Further distinguished from the "Core Metabolism" of fifty years ago, it is within the framework of "Void Metabolism" that the practice of designing small houses in Tokyo's residential areas is a clearly perceivable housing behaviour.'[48]

Embracing sociology, anthropology, and biology, Atelier Bow-Wow's interest in the relationships between nature, human life, and the built environment nurtured a method of study they call 'behaviorology'. This view, based on the observation of living things, ecology, and animal anatomy, is expressed by their signature style 'anatomy drawings' in which section perspectives deliver an empiric approach to materials and living patterns. The building must be conceived as more than the achievement of the mind of a human being, as inherited from the modernist scope: 'the realm of social relationships is expanded to include nature and the whole of the cosmos, resulting in a liberation of the human imagination'.[49] In their writings, buildings are compared to intelligent breathing creatures in search of happiness, who capture various fluxes, from the micro-phenomena of natural elements to the psychological states of human beings.

The idea of orchestrating 'ecological relationships' and various rhythms within the house resulted in a consciousness of the temporality of architecture:

15

16 17

15 Still from *The Crazy Family*, directed
 by Sogo Ishii, 1984
16 Ikimono Architects, concept drawing
 for Atelier Tenyanjima, 2011
17 Keisuke Oka, concept drawing for the
 Arimaston Building, 2005–

'The coordination of these different rhythms can result in various encounters: the past with the future, and the social with the natural, building up a spatial and temporal framework for positioning ourselves in the here and now. Such an overlay resembles the temporal arts, such as theatre and music, and relativizes compositional concepts from the twentieth century, influenced largely by the visual arts of painting and sculpture.'[50] The temporality of the compositional framework expands the concept of architecture to external circumstances and forces such as chaos (Sou Fujimoto), weather (Junya Ishigami and Ikimono Architects; image 16), or parallel time (Hideyuki Nakayama). Advocating that non-professionals should build their own house, Osamu Ishiyama's working method based on continuity and discontinuity along with his belief in improvisation, craftsmanship, and happy architecture influenced the birth of Keisuke Oka's Arimaston Building, which was begun in 2005 (image 17).

Digging the ground for a year and a half, Oka kept thinking about improvisation and his previous life as a Butoh dancer. Still under construction, the house looks like the scaffolding in a building site, with suspended wires, bags of sand, and no real partitions. As he explains, 'I want to discover things as I am building. By doing so, the building will become more and more alive.'[51] Oka keeps a You Tube diary to record the infinite process of self-built architecture. The decorative elements in concrete are casts from domestic objects, plants, and branches, reflecting the organic nature of the name Arimaston: *Ari* is the ant (earth), *Masu* is the trout (water), and *Tombi* is the kite (sky). In his writing on Butoh dancer Min Tanaka, Guattari compares the dancer to a 'body weather', a 'body assemblage' whose posture is neither horizontal nor vertical but transversal. The dynamism of the diagonal shifts the anthropocentric perspective: the dancer is 'wrapped-up like a building in machinic becoming, yet open to diverse "winds" that are formed by fluctuating matters in relation to which the dancer himself is decentred and into whose shifting relations viewers enter'.[52]

The profound relationship between client, architect, and architecture transforms the house into a network of sensitivities. In Moriyama House (2005), the life and behaviour of the client 'Mr Moriyama' overlaps with the architectural thinking of the architect Ryue Nishizawa. The environment of the house in the suburbs of Tokyo is teeming with little alleys, unpaved roads and gardens. Nishizawa was inspired by the specific context of this old residential area and enjoyed the sense in which plants and trees did not feel restricted to a specific property. The semi-anarchic layout of the area is neither a strict grid nor a random pattern. The client Yasuo Moriyama, whose family ran a liquor shop in this neighbourhood, decided to stop working and asked if the house could be divided into multiple units so he could rent some of it. Nishizawa responded with a house that is deconstructed, with individual rooms or suites of rooms that are split into separate buildings. The interspersed paths and courtyard form a checkerboard that challenges the conventional structures of dwelling. 'By dismantling the programs and dispersing them into several boxes', Nishizawa explains, 'the structures turn into a cluster and a concept of the environment or landscape begins to emerge.'[53] In fact, undoing the property generated a form of continuity with the urban fabric rather than a division. The house becomes an environment.

The presence of the owner 'Mr Moriyama' contributes to the elusive, ungraspable character of the house. While a house usually serves as a mirror of the client's status, profession, or activities, Moriyama House is defined by the anti-productivist attitude of the proprietor. Ila Bêka and Louise Lemoine's film *Moriyama-San* (2017; images 18, 19, 20) captures the vibrant artistic and literary inspirations of the owner, whose quiet personality is articulated through the books, films, plants, and garden life. The tiny objects and books on display in little corners, shelves, and steps of staircases within the home echo

18

19

18-20 Stills from *Moriyama-San*, directed by Bêka & Lemoine, 2017

20

Nishizawa's attraction to the 'elusive charm' of architecture studies piling up in his office, which he describes as 'a kind of indescribable hedonism': 'In giving shape to something shapeless, studies undeniably have a continuity from moment to moment, and it is this present-progressive form of creation itself from which architecture arises'.[54] Moriyama's intangible and indefinable life is one of a domestic flâneur who behaves in a similar present-progressive form and reflects Nishizawa's idea of a house as a manifestation of 'acentricity': 'It allows any place to become the center. One might say that this creates both a sense of always being at the center and a sense of multicentricity.'[55] Inspired by the city of Tokyo as a collection of living organisms, Nishizawa conceived the house as a community of little dwellings challenging the idea of ownership and family norms.

    Moriyama House anticipates Nishizawa's interest in the concept of 'plasticity' inspired by the release in 2008 of French philosopher Catherine Malabou's book *What Should We Do with Our Brain?*[56] The architect wished to create a house that would respond to the philosopher's study of the revolutionary discoveries made in neuroscience. While the flexibility of the brain has been appropriated as a mirror of the neoliberal management discourse, Malabou argues for its *plasticity* as a form of disobedience. She writes in her conclusion: 'To refuse to be flexible individuals who combine a permanent control of the self with a capacity to self-modify at the whim of fluxes, transfers, and exchanges for fear of explosion. To cancel the fluxes, to lower our self-controlling guard, to accept exploding from time to time: this is what we should do with our brain.'[57] The plasticity of the brain means it can not only adapt but also change existing circumstances in interaction with the surroundings. Nishizawa thus advocates 'a house with plasticity, not flexibility' as 'the ability to change positively and drastically, rather than just simply adapting to environmental changes'.[58] The architect believes in a house that does not adapt but fuels the 'courage to continue the process of destruction and creation, without compromising to the present situation'.[59] If our brain can change in the course of our lives, why shouldn't our houses?

21 Tosa Mitsunobu, *The Mayfly (Kagero)*,
Illustration to Chapter 52 of *Genji*
(Genji monogotari), sixteenth century

Endnotes

1. Kamo-no-Chomei, *Hojoki: Visions of a Torn World*, trans. Yasuhiko Moriguchi and David Jenkins (Berkley: Stone Bridge Press, 1996), 33.
2. '[So] many subsequent volumes published on Japanese domestic architecture focus on the production and design of homes that are empty of people and their possessions,' writes anthropologist Inge Daniels in *The Japanese House: Material Culture in the Modern Home* (New York–Oxford: Berg, 2010, reprinted 2011), 3.
3. Dana Buntrock, 'Katsura Imperial Villa: A Brief Descriptive Bibliography, with Illustrations', in *Cross-Currents: East Asian History and Culture Review*, 3 (June 2012). PDF available at https://cross-currents.berkeley.edu/sites/default/files/e-journal/articles/buntrock_biblio_lores.pdf. Accessed 2 Oct. 2016.
4. Murasaki Shikubu, *The Tale of Genji*, trans. Royall Tyler (New York: Viking Press, 2001).
5. See Masako Watanabe, 'Narrative Framing in the "Tale of Genji Scroll": Interior Space in the Compartmentalized Emaki', *Artibus Asiae* 58, 1/2 (1998): 116. doi: 10.2307/3249997.
6. According to Doris Croissant, seventeenth-century representations of Genji's consort, the Third Princess, reveal the ambivalent role of distinctly gendered ways of seeing the other sex. See her 'Visions of the Third Princess. Gendering spaces in "The Tale of Genji" illustrations', *Arts Asiatiques* 60 (2005):103–120. doi: 10.3406/arasi.2005.1533.
7. See note 1.
8. I owe the discovery of Chomei's hut to a conversation with curators Pippo Ciorra, Kenjiro Hosaka, and Chief Architectural Advisor Yoshiharu Tsukamoto in Tokyo, April 26, 2016.
9. Kamo-no-Chomei, 71.
10. Kamo-no-Chomei, 61.
11. Wajiro Kon, *Modernologio (Moderunorodio)* (Tokyo: Shunyo-do, 1930), reprinted in Wajiro Kon, *Introduction to Modernologio* (Kogengaku Nyumon) (Tokyo: Chikuma Shobo, 1987).
12. Wajiro Kon, 'Examination of Possessions of a Boarding Student II' (Geshukuzumi Gakusei Mochimono Shirabe II) in *Modernologio (Moderunorodio)* (see note 11, above), 218.
13. Wajiro Kon, 'Diagrams of Traffic in a House' (Jukyo naino Kotsu Zu) in *Modernologio Collection* (Kogengaku Saishu) (Tokyo: Kensetsu-sha, 1932), reprinted in Wajiro Kon, *Introduction to Modernologio*, 328.
14. Izumi Kuroishi and Jilly Traganou, *Design and Disaster: Kon Wajiro's Modernologio*, catalogue for the *Design and Disaster: Kon Wajiro's Modernologio* exhibition (held at the Arnold and Sheila Aronson Galleries, Sheila C. Johnson Design Center, Parsons The New School for Design, curated by Kuroishi and Traganou, March 13–March 27, 2014), 13. See Izumi Kuroishi, 'Visual Examinations of Interior Space in Movements to Modernize Housing in Japan, c. 1920–40', in *Interiors*, 2: 1, 95–123.
15. Yasufumi Nakamori, 'Ishimoto Yasuhiro's Katsura – reexamined and revisited', in *Katsura: Picturing Modernism in Japanese Architecture: photographs by Ishimoto Yasuhiro* (New Haven: Yale University Press, 2010), 20.
16. Hiroshi Misawa, 'The legacy of Antonin Raymond and Junzo Yoshimura for Modern Residential Architecture in Japan', *GA HOUSES*, 100 (Japan VI, 2007), A.D.A. EDITA, Tokyo, 51.
17. Yasufumi Nakamori, 20.
18. *Katsura: Tradition and Creation in Japanese Architecture* (Yale: Yale University Press, 1960).
19. German architect Bruno Taut's famous ethnographic travelogue *Houses and People in Japan* (1938) (reprinted in 1958 by Sanseido Company, Tokyo), promoted the idealized refinement, harmonious simplicity, and geometric proportions of the Japanese house.
20. Noël Burch, 'On Architecture', in *To the Distant Observer: Form and Meaning in the Japanese Cinema* (Berkley–Los Angeles: University of California Press, 1979), 200.
21. The key figures of the 'home drama genre' are filmmakers Yasujiro Ozu, Mikio Naruse, Yasujiro Shimazu, and Heinosuke Gosho. From the 1930s to the late 1950s, their films focus mainly on the relationships between family members, domestic space, and the changes occurring in Japanese society such as the changing role of patriarchal authority and the liberation of women. See Tadao Sato, 'The Family', in *Currents in Japanese Cinema* (Tokyo: Kodansha,1982), 139–144.
22. See Donald Richie, *A Hundred Years of Japanese Film* (Tokyo: Kodansha, 2001), 123; and *Japanese Cinema: Film Style and National Character* (New York: Anchor Books, 1971), 64.
23. On Ozu's post-war 'Japaneseness', see Richie, *Japanese Cinema: Film Style and National Character*, 70; and Richie, *A Hundred Years of Japanese Film*, 124.
24. Yoshishige Yoshida [also Kiju Yoshida], *Ozu's Anti-Cinema* (Ann Arbor: Center for Japanese Studies, University of Michigan, 2003).
25. See 'Habiter', in Shigehiko Hasumi, *Yasujiro Ozu* (Paris: Cahiers du Cinéma, 1998), 85–108.
26. Sato, 126.
27. Yusuke Nakahara, 'Locked-Room Painting' (1956), in *From Postwar To Postmodern, Art In Japan 1945–1989: Primary Documents*, edited by Doryun Chong, Michio Hayashi, Fumihiko Sumitomo, and Kenji Kajiya (Durham, N.C.: Duke University Press, 2012), 81.
28. Under the influence of Kenzo Tange, Metabolism was a group of architects and designers formed in the 1960s including Kisho Kurokawa, Kiyonori Kikutake, and Fumihiko Maki.

Their visions for future cities and strategies for flexible, transformable urban development responded to Japan's rapid economic growth after the devastation of war.

29 Kazuo Shinohara, 'A House is a Work of Art', in *From Postwar To Postmodern, Art In Japan 1945–1989*, 158.
30 One of the first English translations of Abe's novel was *The Woman in the Dunes*, trans. E Dale Saunders (New York: Random House, 1972).
31 Kobo Abe, 'For a new realism: the meaning of reportage' (1952), in *From Postwar To Postmodern, Art In Japan 1945–1989*, 45.
32 Mathieu Capel, *Évasion du Japon: Le cinéma japonais des années 1960* (Paris: Les Prairies Ordinaires, 2015), 262–275.
33 Toyo Ito, 'The Logic of Uselessness', in *Tarzans in the Media Forest*, selected and translated by Thomas Daniell (London: Architectural Association, 2011), 22–32.
34 Toyo Ito, 'White Ring' (1976), in *Tarzans in the Media Forest*, 33–34.
35 Ito, *Tarzans in the Media Forest*, 39.
36 *Provoke* was an experimental photography magazine published from 1968 to 1969 in the wake of violent waves of political protest in 1960s Japan. Photographers Takuma Nakahira, Yutaka Takanashi, and Daido Moriyama, critic Koji Taki, and poet Takahiko Okada were all members of the Provoke group. Rough, blurred, and out of focus, their subversive aesthetic advocated a new photographic expression against the establishment of objective photojournalism.
37 Koji Taki, 'What is Possible for Photography?' (1970), in *From Postwar To Postmodern, Art In Japan 1945–1989*, 217.
38 Taki Koji, *Ikirareta ie* (Tokyo: Tabata Shoten, 1976). The title of Taki's book could also be translated literally as 'the lived house'.
39 Toyo Ito, 'Blurring Architecture', in *Toyo Ito: Blurring Architecture 1971–2005* (Milan: Charta, 1999), 49–61.
40 Interview with Toyo Ito, *Shaking the Foundations: Japanese Architects in Dialogue* (Munich–New York: Prestel, 1997), 94.
41 Toyo Ito, 'A New Architecture is possible only in the Sea of Consumption' (1989), in *From Postwar To Postmodern, Art In Japan 1945–1989*, 360.
42 Toyo Ito, 'Dismantling and Reconstructing the "House" in a Disordered City', in Ito, *Tarzans in the Media Forest*, 69–71.
43 See Aaron Gerow, 'Playing with Postmodernism, Morita Yoshimitsu's *The Family Game* (1983)', in Alastair Phillips and Julian Stringer, eds., *Japanese Cinema: Texts and Contexts* (London–New York: Routledge, 2007), 240–249; and Tom Mes and Jasper Sharp, *The Midnight Eye Guide to New Japanese Film* (Albany: Stone Bridge Press, 2005), 70, 277.
44 Félix Guattari, 'The Architectural Machines of Shin Takamatsu', in *Machinic Eros: Writings on Japan by Félix Guattari*, ed. Gary Genosko and Jay Hetrick (Minneapolis: Univocal Publishing, 2015).
45 Guattari, 'Architectural Machines', 78.
46 Akira Asada and Arata Isozaki, 'From Molar Metabolism to Molecular Metabolism', in *Anyhow*, ed. Cynthia Davidson (New York: MIT Press / Anyone Corporation, 1997), 80–84, quoted by Thomas Daniell in *After the Crash: Architecture in Post-Bubble Japan* (New York: Princeton Architectural Press, 2008), 137.
47 Daniell, *After the Crash*, 143.
48 Atelier Bow-Wow, *Behaviorology* (New York: Rizzoli International Publications, 2010), 13.
49 Atelier Bow-Wow, *Behaviorology*, 11.
50 Atelier Bow-Wow, *Behaviorology*, 15.
51 Rumi Tomiya, 'Why does he continue all alone making a building with no blueprint? The quest of Keisuke Oka, creator of the Arimaston building', *Ignition Int*, September 2014. Article available at https://medium.com/ignition-int/why-does-he-continue-all-alone-making-a-building-with-no-blueprint-a2d11ecf3328#.9tevfr59v.
52 Gary Genosko, 'Pathic Transferences and Contemporary Japanese Art', in Félix Guattari, *Machinic Eros*, 123.
53 Ryue Nishizawa, *Tokyo Metabolizing*, ed. Koh Kitayama (Tokyo: TOTO Publishing, 2010), 88.
54 Ryue Nishizawa, *Studies by the Office of Ryue Nishizawa*, Contemporary Architect's Concept series 4 (Tokyo: LIXIL, 2015), 9.
55 Nishizawa, *Tokyo Metabolizing*, 82.
56 Catherine Malabou, *What Should We do with Our Brain?* (New York: Fordham University Press, 2008).
57 Malabou, *What Should We Do with Our Brain?*, 78–79.
58 Nishizawa, *Studies by the Office of Ryue Nishizawa*, 25.
59 Nishizawa, *Studies by the Office of Ryue Nishizawa*, 25.

Why Houses?
Kenjiro Hosaka

Why houses?
Japanese houses criticize. Though by no means large, they sharply criticize history, the surrounding environment, the city, the concept of family, and the architectural format itself. 'House' in this case refers to a 'single-family dwelling'. We think of a house as something that an architect designs in conjunction with a family – what they design is a method of living for the family, the smallest social unit, to connect with or maintain its distance from the larger society.

Of course, not every Japanese house is 'critical'. Many house makers attempt to differentiate the houses they design from those of others while keeping costs down, which leads to houses that are ostentatious and often lacking in taste, in turn creating (or destroying) the townscape. This is why a significant number of architects design critical houses and locate them in the city. Though the effect might be gradual, they believe that this will bring about a change there.

How are they able to bring about this change? Because there are an unimaginable number of houses made in Japan every year, a situation that stems from the family system implemented by the government after World War II (for details, see part 1 of Fujioka Hiroyasu's essay in this book). This is why the *The Japanese House* focuses on houses since 1945. Even today, many houses are being built in Japan – the total for the 2015 fiscal year alone was 920,000 (including multiple-dwelling complexes). Though this represents a drop of more than 40% from a peak of 1,630,000 houses in 1996, it is still a remarkable number when compared to other countries. For example, the number of housing starts (an important economic indicator) in the US was approximately 1,200,000 in 2015. Considering that Japan is home to 126 million people compared to America's 324 million, the number is truly staggering.

When Arata Isozaki was a graduate student, he and friends wrote an essay titled 'Long Live Small House Designs!' (1958)[1] under the pen name of Toshiya Yada. The paper included the following statement: 'Objective conditions changed around the time of the Korean War. As a result, small house designers and their works and theories ceased to function as the avant-garde.'[2] The government's 1956 *Economic White Paper* also suggested that 'the post-war era is over'.[3] It is important to note that the report was written at a time when post-war reconstruction efforts were beginning to stabilize. In other words, young people were convinced that architects should stop making post-war housing and move on to a new phase. Today, after sixty years, can we really say that that era has ended?

Some renowned architects, including Kenzo Tange, Fumihiko Maki, and Yoshio Taniguchi, almost never designed houses, but the majority of Japanese architects do. And the question we need to ask ourselves is 'why?' Is it because houses are the roots of architecture? That seems like a logical explanation, but, as Joseph Rykwert points out in *On Adam's House in Paradise*, it is surprisingly difficult to determine the roots of architecture. They might lie in a 'found cave' or they might lie in a 'made tent'. Or perhaps they are rooted in creating a space to protect oneself from the elements, or a space (or place) to pray. It is hard to know.

One thing, however, is clear. Though there might be stylistic differences in spaces used for prayer, a special importance is attached to convention. Houses by comparison are much freer. On the other hand, houses must satisfy the private desires of an absolute other (the client), and in this sense they are thoroughly restricted. Architects are clearly attracted by these contradictions. Moreover, in surveying every era and region, we find a nearly infinite number of resources to surmount these contradictions. The moment you decide to use a square in a plan, concrete as a material, or a bay window, you become part of a network of other houses, and the number of these networks is much greater than those generated by prayer spaces.

Why We Need a Residential Genealogy
Genealogy is the key element in *The Japanese House*, which sets out to analyze these complex networks. In this case, however, the word 'genealogy' does not refer to a method of historical research – it is not a question of authenticity or origin. Our focus is, instead, on so-called structural genealogy, a concept developed by Michel Foucault and informed by Nietzsche.[4] Genealogy is neither traditional history nor metaphysics; according to Foucault, the objective of genealogical history is not to rediscover our roots, but conversely to engage a persistent effort to disperse them.

More to the point, however, there is no single root or origin in Japanese houses. In discussing Japanese houses, many people are reminded of features such as *tatami*-mat floors and rooms partitioned with *fusuma* sliding paper doors or *shoji* screens, components that date to the *shoin-zukuri* style developed during the Momoyama Period in the late sixteenth century. This should nonetheless not be seen as the origin of Japanese houses, though, because the *shoin-zukuri* style would never have existed without the *shinden-zukuri* style of the Heian Period (794–1185).

Does this mean that the *shinden-zukuri* style constitutes the origin of the Japanese house? In the sense that the style hinges on fluid spaces with features such as wooden floors and makes use of thin, portable elements such as folding screens and bamboo blinds as partitions it certainly has parallels with contemporary houses. Using a garden to create a lifestyle integrated with nature (or artificially creating 'nature' and distributing it around the living space) were also aspects of the *shinden-zukuri* style, so comparing it to a contemporary house like Ryue Nishizawa's Moriyama House makes sense. On the other hand, it does not make sense to locate the origins of Japanese houses in a style that required an expansive lot and was designed for aristocrats.

Can we instead uncover the origins of Japanese houses in the dwellings of common people such as farmers and fishermen? These pit dwellings were used for centuries, from the prehistoric Jomon Period to the Heian Period, and were made by digging into the ground, erecting dug-standing pillars, and covering them with a large roof that reached down to the ground. A work like Makoto Tanijiri's Primitive Living in Saijo (2007) is a clear reference to these pit dwellings, but it would be difficult to argue that this style was the origin of Japanese houses because it can be found in many parts of the world.

In addition to the lack of a definite origin, the influx of Western architectural concepts and styles in the late nineteenth century led to drastic changes, making it even more difficult to determine the exact lineage of Japanese houses. When we come into contact with an unfamiliar culture, we have a tendency to search for the origins of something as a way of achieving a deeper understanding. The search for origins, however, is often futile. Consider an individual – each of us has a seemingly infinite multitude of ancestors, and the fact that we are living in this particular time and place is simply the result of a long sequence of accidents. The same is true for houses.

This is where genealogy comes into play. Yoshiharu Tsukamoto, who served as an academic adviser for this exhibition, offers the following explanation about the genealogy of houses: 'By introducing a temporal axis to the housing typology and tracing the changes, you can compare actual structures to determine what has changed and what has not'.[5]

A genealogy of houses places parentheses around things such as what the architect said at the time the work was completed and how the house was evaluated at the time (or later on). It attempts to understand what kind of critical relationship the house had with other houses, and to extract it from this complex network.

Here is an example. Due in part to its tower-like form, Tower House (Takamitsu Azuma, 1966) was originally viewed as a small individual fortress attempting to oppose the big city. But is this really the case? Today, having been buried beneath many other buildings, it is no longer a tower soaring above the city. There were other tower-like houses, such as Chicken Coop (Isamu Kujirai, 1973) and Crow Castle (Eiji Ebihara, 1972), built during the same period, but it would be difficult to argue that the potential of this approach has been carried on in the present day. Today, the things that appeal to us about Tower House are the rough, natural texture of the concrete, and the rich dialogue it creates with the surrounding city. There is little doubt that at least as far as the texture is concerned, the architect would agree – despite the fact that this may not have been a theme that seemed worthy of much attention at the time.

The goal of this genealogy is to shed light on the characteristics of things that have become buried in a clichéd discourse. In this essay, I will concern myself with the networks that connect thirteen genealogies of houses.[6] To be more precise, I will employ a matrix based on three periods defining the horizontal axis (1945–1970, 1970–1995, and 1995–2015), and a vertical axis based on three categories: 'style', 'city', and 'industry'.

By referring to this typological matrix, we should be able to determine what was important in each period. For instance, 'style' and 'industry' were the important trends from 1945 to 1970, and 'style' and the 'city' from 1970 to 1995. 'Style' and the 'city' were also important from 1995 to 2015, as was a fusion of the two. Needless to say, there were also changes in the platforms that supported architectural practice. The first period, for example, was marked by the formation of groups and associations like the New Architects' Union of Japan (NAU), the second saw the rise of magazines such as *Toshi jutaku* (Urban House), and over the last two decades various loose associations between individuals have grown out of projects and symposiums.

Next, I would like to present a brief overview of the critical spaces that have emerged from the three trends of style, city, and industry.

Industry

During post-war reconstruction, architects designed housing prototypes based on a sense of duty. The use of building methods such as prefabrication and assembly – as seen in works like PREMOS (Kunio Maekawa, 1946–1951) and Yotsuya Kano House (Junzo Sakakura, 1950) – suggested the potential for mass production, but unfortunately these approaches did not prove to be a success. Though it was essential to create a system of mass production that included marketing, architects remained indifferent to such concerns.

They were better at proposing ideal models. House No. 3 (Kiyoshi Ikebe, 1950) and Masuzawa House (Minimum House) (Makoto Masuzawa, 1952) are prime examples. And as with SH-1 (Kenji Hirose, 1953), there were also attempts to standardize and normalize new materials (which in this case meant light-gauge steel). In many instances, however, the houses had the undeniable quality of a handmade article rather than an industrial product.

Architects did not simply design actual houses – developing concepts for houses was also a key part of their work. The *Feudalism of Japanese Houses*[7] by Miho Hamaguchi (who might be seen as Japan's first female architect) is a particularly notable example. In Hamaguchi's analysis, Japanese houses of the past had been designed to allow the members of one family to receive the members of another (in other words, houses were based on a patriarchal, feudalistic notion). Moreover, Hamaguchi proposed that the *tokonoma* (alcove) be eliminated and the term *genkan* (threshold) be replaced with the more neutral *deiriguchi* (doorway). The late 1940s were an era of women's liberation (the first female Diet member took office in 1946), and woman's freedom from the home was also an important theme for architects.[8]

In the end, one might say that the people who were actually responsible for post-war housing prototypes were the so-called 'house makers'. Japan is unusual in that it is one of the few places in the world where prefabricated houses or 'prefabs', assembled on-site out of factory-made components, proved to be such a successful business. One distinctive feature of the industry is the involvement of automobile companies (Toyota Home) and electronics manufacturers (PanaHome, which is part of the Panasonic Group). Sekisui Heim, which produced Sekisui Heim M1 on the advice of the young researcher Katsuhiko Ono, was originally a division of the Sekisui Chemical Company.

Ultimately, the houses produced by this industry shaped people's ideas of what a house should be. Though many architects and some clients tried to resist this tendency, the majority of the houses were mediocre and kitsch. One person who attempted to deal with this face-to-face was Kazunari Sakamoto. Sakamoto addressed the situation in his doctoral dissertation on architectural images.[9] His research, which set out to understand the average person's architectural preferences and desire in reference to own their own home, concluded that it was pointless to simply criticize consumer society. In 1989, Toyo Ito published an essay titled 'A New Architecture is Possible Only in the Sea of Consumption'.[10] These concerns led Sakamoto and Ito to become involved in the Is Prêt-à-Porter project undertaken by the house maker Sekisui House from 1989 to 1992 (other participants included Kunihiko Hayakawa, Tsutomu Abe, Itsuko Hasegawa, Yoshihiro Masuko, and Hiroshi Naito).

House makers have also been subjected to criticism. A case in point is Osamu Ishiyama's book *Thinking about Houses from an Akihabara Perspective* (1984),[11] where the author alleges that the lack of transparency in housing production and distribution, and the overemphasis on image, wrongfully led houses to become big-ticket items. Moreover, he argues that just as you could obtain electronic parts in Akihabara (a district of Tokyo known for its electronics shops) and build your own radio and other electrical appliances very cheaply, you should be able to build cheaper and stronger houses. Ishiyama's ideas have lost none of their power, as evidenced by an intriguing work like the Arimaston Building (Keisuke Oka, 2005–). Kyohei Sakaguchi, one of Ishiyama's students, also proposed the idea of a 0-yen house, inspired by his research on homeless people's 'houses'. This led him to produce a prototype for a 'mobile house', which he patented and provided to the public through books.

While recognizing the importance of such idealistic and anti-establishment ideas, most people are really looking for something that is easy to understand and comfortable, and when it comes to actually building a house, they do not always have a clear idea about what they want. Though some people might harbour a vague sense of dissatisfaction about house makers and the opaque nature of the industry, for the most part their feelings do not quite extend to the Akihabara level.

The Box House series (Kazuhiko Namba, 1995) might initially seem rather plain, but one might say that they are new houses designed for this kind of person. The series makes use of an easily comprehensible form (a box) and a clear concept (a single-room house). In addition, the use of completely standardized components and construction methods keeps the cost reasonable. As a result, the architect can design a house even if the client only has a vague idea what they want, and the client can develop their own image of the family as they occupy and live in the house. In fact, to order the house, the client must take the fairly large step of deciding to move the family into a one-room house with a large atrium. The key point is that the prototype has been developed to such a degree that this decision does not seem like such a big step.

At this point, I should say something about the earthquake because it is extraordinary times like these that lead to greater standardization in houses. Japan is an earthquake-prone nation, and in recent years we have experienced two major disasters – the Great Hanshin-Awaji Earthquake of 1995 and the Great East Japan Earthquake of 2011. Temporary houses are built after a disaster strikes, but the cost and specifications are determined by the Ministry of Land, Infrastructure, Transport, and Tourism. This only allows for housing that can be built quickly, is stable, and lasts for a few years, and the entire order is therefore filled by an industrial group. Due to the fact that the stricken area in the Great East Japan Earthquake was not in the city, and a large number of temporary houses were needed, wooden units unlike anything in the past were installed through the co-operative (and largely volunteer) efforts of local governments, builders, and architects. This project, propelled by people with on-site capabilities and undertaken in a regional area rather than an urban centre, promises to exert an influence on the future standardization of houses.

Style

After the war, in the midst of an increased need for housing and an abruptly Westernized lifestyle, architects began to re-examine Japanese-style spaces and structures by fusing them with Western modernist architecture.

There were also architects who turned to concrete, a material that was both old and new, as a familiar rather than a foreign element in people's lives. Though it was originally uncommon to use concrete for small houses, this changed when many Japanese cities were reduced to ashes in the war. For example, the fact that most of the buildings that survived the atomic bomb in Hiroshima were made of reinforced concrete apparently led to a new confidence in the material. As this might suggest, it is important to remember that the use of concrete in Japanese houses was not simply related to form, but also to content, and that is to how the houses behaved.

While on the one hand a new sensibility emerged in regard to Japaneseness and materials used in the construction of houses, during the period of high-economic growth that continued from the mid-1950s to the mid-1970s, traditional Japanese *minka* (private houses) began disappearing all over the country.[12] It was during this period that Teiji Ito published *Minka Were Alive* (1963).[13] In the book, Ito notes that the *sukiya-zukuri* style of residential architecture, which was influenced by teahouses, was based on a layout that made it similar to contemporary architecture. At the same time, Ito points out that minka were based on a logical, column-and-beam structure. In effect, he analyzed the architectural value of *minka*.

The reappraisal of architecture such as *minka* that were designed by anonymous architects became a worldwide trend. Bernard Rudofsky's 1964 text *Architecture Without Architects*[14] was translated into Japanese in 1976, and in 1966 Mayumi Miyawaki launched a series of design surveys, the first of which focused on Kurashiki in Okayama Prefecture. In the 1970s, the focus of such fieldwork, which had recently been rediscovered, extended to foreign countries, most notably the surveys architect Hiroshi Hara conducted in Asian and African villages. Among the graduate students who assisted him in this project were future architects Riken Yamamoto and Kengo Kuma. The surveys inspired Yamamoto to approach houses from a schematic perspective as a collection or rooms rather than a physical form, and the results are evident in a work like House in Okayama (1992).

This interest in foreign houses was rooted in a push toward stylistic relativization, and was in turn related to the playful spirit of postmodernism. Strictly regulated applications – such as repetition, nested structures, and symmetry – have a tendency to alienate the people living inside a structure, but the interior plans in such houses are actually quite conservative. In the first decade of the twenty-first century, architects overrode these regulations to create interior spaces that were simultaneously logical and emotional.

While interest in architecture all over the world led to the frequent use of the word 'vernacular', this focus was tinged with a kind of exoticism. In Japan, there has been an awareness that this turn to the 'vernacular' is often limited to superficial stylistic concerns rather than engaging with the inherited knowledge and skill contained within traditions. Japanese architects of the twenty-first century are trying to reinterpret the vernacular as a database of nature-related wisdom. In some cases, the city is conceived as a form of nature,[15] and an effort is made to apply the wisdom of nameless architects, and the wisdom that has been ceaselessly maintained, albeit non-verbally, in the community to give shape to an appropriate townscape. In other words, vernacular concerns are used to form links with the environment and buried in the landscape instead of highlighting them.

The City

While on the one hand architects re-examined Japaneseness after the war, there was also an effort to standardize materials, building methods, and floor plans in order to build large numbers of houses. During this period, there was a need for architects who were also enlightened historians and technicians.

But in the 1970s, as the housing industry began producing houses with a superior performance, there was no longer any place for technicians. And with the rapid relativization of style, there was no longer any compelling reason to re-examine Japaneseness.

In these circumstances, Kazuo Shinohara proposed a new kind of architect. Exemplified by the axiomatic, declarative statement, 'A house is a work of art', Shinohara attempted to model the architect after a mathematician or thinker (it should be noted that he made no effort to make the architect an artist).

House in White (Kazuo Shinohara, 1966) is in effect a dialogue between history and technology: the tile-covered pavilion roof is reminiscent of the traditional Japanese *minka*, but when you walk inside you find that the eaves are painted white; the interior contains a central pillar, but there are no beams (though they are not visible inside, the roof is actually supported by diagonal members rather than beams); and the house eschews the column-and-beam or framework structure found in traditional Japanese architecture. While referencing history and technology to construct an abstract space, Shinohara adopted a method that was completely at odds with them.

Interiors are not the only things that have been abstracted, however. Houses, for example, are disconnected from their surroundings – the city – and Shinohara himself declared that he had no interest in either the site or the client's opinion. The interiors that emerge from this viewpoint are not only extremely abstract, but are reflective spaces that encourage the resident to consider a variety of things. This explains why so many of Shinohara's clients were artists and writers. Ignoring practical concerns such as comfort, Shinohara's methods, which stressed aesthetic values based on canonicity, might be seen as an example as what Alexandre Kojève referred to as 'Japanese snobbery' (he used the expression about traditional arts like tea ceremony and *ikebana* in his *Introduction to the Reading of Hegel*[16]). In later years, Shinohara also made works like House under High-Voltage Lines (1981), in which the interior space is boldly regulated in correlation with an invisible force (the house had to be built within a circular range determined by the high-voltage power cables overhead). In other words, the more Shinohara became aware of the magnetic power of the urban context, the more thoroughly he ignored it in his quest to attain an autonomous space. In trying to create a correlation with this situation, Shinohara chose to boldly regulate the space without any concern for inconvenience or ugliness.

Architects born in the 1940s – such as Tadao Ando, Toyo Ito, and Itsuko

Hasegawa – engaged in an aggressive criticism of the city with houses made up of self-sufficient, closed spaces. For example, in a 1973 text titled 'Urban Guerrilla Housing', Ando referred to one of his houses as 'a guerrilla hideout'.[17] Fumihiko Maki, part of an older generation, called this a movement of 'stray samurai' in an essay published in 1979.[18] It is interesting to note that while Ando's discussion appeared in *Toshi jutaku* (Urban House), a magazine that had been launched a few years earlier in 1968, Maki's appeared in *Shinkenchiku* (New Architecture), a historic publication that dated back to 1925. In contrast to *Shinkenchiku*, which dealt solely with trends in Japanese architecture, there were magazines such as *Kenchiku bunka* (Architectural Culture, 1946–2004), which saw architecture as culture and introduced various foreign trends, and *SD* (Space Design, 1965–2000), which focused on a wider range of interests, including the city, art, and design. Based on the existence of these publications, the 1970s were an era in which architectural criticism reached new heights. Koji Taki's *Lived-in Houses*, published in 1976,[19] exerted a particularly strong influence on architects of the period.

The architects who became physically entwined with the city were part of the generation who followed the 'stray samurai'. This included the Iryuhin Kenkyujo (Research Institute for Things Left Behind), formed in 1968 by a group of students from Isozaki Arata's seminar at Musashino Art University (Tokyo) who remained active until 1974. In 1969, one of the group's members, Tomoharu Makabe, began making 'urban frottages' in which he collected various textures from the city by making rubbings of things like street surfaces, manhole covers, and the walls of buildings.

By the late 1960s and the early 1970s, the problem of isolation and the city was no longer limited to architecture. For example, *The Ruined Map*, a 1967 novel by Kobo Abe,[20] is renowned for its thematization of, to paraphrase the author, 'becoming free in the city' rather than 'becoming free from the city'. Abe explored this theme further in his 1973 novel *The Box Man*,[21] where the protagonist places a box over his head to prevent anyone from looking at him. At the same time, he divests himself of all social attributes and reaches the point (or perhaps it is merely an illusion) where his existence is determined by the gaze of the city. If the box is a metaphor for the smallest possible house, the Box Man might well be a distorted being who attempts to irrevocably blend inner life and home.

White U (Toyo Ito, 1976) can be seen as an architectural attempt to turn an interior space into something mental. The house was designed for a family composed of a widow and her two daughters. Ito, the woman's younger brother, created a space that shut out any view from the outside, and gave rise to pools of light in various places around the house. This space, which could only be called sensorial, was part of a reactionary tendency in the 1970s, an era of continued high-economic growth, and the first decade of the twenty-first century, an era in which society became increasingly information-driven.

There are also architects who are fond of lightness. House in Kuwabara, Matsuyama (Itsuko Hasegawa, 1980), for example, is a bold attempt to embrace lightness through the use of an industrial material (punching metal). In another work, A Small Bathhouse in Izu (Kengo Kuma and Satoko Shinohara, 1988), the architects set out to create a contemporary barracks that is also semantically light by combining a traditional, anti-urban material such as bamboo with an industrial, urban material such as galvanized iron. In the 1980s, this type of lightness often involved a correlation with the material.[22] The 2010s saw an even greater desire for lightness with a closer correlation to the city. Examples include House in Rokko (Yo Shimada, 2012), which attempted to make a connection between a residential space that was separated from the ground and the urban landscape below by mediating the sightline; and Garden and House (Ryue Nishizawa, 2013), in which living plants and people had an equal relationship in the city.

To return to a slightly earlier period, the 1990s saw the revival of an urban-core movement in the wake of the collapse of the bubble economy of the 1980s. Unable to purchase large lots, clients were forced to build houses on what could only be described as 'gaps' of land, which led to the birth of even smaller gaps. But this was not as grievous as it might sound. The city is an aggregate where gaps and buildings are organically entangled and enmeshed, making it unclear which is the figure and which is the ground. The situation is akin to a Giambattista Nolli map. The important thing is to take note of these gaps and give them meaning – there have been many attempts to design houses based on this viewpoint since the late 1990s. This approach attempts to connect us to the city by using gaps as an intermediary. Another approach set out to re-evaluate *machiya*, a traditional type of house that is connected to the city without any gaps. The methodology was rooted in the fear that the townscape, made up of towering houses from the bubble era, was in danger of being destroyed.

The primary difference between a city and a farming village is that the former is a social space formed by a collection of nuclear families and individuals who are living away from 'home'. The fact that the residents do not strive for a unified set of values or take any particular responsibility for the context plays some part in the destruction of the townscape. On the other hand, the city is a space occupied by a collection of people searching for a family that is not based on blood ties and for a new style of working. All houses have to do is stimulate and sustain this type of human dynamism and create a connection with the city. Resolving these issues necessitates further study of residential genealogy.

Endnotes

1. Toshiya Yada, 'Shojutaku kenchiku banzai! (Long Live Small House Designs!)', in *Kenchiku Bunka* (Architectural Culture) (Tokyo: Shokokusha, April 1958), 4–9. This essay was included in the April 1958 issue of *Kenchiku bunka* (Architectural Culture) whose feature was titled 'Problems with Small House Designs'. This issue also contained 'White Paper on Small House Designs' (11–15) by Kiyoshi Ikebe, and 'Can Architects Make a Living by Designing Houses?' (43–44) by Kazutoyo Ueda, the Research Institute of Architecture (RIA), which expressed an opposing view from Isozaki's.
2. Toshiya Yada, 'Shojutaku kenchiku banzai! (Long Live Small House Designs!)', in *Gendai kenchiku gusakuron* (An Essay on Contemporary Architecture is a stupid stunt) (Tokyo: Shokokusha, 1961), 26.
3. Economic Planning Agency of Japan ed., *Showa 31 nendo Nenji Keizai Hokoku* (Economic White Paper of the year 1956) (Tokyo: Shiseido, 1956), 42.
4. See Michel Foucault, 'Nietzsche, Genealogy, History', *The Foucault Reader*, ed. Paul Rabinow (New York: Pantheon, 1984), 76–100.
5. Yoshiharu Tsukamoto, 'Commonality in Architecture', *Commonalities: Production of Behavior* (Tokyo: LIXIL, 2014), 13.
6. Of course, discussing every type of Japanese post-war house based solely on these thirteen genealogies is impossible. Unfortunately, it was necessary to exclude works such as Lambda House (Research Institute of Architecture, 1960), Matsukawa Box (Mayumi Miyawaki 1971, 1978, 1991), and Hara House (Hiroshi Hara, 1974), which were important in terms of the history of Japanese residential architecture but did not fit into the genealogies.
7. Miho Hamaguchi, *Nihon Jutaku no Hokensei* (The Feudalism of Japanese Houses) (Tokyo: Sagami shobo, 1949).
8. Incidentally, in the late 1950s Hamaguchi designed stainless steel sinks for the large number of apartment buildings constructed by the Japan Housing Corporation; these sinks became an even more popular symbol of modern living than light-gauge steel and atriums.
9. Kazunari Sakamoto, *Images and Its Function in Architecture: On the Role of Images in Architectural Space and the Function of the Architectural Images in Society* (Ph.D. dissertation: Tokyo Institute of Technology, 1983).
10. Toyo Ito, "Shohi no umi ni hitarazu shite atarashii kenchiku ha nai (A New Architecture is Possible Only in the Sea of Consumption)," *Shinkenchiku* (New Architecture), no. 64, Shinkenchiku-sha, Tokyo (November 1989): 201–204.
11. Osamu Ishiyama, *Akihabara kankaku de jutaku wo kangaeru* (Thinking about Houses from an Akihabara Perspective) (Tokyo: Shobunsha, 1984).
12. In 1966, the Agency for Cultural Affairs conducted a National Emergency Survey on *minka*, and a project to preserve these houses was launched in the 1970s.
13. Teiji Ito, *Minka wa ikiteita* (Minka Were Alive) (Tokyo: Bijutsu Shuppan-sa, 1963). This book was based on a ten-volume series of photo books called *Japanese Minka*, which was published by Bijutsu Shuppan-sa from 1957 to 1959. The photographs were taken by Yukio Futagawa, who would later become the publisher of the magazine *GA* (Global Architecture), and the texts were by Ito. *Minka Were Alive* was a revised version that only included the texts.
14. Bernard Rudofsky, *Architecture Without Architects: A Short Introduction to Non-Pedigreed Architecture* (Albuquerque: University of New Mexico Press, 1964).
15. As this refers not to nature itself but to things that naturally exist in a place, the Japanese word *shizen*, which corresponds to 'nature', is often used in Japan.
16. Alexandre Kojève, *Introduction to the Reading of Hegel*, ed. Allan Bloom, trans. James H Nichols, Jr (Ithaca, New York: Cornell University Press, 1980), 158–159; original in Alexandre Kojève, *Introduction à la lecture de Hegel* (1947; Paris: Gallimard, 1979), 434–435.
17. Tadao Ando, 'Toshi Gerira Jukyo (Urban Guerrilla Housing)', Toshi jutaku (Urban Housing) special issue no. 7307, Kajima Publishing, Tokyo (July 1973): 18–19.
18. Fumihiko Maki, 'Heiwa na jidai no nobushitachi (Stray Samurai in a Peaceful Time),' *Shinkenchiku*, Shinkenchiku-sha, Tokyo (October 1979): 195–206.
19. Koji Taki, *Ikirareta ie* (Lived-in Houses) (Tokyo: Tabata Shoten, 1976).
20. Kobe Abe, *The Ruined Map*, trans. E Dale Saunders (New York: Vintage International, 2001).
21. Kobe Abe, *The Box Man*, trans. E Dale Saunders (New York: Vintage International, 1974).
22. Kuma is an architect who strives for semantic lightness, and his spirit is clearly evident in his statements and texts. Take, for example, *Jutaku ron: Jusshurui no Nihonjin ga sumu jusshurui no jutaku* (Ten House Theories: Ten Types of Houses for Ten Types of Japanese People) (Tokyo: Toso shuppan, 1986). As the subtitle suggests, the book divides Japanese houses into ten types and analyzes what kind of person would want to live in them. For example, a person who hires an architect to design a house wants a house, but at the same time they want to engage in intelligent communication with the architect. The fact that the pronunciation of the book's Japanese title is the same as Kazuo Shinohara's important work *Jutaku ron* (House Theories) (Tokyo: Kajima Publishing, 1975) suggests that it is a kind of polemic. In another book, Kuma expresses an extremely candid view of Row House in Sumiyoshi (Tadao Ando, 1976), which might be seen as a form of resistance to the city. Kuma says that when he saw a bunch of tennis rackets hanging on the wall of the house, he felt disappointed by the work's lack of urban resistance.

Houses

Japaneseness

In the years that followed Japan's defeat in World War II, the centrality of tradition in Japanese architecture became uncertain. For many, tradition was tainted by its associations with nationalism and the catastrophe wrought by the state's wartime activities. In 1955, however, tradition re-entered public discourse as part of a debate between architects, artists, critics, and historians – the so-called *dento ronso* (tradition debate). The wide-ranging debate was perhaps motivated by the rekindling of Japanese patriotism and pride after the 1952 treaty of San Francisco saw the end of the seven-year Allied Occupation and the restoration of Japan's national sovereignty.

Central to the debate in architectural circles was the question of which historical style could represent Japanese tradition in the modern age. One was *shinden-zukuri*, a style associated with Heian-period palace architecture and characterized by raised floors and open spaces. Another was the style of rural houses (*minka*), which typically contained earthen floors topped with sturdy columns and large roofs. Whereas the former originated in aristocratic society and bore an affinity with the modernist preference for transparency and geometry, the latter originated in the agricultural and samurai classes and related more to the pit-dwellings of Japan's prehistoric Jomon period (10,500–300 BCE). The concept of traditional Japanese space in the middle of the twentieth century came to waver between two possibilities – one that seemed to anticipate modernist architecture, the other that traced its roots to a prehistoric time before even the introduction of rice cultivation in Japan. Would the revival of tradition entail a synthesis with Western modernism, or a return to unique roots without recourse to Western influence? Much of the debate occurred in the pages of *Shinkenchiku*, which during the 1950s focused both on contemporary and historical Japanese architecture. Both Kenzo Tange and Noboru Kawazoe (the magazine's editor), made a plea for the importance of *shinden-zukuri* in contemporary design, while Seiichi Shirai powerfully advocated the rougher, more rustic and 'Jomonesque' spirit of *minka*.

On the one hand, in Kenzo Tange's own house (1953) the light and open quality of *shinden-zukuri* was reinterpreted through modern architectural methods – the raised first floor, extensive *engawa*, and *tatami* flooring continuous throughout the space could be said to aspire to the same unrestricted nature and uniformity of Mies van der Rohe's architecture. Similarly, Kiyoshi Seike's modular, minimal houses of the 1950s offered an eloquent example how the light, transparent qualities of *shinden-zukuri* could be incorporated into a modern design philosophy. In the House for Prof. K Saito (1952), the way the house projects over its concrete foundations gives it a sense of floating reminiscent of palace architecture, despite the house's humble scale. This synthesis inflects even the smaller details of the house, particularly the movable *tatami* mats raised on casters, which allowed the resident to strike a happy balance between Western, chair-sitting lifestyles, and the floor-sitting behaviours of Japan.

In Seiichi Shirai's House in Kureha (1965), meanwhile, an alternative interpretation was offered, characterized by an earthy, textured, and closed quality very different to that proposed by Tange or Seike. Featuring low flooring, limited openings, thick columns, and plastered earthen walls in the place of *engawa*, raised flooring, and other elements of *shinden-zukuri* architecture, the house is neither open nor light. Rather, it is as if columns have been erected and a floor built on top of the pit of a prehistoric pit-dwelling. Utilizing the language of 'Jomon-ness', Shirai demonstrated that 'Japaneseness' could be drawn on to very different ends than the light, clean modernism of other architects of his generation.

The ideological debate between the advocates of *shinden-zukuri* and *minka* architecture were not the only terms with which Japaneseness was debated. Antonin Raymond's own house and studio (1951), for example, appears thoroughly Japanese, with its use of wood, its single story, and its emphasis on the horizontal, but within this framework he made a number of significant alterations that assumed an American or Mediterranean lifestyle in which the relationship between interior and exterior is fundamentally altered. Between the living and dining room is a covered, semi-outdoor space which formed the backdrop for a photograph of Raymond and his wife enjoying an outdoor meal. This use of the exterior space for dining marks a significant departure from the traditional Japanese *engawa*, transforming it into something more like the European loggia. A Japanese structure thus becomes modified by the Western behaviours of the residents. This point of contact between divergent behaviours and traditions was also explored in Tsutomu Ikuta's House with Chestnut Trees (1956), in which a wing of Japanese-style rooms and one of Western-style rooms converge on a semi-exterior space which once again combines *engawa* and veranda. The veranda area, which the architect envisioned as a continuation of the Western-style rooms with Western-style furniture, has a low handrail while the *engawa* does not. This space therefore ensures the connection between the two spaces is smooth, facilitating an act of mediation between two cultures that might otherwise collide.

Antonin Raymond
Raymond House and Studio in Azabu, 1951

1

In 1949, Czech-born American architect Antonin Raymond and his wife Noémi (a designer of interiors, furniture, and textiles) returned to Tokyo from America, where they had spent the war years. Raymond intuited that the most effective response to the post-war housing crisis would be based on a synthesis of Western modernism with Japanese craft. His own house offered a clear example of the potential of simple, efficient design using effective, readily available materials. The house incorporated traditional Japanese carpentry, but the structure was built with the kind of unplaned, lightweight logs known as *ashiba maruta* that were usually used only for scaffolding. Raymond's design was based on *ken*, a Japanese module derived from *tatami*, which he identified as a local (and thus easily communicable) equivalent to modular design. The Raymonds admired the openness of the Japanese house to nature, and throughout the building they utilized translucent sliding screens covered in paper (*shoji*) while also incorporating a paved, sheltered terrace like those found in many American homes. The humble minimalism of the design expresses what Noémi Raymond called the 'efficient beauty' of Japanese houses – 'do away with what you do not need and let the necessary things be simple and beautiful'.*

Location: Minato, Tokyo (demolished)
Total floor area: 541.2 m^2

1   Noémi and Antonin Raymond dining on the terrace
2   Detail of paving
3   Dining room leading to terrace
4   Exterior with living room (left) and terrace (centre)
5   Dining room leading to terrace

*   Noémi Raymond, 'On the Design of Interiors' (1953), republished in Kurt G F Helfrich and William Whitaker, eds., *Crafting a Modern World: The Designs of Antonin and Noemi Raymond* (New York: Princeton Architectural Press, 2006), 306.

2

3

4

5

Kiyoshi Seike
The House of Prof. K Saito, 1952

1

The post-war period saw an increasing preference for the Western-style division of rooms in Japanese houses, prompting Kiyoshi Seike to design a series of minimal houses that advocated the continuing effectiveness of the multi-use, open floor plan of Japanese homes for modern living. The House for Prof. K Saito is a simple, wooden-frame structure raised atop a concrete podium, with one end cantilevered above ground level. Within the walls, two raised *tatami* rooms flank a wide, open living room floored in wood. Seike used minimal partitions on the interior to create a fluid relationship between the spaces, while sliding doors can be opened in order to establish a high degree of continuity with the outside. One of Seike's most distinctive inventions was a moveable furniture unit topped with four *tatami* mats which performed as a multi-use device which could bridge the gap between the floor-sitting lifestyles of Japan and the Western use of chairs and tables. This simple and portable design also allowed for the flexible reorganization of space. The architect's quiet designs were influential for their simultaneous internationalism and introversion, based on a deep appreciation for Japanese craft (especially wood joinery) and a cosmopolitan engagement with the developments of European architecture.

Location: Ota, Tokyo (demolished)
Total floor area: 71 m²

1   Exterior
2   Man sitting on *tatami* unit, viewed from exterior
3   Living room with movable *tatami* unit and Western-style chairs

2

3

Kenzo Tange
A House, 1953

1

For Kenzo Tange, the return to tradition involved not a nostalgic attachment to the past but a dialectical process of creation. His own house formed an early instance of his synthesis of Japanese history with the expressive vitality of late modernism. The building was raised dramatically above the ground, a device that simultaneously recalls the *piloti* of the international style and the raised platforms of Ise Grand Shrine and Katsura Imperial Villa, the paradigmatic classics of Japanese architectural history. (Tange would later publish books on both these buildings, implicitly casting them as historical precedents for his own work.) The house, unusually for Tange, was a wood-frame structure. In an explicit rejection of the Western arrangement of domestic spaces, it consisted of one undivided, *tatami*-floored room – nevertheless furnished with a mixture of Japanese objects and mid-century Western furniture. The abstract grid of Tange's plan for the house indicates that for the architect it was not altogether clear where Japanese space ends and the modernist 'universal space' of Mies van der Rohe begins. The house thus forms an eloquent argument for the idea that in Japan tradition was already modern.

Location: Setagaya, Tokyo (demolished)
Total floor area: 140 m²

1 Exterior
2 Interior with Akari lamp by Isamu Noguchi
3 Site plan
4 Kenzo Tange and his family outside of house, next to ceramic figurine by Taro Okamoto
5 Interior, with Kenzo Tange sitting on a lounge chair of his own design (T-7304KY-NT)

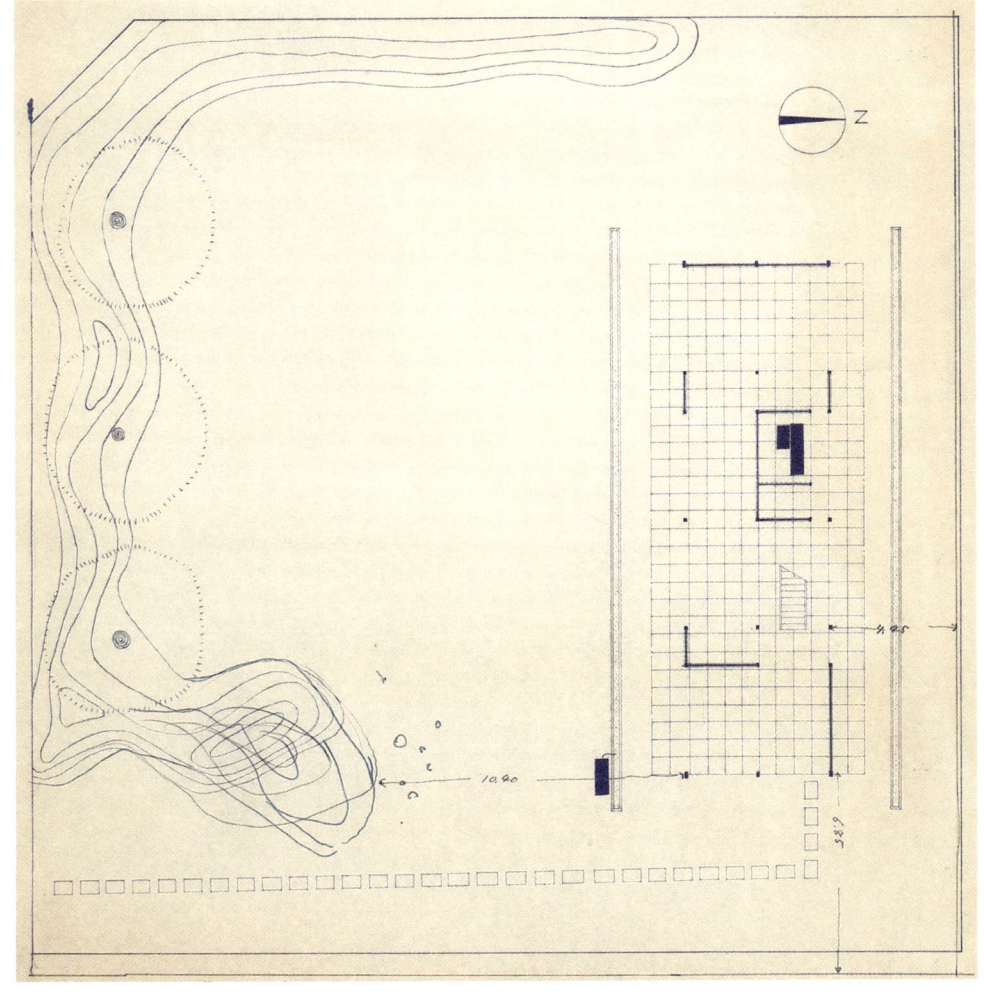

2

3

4

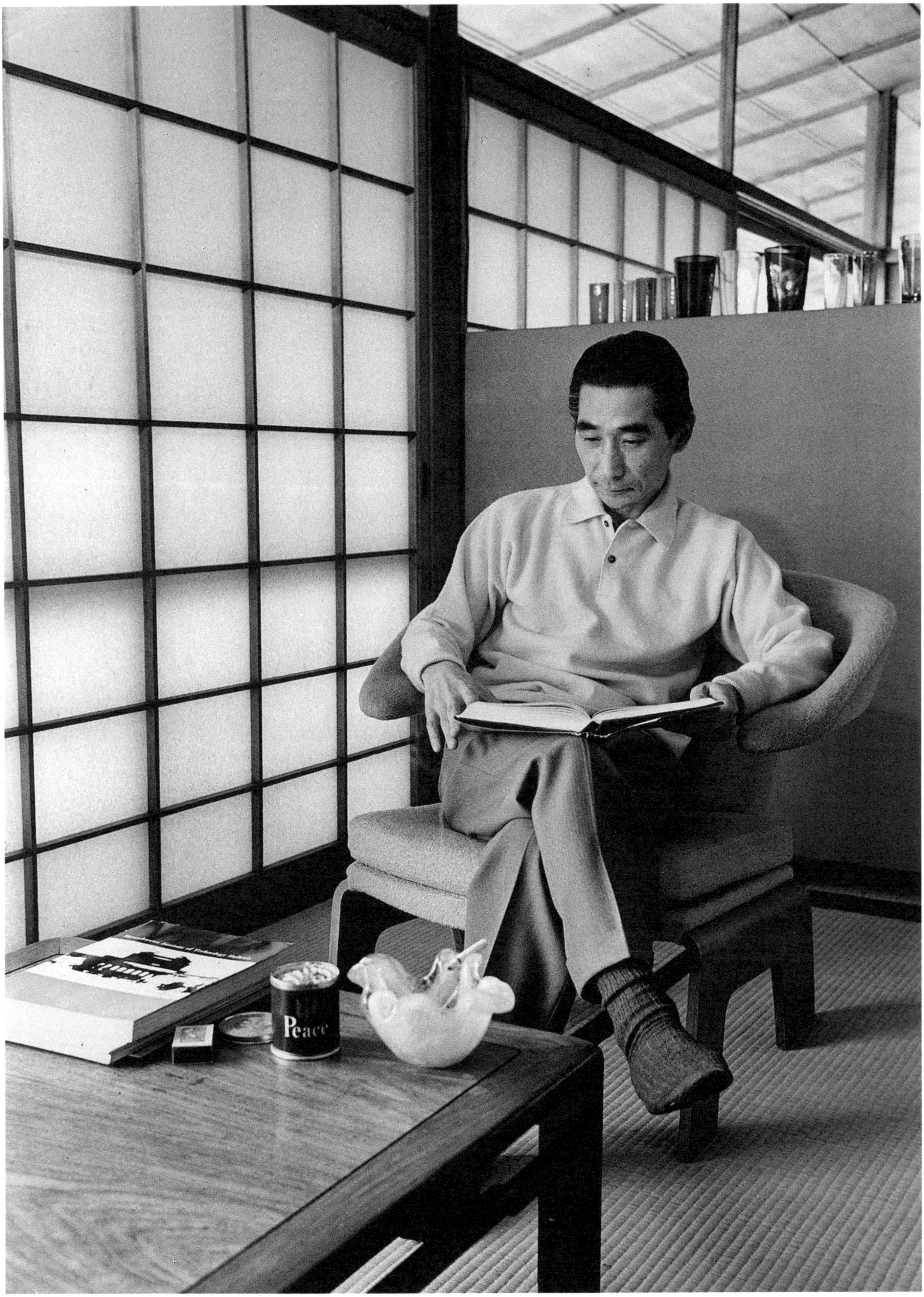

5

Tsutomu Ikuta
A House with Chestnut Trees, 1956

1

The house is a one-storey, wooden residence built in the west of Tokyo. It consists of a large space and a smaller one arranged in an L shape, each covered with a gabled roof. Ikuta's task (he had translated Lewis Mumford into Japanese and was an admirer of Frank Lloyd Wright) was to combine a modern lifestyle with the traditional form of a Japanese house. The larger space gathers the most 'public' part of the house – entrance, living, and dining areas and the kitchen. The smaller space houses the two bedrooms (both Japanese style) and a children's room (Western style). The two parts of the house are both facing the garden and are connected by an L-shaped terrace, again divided into two sections. The roughly square section facing the public space is a so-called 'Western-style' terrace with a handrail. The long, narrow section facing the private space is a Japanese-style terrace, or *engawa*, and does not have a handrail. Through this terrace, built around a chestnut tree, Ikuta brings together the heterogeneous duplets of public and private, Western and Japanese, in a way that seems perfectly natural. In 1968, when the latest trends in Western architecture were introduced in Japan, this building, concealing a strong will within its simple, taciturn form, was re-evaluated as a residence strongly tied to the Japanese tradition.

Location: Koganei, Tokyo (demolished)
Total floor area: 79.4 m²

1 Exterior, showing terrace leading to Western-style (left) and Japanese-style (right) rooms
2 Floor plan
3 Western-style living room viewed from *engawa*

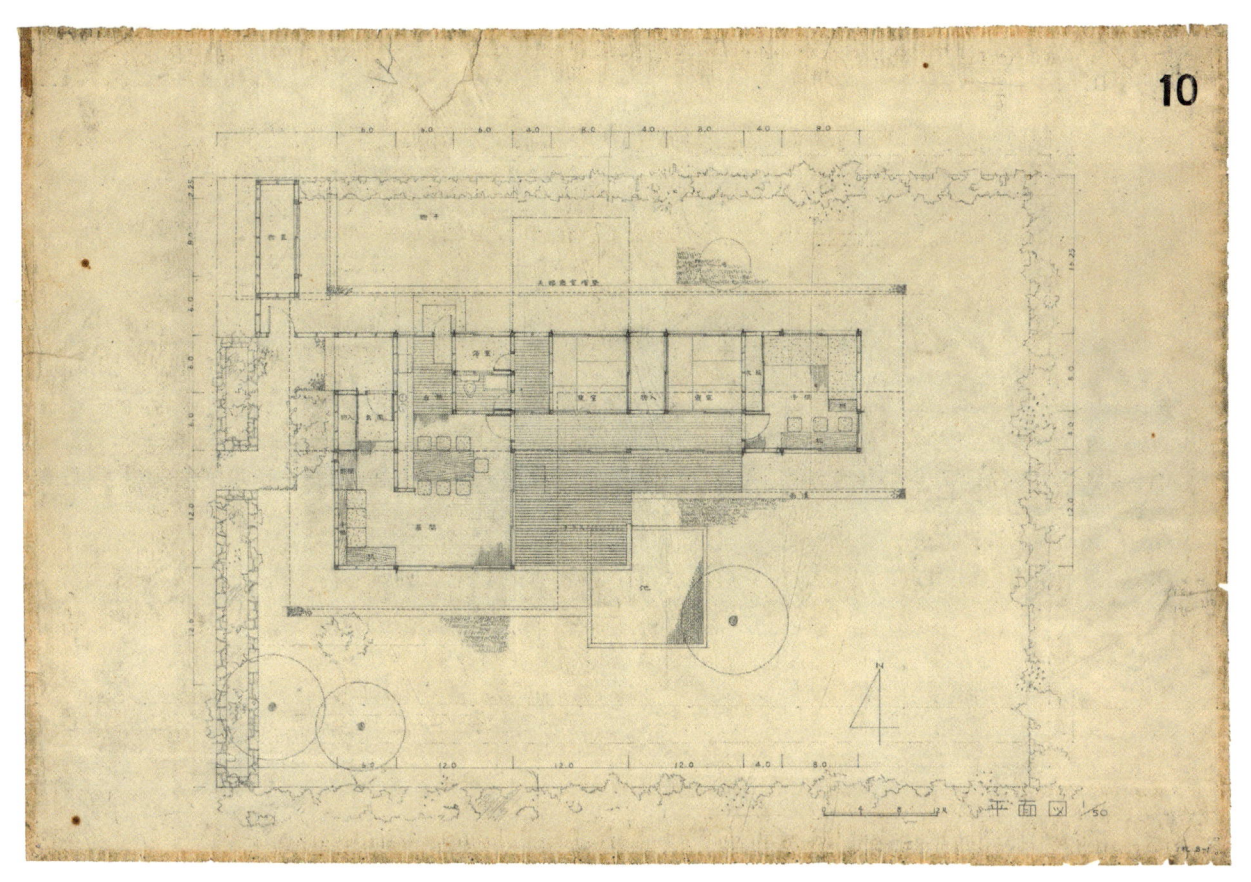

2

3

Seiichi Shirai
House in Kureha, 1965

1

The House in Kureha consists of separate, low-lying buildings containing the main house, gatehouse, and study. The main house sits only 18 cm from the ground, and has an *inubashiri* (a narrow, semi-open terrace-like area) covered in pebbles as well as short, round chestnut columns supporting deep eaves. In the study, a tiled floor is accompanied by a raised *tatami* area and a thick, almost fluted column. With its weighty columns, solid proportions and emphasis on varied, earthy textures, the house evidences the architect's interpretation of tradition from a perspective that is neither abstract nor functionalist, but emotive and material.
A devotee of Kantian philosophy, Seiichi Shirai studied philosophy in Heidelberg in the 1930s, where he explored not the modernism of the Bauhaus but the sublime interiors of Gothic cathedrals. During the tradition debate of the 1950s, Shirai objected to the ways in which Japanese tradition had been co-opted by various groups – the Imperial state who had employed it for nationalist propaganda; the modernists who had retrospectively interpreted it in terms of geometry, abstraction, and simplicity; and finally the Europeans who imagined a kitsch *japonica* privileging subdued delicacy and refinement. He argued for an understanding of tradition as a 'desperate pulsation' within the human spirit, a dynamic and living force that could be sourced in neither typological forms nor superficial details.

Location: Toyama, Toyama
Total floor area: 252.9 m²

1   Main house, detail of exterior column and eaves
2   Study, view of raised *tatami* area with *tokonoma*
3   Main house, view of garden from *tatami* room
4   Floor plan of study
5   Main house, view of guest room

2

3

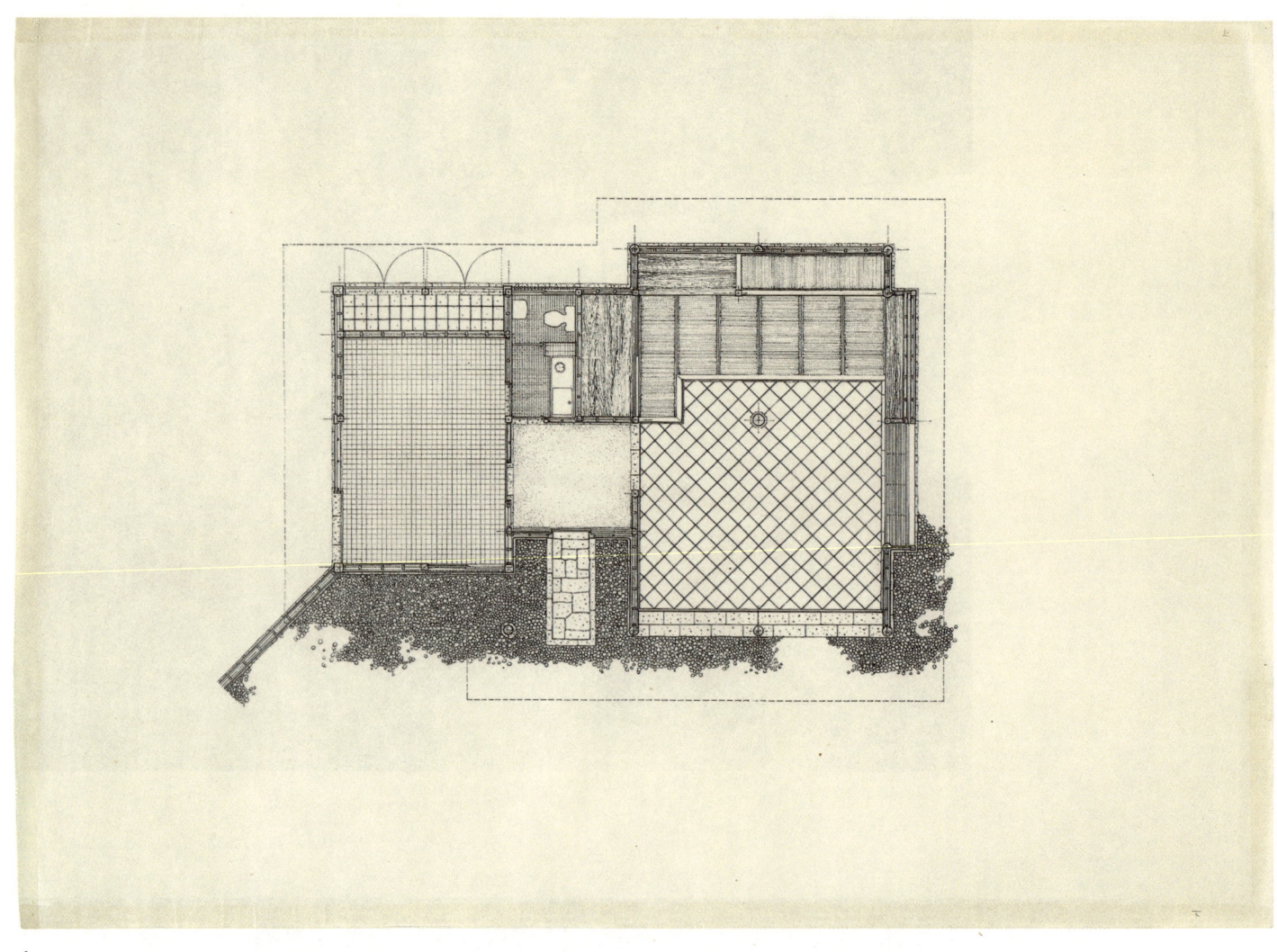

4

5

Mass Production

In 1945, as Japan surrendered to defeat in World War II, the nation was faced with a housing shortage of critical proportions. The war's effect on Japanese infrastructure was calamitous, and approximately fifty per cent of Tokyo had been destroyed by US firebombing. Across the country, an estimated 4.2 million houses had been lost. People sheltered in makeshift, temporary structures; to rebuild itself, Japan had no choice but to develop an efficient, cost-effective method of rehousing the population.

    Many notable architects directed a considerable amount of effort towards reconstruction and housing, determining that the solution to the housing crisis lay in standardized, modular design using prefabricated elements. There were international precedents for this strategy. The second Congrès internationaux d'architecture modern (CIAM II) in 1929 had revolved around the theme of the 'minimum' dwelling – a housing form that could meet the needs of its occupants with the minimum means, deploying industrial technologies and methods to do so. In the report they submitted to the conference, Le Corbusier and Pierre Jeanneret proposed the efficiency of Taylorist and Fordist methods of production as precedents for a new approach to functional, economical design. It is no coincidence, then, that two of Le Corbusier's former employees – Kunio Maekawa and Junzo Sakakura – were at the forefront of establishing a form of minimum housing suitable for the Japanese context. Both architects developed strategies for prefabricated houses that build on wartime infrastructure and technologies – Maekawa's PREMOS, for example, was assembled from wood panels produced in a factory that had manufactured wooden airplanes for the war effort.

    While the discussions at CIAM II had mainly been concerned with multiple-dwelling housing complexes, however, the Japanese focused primarily on freestanding, single-family homes. This established a tradition within modern Japanese architecture that was to strongly influence the development of Japanese cities throughout the twentieth century. In the 1960s, the concepts of prefabrication, standardization, and technology were explored theoretically by the architects of the Metabolist group – particularly in the work of Kisho Kurokawa, who famously proposed the idea of a 'capsule' architecture composed of small-scale standardized transportable units from 1969 onwards. Prefabricated housing flourished once again in the 1970s, meeting the housing demands of the baby boomer generation as they reached working age. Sensing a gap in the market, various companies entered into the housing industry, including Toyota and Panasonic. In 1970, the Sekisui Chemical Company, a manufacturer of plastics, commissioned Katsuhiko Ono to create Sekisui Heim M1, an important example of prefabricated architecture.

While Japanese architects have been at the forefront of prefabricated, mass-produced housing, however, there has been considerable resistance among much of the Japanese public for the products of these experiments, due largely to a widespread preference for customized, individualized homes. Alongside more rigorous experiments in standardization, therefore, there has developed a trend for factory-made houses with an emphasis on customization and stylistic difference from competing products, much like other commodities.

Kunio Maekawa
PREMOS (Prefabricated Housing), 1946–1951

1

A former employee of both Le Corbusier and Antonin Raymond, Kunio Maekawa was a central protagonist of Japanese modernism. Maekawa was increasingly frustrated at the lack of adequate housing in the country, arguing that not only were there not *enough* homes but that the houses that did exist were stylistically and functionally retrogressive. Maekawa had a chance to put his criticisms into practice when he was contacted by the Manchurian Aircraft Company for advice on how to use San'in Manufacturing, one of their factories that had been made redundant after the war. The first two PREMOS units were completed in 1946, each with a floor area of 52 m² and three individual rooms. The houses were constructed from self-supporting honeycomb panels, designed by structural engineer Kauru Ono, which were covered in plywood sheeting. They were produced throughout the 1940s, primarily as housing for Occupation soldiers, railroad workers, and miners. Manufacturing, however, was plagued by problems including scarcity of materials, labour disputes, and inadequate technology, and the program ended around 1951.

1   Exterior of PREMOS model 721, housing for workers in Urahoro coal mine, 1950–1951

Junzo Sakakura
Yotsuya Kano House, 1950

1

Between 1931 and 1939, Junzo Sakakura worked in the Paris office of Le Corbusier and, alongside Kunio Maekawa and Takamasa Yoshizaka, was pivotal in transmitting the central principles and practices of international modernism to the Japanese context. During the war, he was commissioned by the Japanese Imperial Navy to produce various prototypes for prefabricated wartime structures, including factories and barracks. His designs were based on drawings of temporary wartime shelters by Charlotte Perriand, Le Corbusier, and Jean Prouvé, which were gifted to him by his friend Perriand when she visited Japan in 1940. In the post-war period, he adapted these designs to housing, most notably in the 1950 house he designed for Hisa-akira Kano, the first governor of the Japan Public Housing Authority. Facing material shortages, the house incorporates a lightweight wooden A-frame that bears much of the house's weight and so utilizes minimal materials. The house could be assembled and even disassembled relatively easily, exemplifying Sakakura's lucid and rational practice, which emphasized clean lines, simple composition, and efficient production.

Location: Shinjuku, Tokyo
Total floor area: 60 m²

1 Exterior
2 'War Assembling Architecture', list of types

戰建 0001

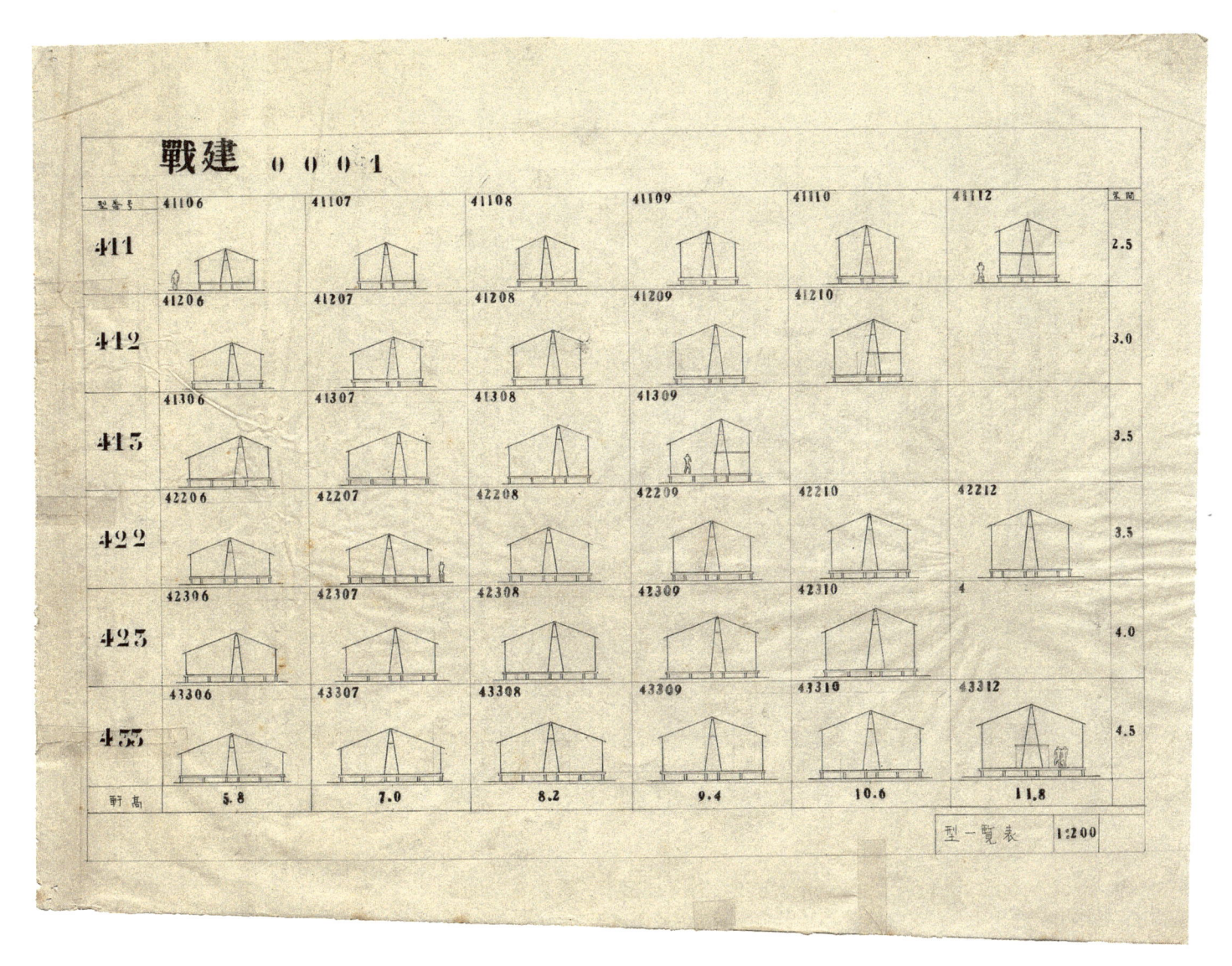

型番号	41106	41107	41108	41109	41110	41112	桁間
411							2.5
	41206	41207	41208	41209	41210		
412							3.0
	41306	41307	41308	41309			
413							3.5
	42206	42207	42208	42209	42210	42212	
422							3.5
	42306	42307	42308	42309	42310		
423							4.0
	43306	43307	43308	43309	43310	43312	
433							4.5
軒高	5.8	7.0	8.2	9.4	10.6	11.8	

型一覧表 1:200

Kiyoshi Ikebe
Residence No. 3, 1950
Residence No. 76, 1965

1

As Japan underwent rapid modernization in the twentieth century, traditional units of measurement such as the *shaku* were considered ill-suited for an emergent industrial nation. Varying from region to region, they resisted the standardization necessary for industrial production. In the post-war period, Kiyoshi Ikebe led the way in formulating a simple, standardized national module, which was for him an essential prerequisite to improving living standards and achieving a solution to Japan's housing problem. In his Residence No. 3 (1950), he employed a 3 m module based on the work of European modernists. Applying this module three-dimensionally, he designed a minimal house with built-in desks, windows, stairs, and kitchen facilities in a Western style (facilities intended by the architect to alleviate housework and improve the living standards of women in particular). His economical designs were partly an attempt to contradict the prevailing belief that Japanese-styles houses were cheaper and easier to construct than Western houses. As Japan's economic base shifted from industrial manufacture to information technologies at the close of the 1960s, architects began to move away from an interest in modular design towards a more image-oriented architecture, and the concept of the module was dismissed as restrictive and technocratic. Ikebe continued defending the importance of a modular approach, and with houses such as Residence No. 76 (1965), with its serpentine configuration of hexagonal units, he demonstrated that modular design could form a functional framework for an expressive, human architecture.

Residence No. 3
Location: Shinjuku, Tokyo (demolished)
Total floor area: 47.9 m^2

Residence No. 76
Location: Nerima, Tokyo (demolished)
Total floor area: 85 m^2

1   Residence No. 3, exterior
2   Residence No. 76, exterior

2

Makoto Masuzawa
Masuzawa House (Minimum House), 1952

1

The Housing Loan Corporation, established by the government in 1950 to assist landowners to build their own homes, only awarded loans to houses with a building area of 15 *tsubo* (around 50 m²) or less – a figure retained from post-war restrictions on construction due to material shortages. Responding partly to these constraints, Makoto Masuzawa explored the absolute minimum size for a home, developing an experimental prototype for a house of just 9 *tsubo*. His design for his own home emphasizes standardization and simplicity, formed of a cube measuring 3 × 3 *ken* (a traditional Japanese measurement for buildings) with a low pitched roof. Within this cube he arranged an open-plan kitchen-living space, bedroom, and small bathroom on the ground floor, with dining room and study on a mezzanine first floor. A central void spans the height of the building, allowing for a sense of openness within otherwise constrained dimensions – Masuzawa made use of sliding *shoji* screens on the exterior in order to further open up the space. The house sat on a spacious 660 m² plot of land, but its clever handling of space within a minimal volume has become an important precedent in recent decades for architects confronted with the severe space constraints of contemporary Tokyo.

Location: Shibuya, Tokyo (demolished)
Total floor area: 49.5 m²

1 Exterior
2 Ground floor interior
3 Ground floor, viewed from mezzanine
4 Section drawing

2

3

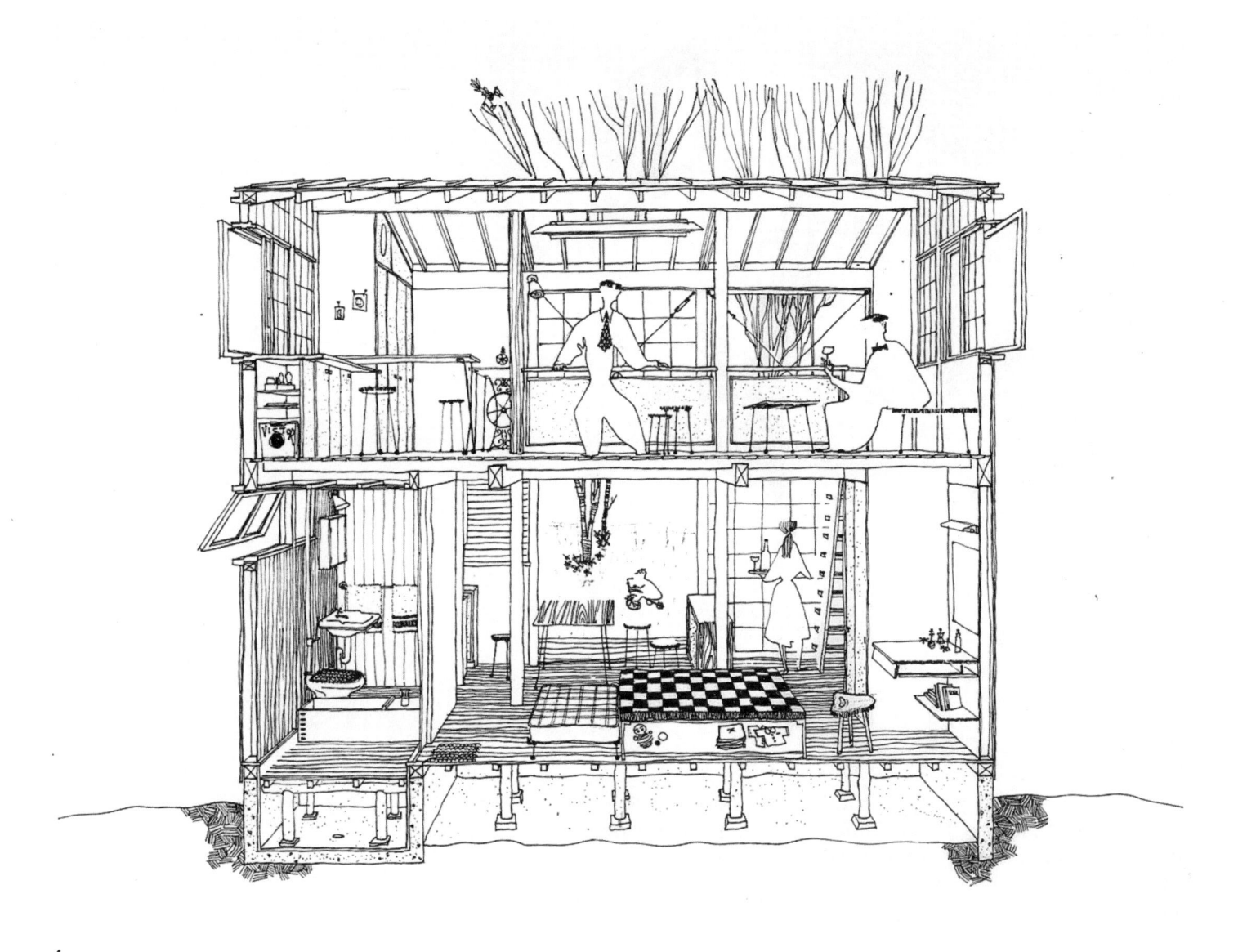

4

Katsuhiko Ohno
Sekisui Heim M1, 1970

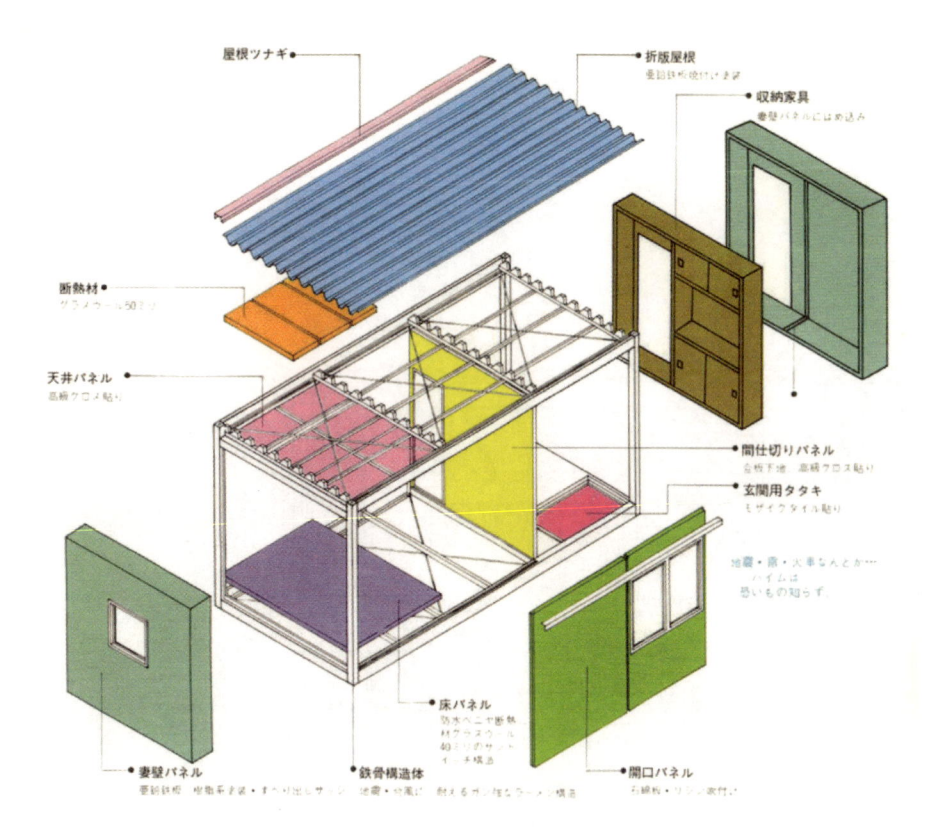

1

The post-war housing shortage had led to the introduction of policies that facilitated the construction of housing on a massive scale, a trend that would continue well after the end of post-war austerity and right through the years of rapid economic growth in the 1950s and 1960s. In 1970, Katsuhiko Ohno criticized this situation, which had prioritized quantity over quality and had, for the most part, created an inferior built environment ill-suited to the needs of most people. Commissioned by the Sekisui Chemicals Company to design a prototype for a mass-produced house, he attempted to attain the highest levels of durability, comfort, and practicality with minimal costs. His system consisted of modular steel boxes that could be simply stacked to produce larger units. In order to establish a highly efficient process, as much as possible of the units' production was brought into the factory – the savings were then redirected to improve the house's performance in terms of durability, warmth, and earthquake resistance. The rigidity of the production process allowed for more flexibility on the part of the consumer – the units could be configured into houses of various sizes or affixed to pre-existing architecture, while their nondescript interiors formed a blank canvas for customization. Today, Sekisui House is the leading prefabricated house manufacturer in Japan, and approximately 10,000 homeowners still live in Sekisui Heim M1 units.

1,2 Promotional brochure for the Sekisui Heim M1

自動車生産と同じベルトライン方式 ―――
工場生産比率じつに95％
日本で初めての
ルームユニット工法です。

ルームユニット工法をひと口でいえば箱型のユニットを構造・内外装・設備いっさいを含めて、工場で生産し、現場に輸送し、ユニットをつないで住宅をつくる方法です。

**広さ13.2㎡（4坪）の
ルームユニットを工場生産。**

住まいは、リビングルーム、キッチン、サニタリー（トイレ・浴室）などのパブリックスペースと書斎、寝室、子供部屋などのプライベートスペースによって構成されます。

これらを機能別に、それぞれ独立したユニットとして工場で完成し、建築現場で連結して、一軒の住まいをつくりあげようという考え方です。

ルームユニットの規格は、巾2.4m・長さ5.6m・高さ2.7m。広さは13.2㎡（4坪＝8畳）です。

鉄骨構造体に、屋根・床・天井・間仕切りの各パネルを組みつけ、次ぎに内装を仕上げます。厨房セット、浴室、トイレなどの諸設備、電気配線、給排水配管までいっさいを組みこみ、部屋ごとそっくり、工場でつくりあげてしまうのです。

完成したユニットは、厳しい最終検査のあとで、工場から建築現場へトレーラー1台に1ユニットずつ乗せて、運ばれます。あらかじめ基礎打ちされた現場では、設計プラン通りにユニットとユニットを接続するだけ――据付け・仕上げ工事だけなら、わずか3日間ですみます。

トレーラーで
運んで
クレーンで吊って…
家づくいの
気苦労はありません。

Kisho Kurokawa
Nakagin Capsule Tower, 1972

1

In 1969, Kisho Kurokawa – the youngest of the Metabolist architects – envisioned the emergence of *homo movens*, a society based on perpetual movement and information exchange. His polemic 'Capsule Declaration'* announced an architectural form for this mobile society – the capsule. Three years later, the Nakagin Capsule Tower was erected over just one month in Tokyo's lively Ginza district. The structure consists of two central 'cores' containing stairwells and elevators into which 144 concrete capsules (each measuring 2.3 × 3.8 × 2.1 m) were attached by four bolts. The capsules were prefabricated by a company that had previously produced shipping containers, and were designed so as to be easily replaced with newer models in the future. They were intended for suburban salarymen working in central Tokyo, who would use them during the week. For Kurokawa the tower was a herald of things to come: 'the landscape of future cities will be determined not by expressways or skyscrapers, but by a colossal aggregation of individual unit spaces'. Furthermore, the capsule would 'institute an entirely new family system centred on individuals [. . .] The housing unit based on a married couple will disintegrate.'**

Location: Ginza, Tokyo
Total floor area: 3,091 m²

1 Exterior
2 Capsule interior, with bathroom

* *SD*, no. 3 (March, 1969).
** Kisho Kurokawa, 'Capsule Declaration' (1969), quoted in Rem Koolhaas & Hans Ulrich Obrist, *Project Japan: Metabolism Talks* (Cologne: Taschen, 2011), 388–389.

2

Kazuhiko Namba
Box Series (1–140), 1995–

1

Kazuhiko Namba's Box Series is an ongoing attempt to produce an efficient, effective, and environmentally sustainable design methodology. His intention has been to produce an urban house that performs with the minimum of means. For Namba, the box represents the minimal conditions required to establish a place – 'a box is primarily place grown out from a space where there was nothing'.* Box House 1, built in 1995, formed the prototype for the series, an experiment in discarding any arbitrary or unnecessary factors and maintaining only the 'prototypical elements'. From this prototype, Namba developed the 'first stage' of the series, which focused on the standardization of materials, dimensions, and room configurations. Once this process of standardization was complete (with Box House 21), the architect began the second stage, which concentrated on 'differentiation' and explored variations on his standardized structural systems.

1   Box House 1, 1995, exterior

*   Kazuhiko Namba, *Namba Kazuhiko: The Box-Houses Under Construction* (Tokyo: TOTO Publishing, 2001), 2.

Kazuhiko Namba + Kai Workshop + MUJI
MUJI + INFILL: Wooden House, 2004–

1

MUJI was founded in 1983 as Mujirushi Ryohin, which roughly translates as 'no-brand, quality goods'. Across a range that includes home goods, clothing, and stationery, their distinctive aesthetic emphasizes plain packaging, clean design, and usefulness. In 2004, they produced a house with Kazuhiko Namba, who based his design on the principles he had developed as part of his Box Series. With its concrete slab foundation, wood-structure frame, and infill, the structure is designed to be both cost effective and quick to assemble. The house is open-plan, with kitchen–dining–living facilities on the ground floor, and sleeping and study spaces on a first-floor mezzanine. The house comes in variants, with additional facilities including a first-floor balcony available at a greater price. Detailing throughout the house is minimal but warm, recalling many of MUJI's products. Several other houses are now available to purchase from the company, with designs by architects including Kengo Kuma.

1   Exterior

Earth and Concrete

Two-thirds of the Japanese archipelago, situated in the Asian monsoon zone, is covered in forests. From its humid climate, fertile soil and resilient trees, Japan has produced a thriving 'wood culture' reinforced by advanced wood fabrication technologies and skilled carpenters. The reinforced concrete that was introduced to this culture during the process of industrialisation seemed entirely dissimilar to wood, from textures to construction methods. Attempts to use this foreign material, however, resulted in it being incorporated within the wood culture, which had remained a central element of everyday life. This led to the development of uniquely Japanese interpretations of concrete, which can be considered similar to the way brutalist architects used concrete in a way that was reminiscent of rough masonry in order to speak to Europe's 'stone culture'.

Concrete was introduced to Japan from the west in the early 1900s. Due to its impressive resistance to earthquakes, reinforced concrete was very quickly adopted by the Japanese architectural profession (as opposed to Europe and the USA, where for a long time it was considered an industrial material for use by engineers rather than architects). Japan became rapidly proficient at concrete production, pursuing new methods and techniques for mixing and pouring concrete, and achieving an internationally recognised standard of quality. Today, Japanese concrete is most associated with the work of Tadao Ando, characterized by hard-edged geometric compositions, smooth surfaces and a level of technical perfection. Ando's approach is not the only interpretation of concrete in Japan, however.

Antonin Raymond's Reinanzaka House (1923), one of the earliest exposed-concrete houses in Japan, was characterized by the architect's collaboration with skilled Japanese carpenters, which resulted in surfaces imprinted with the joints and knots of the thin cedar-board formwork. This effect transfers to concrete something of the organic quality of wood, evidencing an approach to concrete construction that forms a strong tradition within Japanese architecture that expresses, in the words of post-war architectural critic Yasugoro Yoshioka, 'a certain kinship with the practice of using gnarled tree trunks and resinous pine slabs in Japanese-style interiors.'[1] This understanding of the affinity between concrete and natural materials was particularly influential for those architects who worked under Raymond, including Junzo Yoshimura. In Yoshimura's Mountain Lodge at Karuizawa, a lage, airy timber structure is elevated atop tall concrete foundations. Instead of separating the house from the ground in the manner of *piloti* or stilts, the architect treated the concrete as a being continuous with the ground. In this way he explored the potential for a modernity that was not divorced from nature.

A second strand was introduced into Japan through the work of Takamasa Yoshizaka. Yoshizaka had worked for two years in the Paris office of Le Corbusier, who at the time was exploring the expressive potential of raw-surfaced concrete in such seminal projects as the Unité d'habitation in Marseille. He used raised concrete platforms to establish a flexible 'artificial ground' which could support a great variety of changing lifestyles. Takamitsu Azuma also employed concrete as a means of sustaining urban living, using it in his own house to establish a defensive structure that remains resilient amidst a constantly changing city.

The architect could not afford any finishing on the concrete, and the interior surfaces are heavily marked by the grains, knots and bulges of the formwork and other irregularities created during the construction process. These surfaces have been polished by its residents' hands and feet and 'weathered' by leaks and condensation over the past fifty years. Its interior brings to mind a cave, which can be studied as a 'geological' subject carrying a layered record of its construction and inhabitation. These architects share with works by Raymond and Yoshimura a sense of concrete as a warm, organic material rather than a tool for industrialisation.

These houses all propose an interpretation of concrete as 'earth', an understanding of it as an organic material that can be considered to have emerged from Japan's wood-centric building culture. These explorations of the aesthetics of concrete through the perspective of the traditional wood culture still feel refreshing for contemporary Japanese society, in which people feel increasingly suffocated by the constraints and pressures of living in an advanced industrial society.

---

1   Quoted in Ken Tadashi Oshima, 'Characters of Concrete', Kurt GF Helfrich and William Whitaker, eds, *Crafting a Modern World: The Designs of Antonin and Noémi Raymond* (New York: Princeton Architectural Press, 2006), 74.

Takamasa Yoshizaka
Yoshizaka House, 1955

1

When Takamasa Yoshizaka returned to Japan after working in France, he set about building a home for his family in post-war Tokyo. He created an elevated concrete 'artificial ground', on top of which a domestic space could be built little by little in response to the family's needs. Yoshizaka's family were known for their open and relaxed lifestyle – contrary to Japanese custom they did not require guests to take off their shoes on entering the house, and over the years even let small animals make their home within the structure. A spirit of inclusivity was apparent throughout. Visually, the building had the character of a bricolage, with a number of disparate decorative elements incorporated into the structure. With private spaces raised to the first and second storeys, the ground level was given a more public dimension. Yoshizaka declined to include fences or gates at the edge of the property, refuting the division between public and private land, and built an atelier and library on the site. The house is thus a realization of the architect's declaration that 'a house must exist on the borderline of individual freedom and collective benefit'.*

Location: Shinjuku, Tokyo (demolished)
Total floor area: 72 m²

1 Model, plaster, cement, acrylic, and wood
2 Exterior, photographed in 1982
3 Site plan, showing (left to right) library, house and studio, c. 1982

* Takamasa Yoshizaka, quoted in *Dis-Continuous Unity: The Architecture of Yosizaka Takamasa and Atelier U* (Tokyo: National Archives of Modern Architecture, 2015), 7.

2

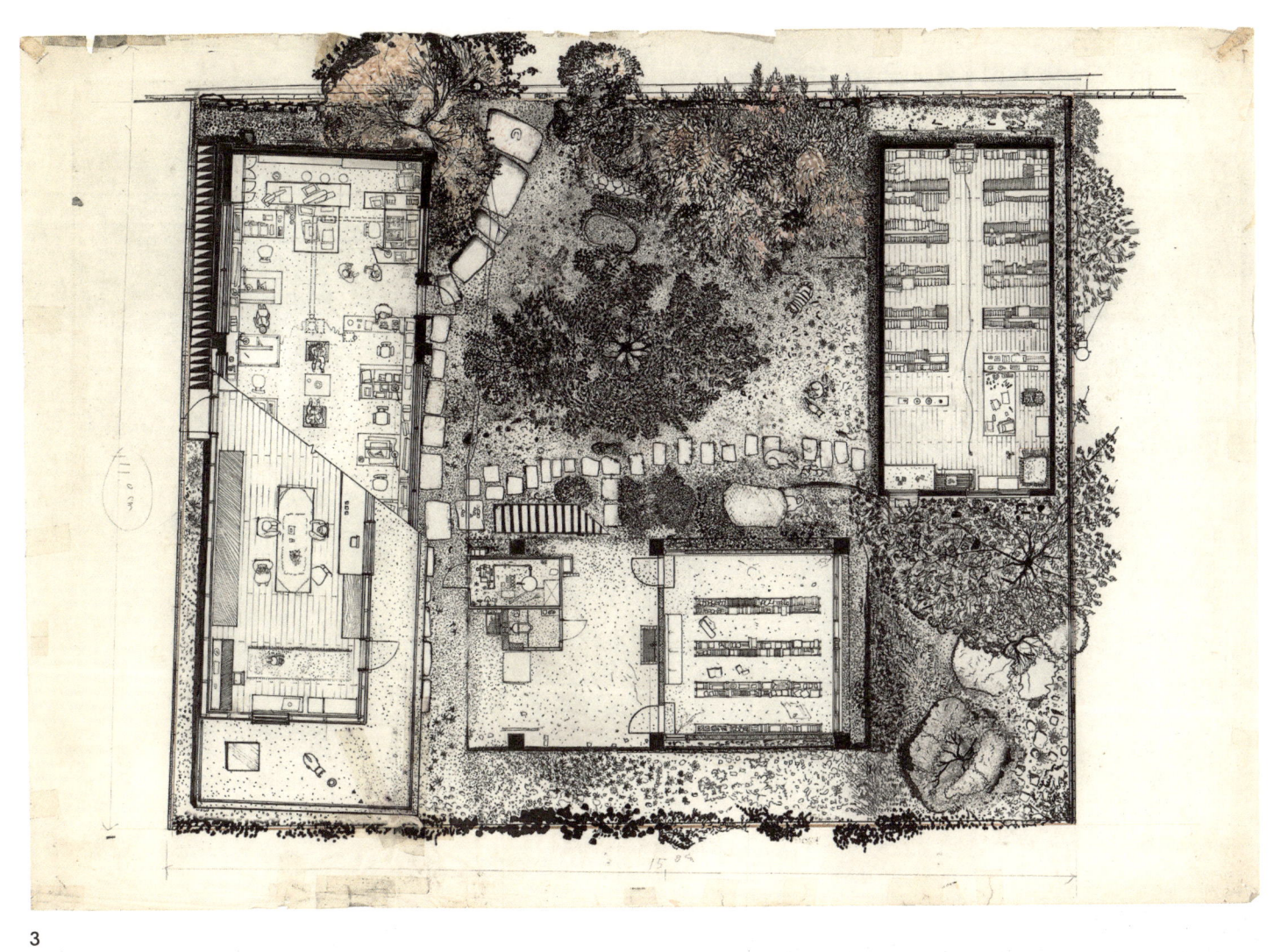

3

Junzo Yoshimura
Mountain Lodge A at Karuizawa, 1963

1

Junzo Yoshimura built this lodge for his own use in Karuizawa, a fashionable retreat outside of Tokyo. The area is also the home of the Summer Cottage (1933) by the architect's former employer Antonin Raymond. Raymond's house, with its combination of exposed concrete base and wood structure and its use of *shoji* to create a permeable boundary between house and garden, is an important precedent for the Mountain Lodge. Responding to the humidity of the forested site and the security needs of the holiday home (which would remain unoccupied for extended periods of time), Yoshimura raised the wooden structure of his house above ground level and sat it on a concrete base housing a vestibule, stairway, and utility space. The concrete foundations are treated as continuous with the forest floor, while the living spaces are situated at the canopy level of the surrounding trees and include large sliding windows that can be opened in order to create a space open to the forest.

Location: Karuizawa, Nagano
Total floor area: 87.7 m²

1   Exterior, detail of concrete foundation block and porch
2   Exterior
3   Section
4   Exterior

2

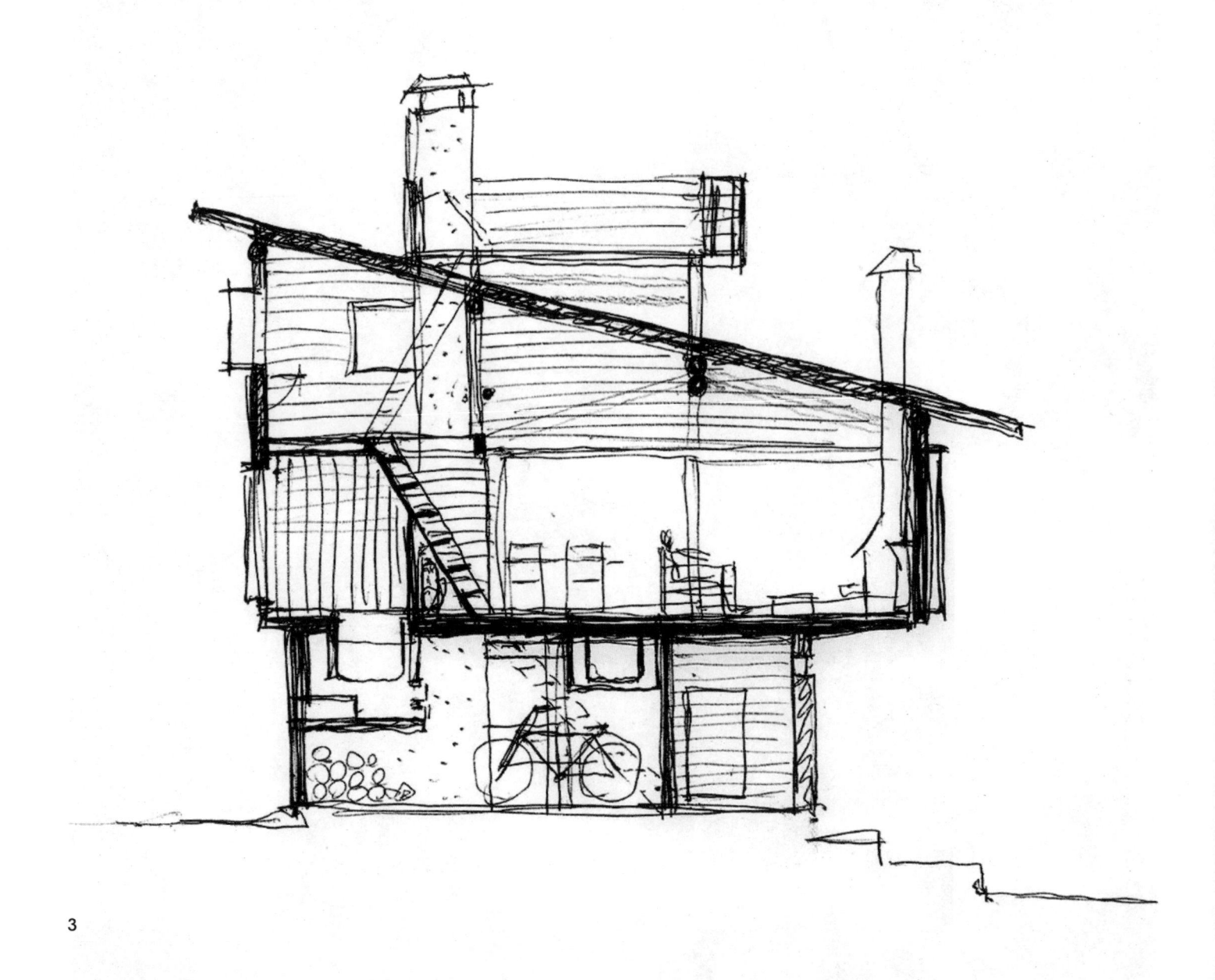

3

4

Takamitsu Azuma
Tower House, 1966

1

In the post-war period, Japan underwent a significant population boom which led to increased pressure on urban space. Takamitsu Azuma, moving to Tokyo with his family and desiring to live in the centre of the city rather than the suburbs, could only afford a 20 m² plot on an awkward, triangular plot created by the building of a large new road for the 1964 Olympics. The traditionally horizontal orientation of Japanese homes was impossible under such space constraints, so Azuma stacked the internal rooms one on top of another. The result, a four-storey structure, was unusually high for contemporary Tokyo residences. The interior is essentially one continuous space arranged around a spiral staircase – there are no doors or internal walls. The rough concrete textures exposed throughout give the house a defensive quality, rendering it a defiant embodiment of the architect's desire to live in the city.

Location: Shibuya, Tokyo
Total floor area: 65.05 m²

1 Exterior
2 Ground floor kitchen, viewed from first floor landing
3 Stairs, viewed from kitchen
4 Takamitsu Azuma and his daughter in kitchen
5 Model, polystyrene board, wood, and newspaper
6 'Interior Geology' studies made as part of a research project by Yoshiharu Tsukamoto Lab, showing details of fixtures and concrete surfaces

2

3

4

5

6

A House is a Work of Art

In 1962, architect Kazuo Shinohara declared that 'a house is a work of art'. Japan was experiencing the benefits of an 'economic miracle' that saw it leap from post-war defeat to the world's second largest economy. His polemic was targeted at mainstream architecture's impulses towards industrialization, positing instead an architectural space that would critique prevailing worldviews. Originally a mathematician, Shinohara was one of the most influential theorists and practitioners in twentieth-century Japanese architecture. Until late in his career he focused exclusively on single-family houses which established the parameters of architectural debate for the succeeding generations of architects (many of whom he directly mentored in his role as Professor at the Tokyo Institute of Technology). His architecture and writing form a complex body of work that foregrounds design's potential as a critical art form.

    Shinohara's critical method is already evident at an early stage in his 1960 essay 'Nihon Dentoron' (Theory of Japanese Tradition), in which he considers many important historical buildings. His analysis attempts to return to the historical context in which the works were created, imagining their social and technological settings and demonstrating that contemporary assessments of tradition included various misunderstandings that had arisen over time. For example, a melancholic, windswept quality may seem like *wabi-sabi*,[1] while a rectilinear, idiosyncratic composition of columns and beams may seem to anticipate Mondrian's grids. Shinohara asserts, however, that these impressions are anachronisms.

    Using a wide range of buildings, Shinohara attempted to illustrate a 'method of Japanese architecture', discussing architectural composition, religious belief, and power, living amidst nature, authority, and irrationality. He identified an irrationality in Japanese architectural styles and spaces, and reasoned that the irrationality within dwellings can provide a potent means of resisting the fragmentation of the psyche and the community resulting from the relentless pursuit of rationality.

    Shinohara's strongest examples concern the space of rural *minka*, the traditional homes of commoners, particularly the role of the *doma*, the spacious, earth-floored entrance areas where residents work. He characterized the *doma* as a 'non-open space', in contrast to the open verandas and garden pavilions of aristocratic dwellings. It was also a space that, unlike aristocratic residences, was associated with production and labour. According to the architect, the opposition between the *blackness* of the *minka*'s sooty columns and log beams and the *whiteness* of the aristocratic house's sawn Japanese cypress columns and Japanese cedar boards is reflected in a parallel opposition between the *practice* of those who performed their own housework and tended fires in their living rooms and the *authority* of those who entrusted the work to others. Shinohara analyses the points at which these oppositional categories blend together, giving rise to multiple architectural housing types in Japanese architecture. House in White (1961) can be understood as deconstructing this opposition, recomposing the respective characteristics of *minka* and aristocratic dwellings through an unprecedented combination of abstract whiteness and non-open space. Shinohara did not concern himself with functional theory, which was hotly debated in the 1960s in relation to small houses. Instead, he dealt with the question of whether an individual living in the present could design a house within the critical space of tradition.

For the architect, the cube that emerged in the House in White's main room was a 'personal cube', distinct from the rational cubes of modernism. The house forms a turning point between what Shinohara considered his 'first style', characterized by dwellings in dialogue with tradition, and his antithetical 'second style'. This phase was predominated by cubes and 'fissures', in an attempt to express a dry, inorganic 'anti-space'. With 1974's Tanikawa Villa, his design practice took yet another turn, instigated by the 'slippage' between its exposed dirt floor and the geometric structural system of columns and roof. He accepted this assemblage of naked elements as a 'savage machine' in which the juxtaposition of contradicting factors could produce new meanings. This savage machine propelled his third phase, in which his interest in chaos and savagery led him to actively pursue new connections with the city. In Tokyo residences such as House in Uehara (1976) and House under High-Voltage Lines (1981), he amplified the moments of slippage, conflict, and anarchy.

Despite the radical shifts in his practice, Shinohara's belief in the house as a work of art remained a constant throughout his career. Behind it lies a perception that architectural production has become increasingly industrialized, large in scale, and controlled by corporate forces. In contrast, the design of individual houses remained relatively unproductive, economically speaking, and could therefore be recognized as art. He situates house design as a form of cultural criticism that directly participates in cultural creation and is unrelated to social production. With his belief that 'freedom appears before us', Shinohara has inspired generations of younger architects who, at the fledgling stages of their careers, have no choice but to concentrate on the design of small houses.

1   *Wabi-sabi* is an aesthetic ideal privileging simplicity, imperfection, and the passing of time. It is often considered a uniquely Japanese aesthetic, both internationally and in Japan.

Kazuo Shinohara
House in White, 1966

1

House in White marks the climax of the first phase of Kazuo Shinohara's practice, which involved isolating the syntax of traditional Japanese architecture to reach a level of geometric abstraction. For Shinohara, the Japanese approach to form was fundamentally concerned with frontality rather than three-dimensionality, and was composed through a process of dividing a whole rather than connecting individual spaces, as in Western architecture. House in White is essentially a white-walled cube housed within a traditional pyramidal roof. The architect divided the square plan so that more than half of the space is allocated to a single room. The roof is supported by a cypress log that stands at the centre of the plan, but the architect concealed its truss beams above a smooth white roof so that it is given a symbolic force detached from its structural purpose. The geometric abstraction of the House in White is divorced from the functionalist principles of modernism. It is instead an expression of Shinohara's desire to create a space detached from that of mechanical civilization by reintroducing elements of the symbolic and the non-everyday –a strategy that Koji Taki has referred to as the 'sacralization of the dwelling'.*

Location: Suginami, Tokyo
Total floor area: 141.3 m^2

1 Exterior, with *shoji* screens open to living room
2 Living room with central cypress log column
3 Elevation
4 Living room, viewed from kitchen
5 Bedroom

* Koji Taki, 'Oppositions: The Intrinsic Structure of Kazuo Shinohara's Work', *Perspecta*, vol. 20 (1983), 50.

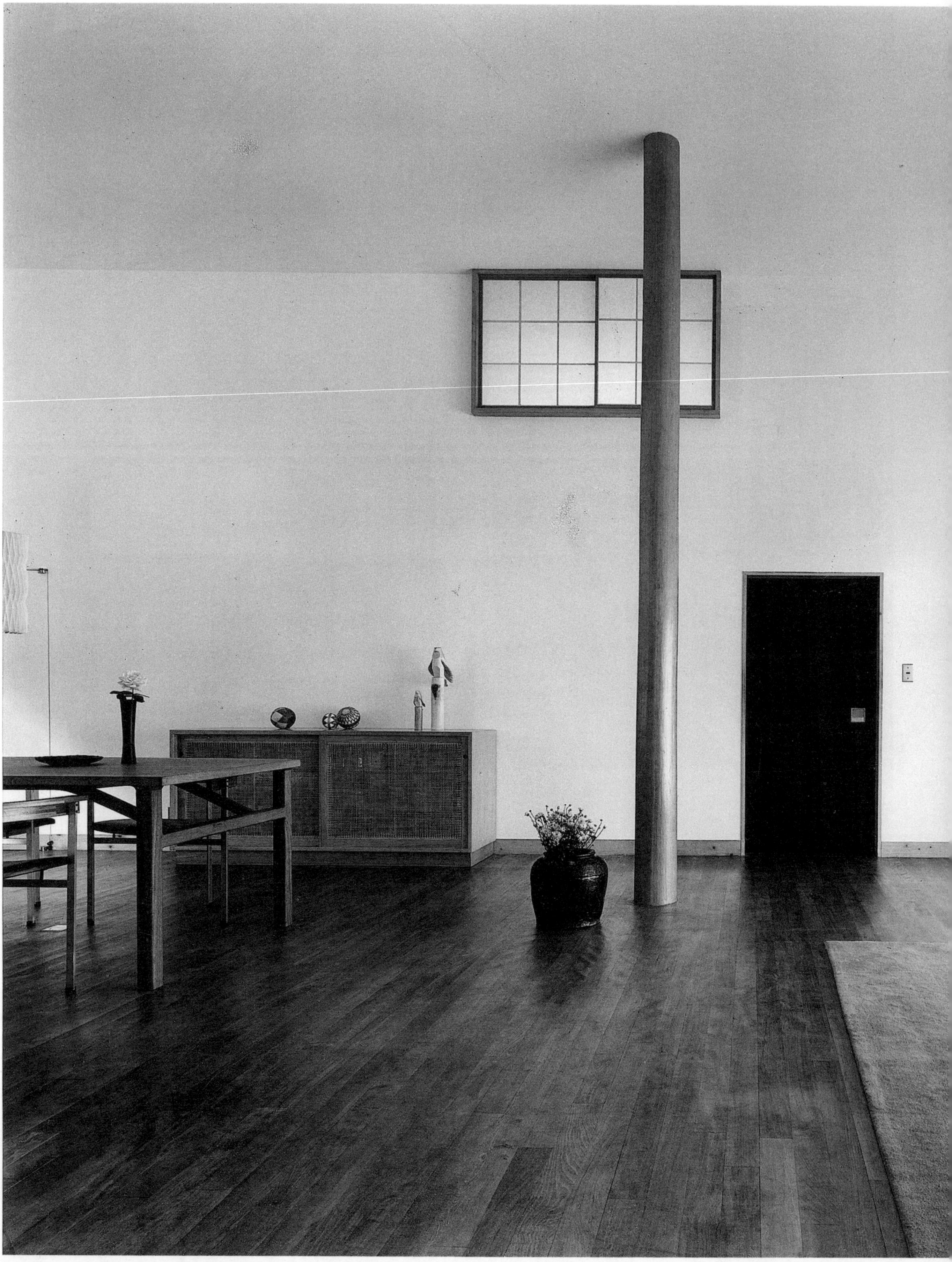

2

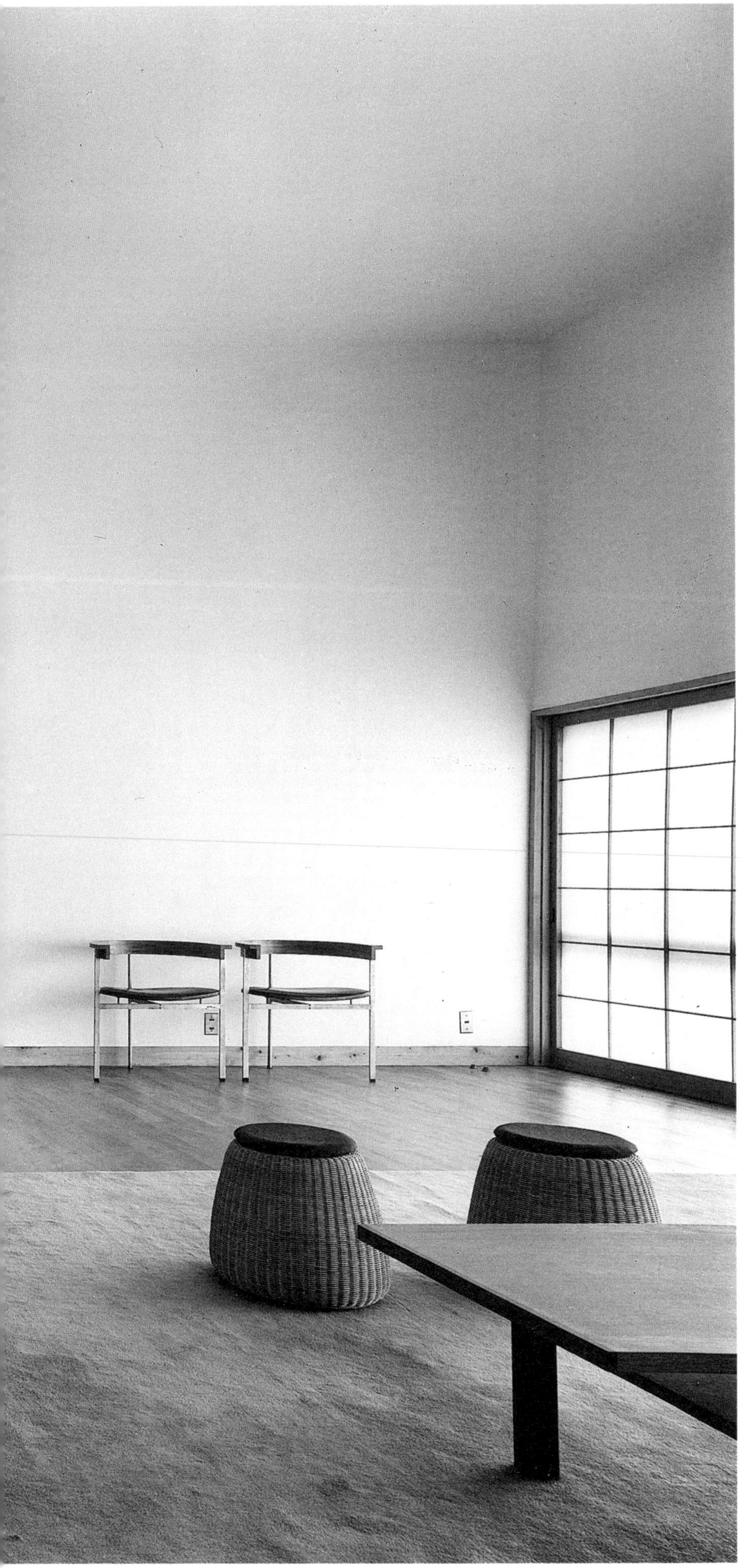

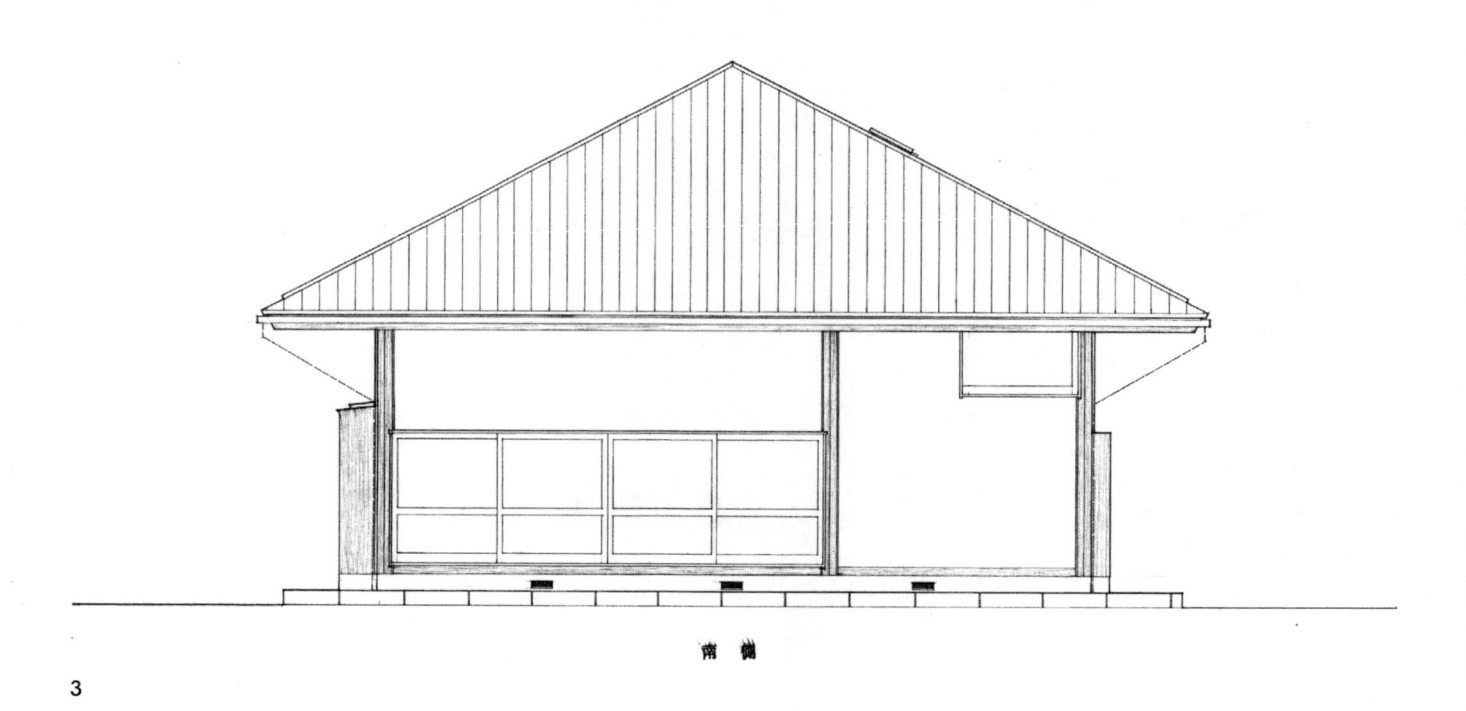

3

南 側

124

4

5

Kazuo Shinohara
Tanikawa Villa, 1974

1

Tanikawa Villa was built in a rural, forested site for Shuntaro Tanikawa (b. 1931), one of Japan's most acclaimed poets. The client had written his request as a poem, specifying that the building should be both a 'winter house or pioneer cabin (house)' and a 'summer space or church for a pantheist (need not be a house)'.* Shinohara's design is one of his most uncompromising residences. With its sloped roof and resemblance to vernacular structures, the house appears as a rereading of the House in White and, as with that earlier building, Shinohara allocated a majority of the plan to a single, symbolic space. Whereas the large space of House in White retained some ordinary functions (it contained the kitchen, dining, and living spaces), Tanikawa Villa is remarkable for its rejection of the everyday. The slope of the hill on which the house sits is entirely incorporated into the interior space, which is floored with dark, moist soil (unrelated to the dry compacted earthen floors of traditional architecture). Three supporting wooden posts recall the cypress column of House in White, but here the fiction is stripped away and their structural elements are laid bare. This represents an important shift in Shinohara's architecture, away from the abstract symbolism of earlier projects towards a desire for raw, 'naked' space in which each element expresses only itself.

Location: Naganohara, Gunma
Total floor area: 185.48 m^2

1   Exterior
2   Main space, with exposed dirt floor and wooden columns
3   Exterior
4   Main space, with sloped dirt floor
5   Main space, details of columns

*   Quoted in Kazuo Shinohara, 'When Naked Space is Traversed', JA, no. 288 (February, 1976), 55.

2

3

5

4

Kazuo Shinohara
House in Uehara, 1976

1

House in Uehara was built for the photographer Kiyoji Ohtsuji on a very small Tokyo site. Earlier in the 1970s, Shinohara had designed a series of abstract, cubic houses in cast concrete, including Uncompleted House (1970). House in Uehara develops this theme, incorporating the 'naked' elements of Tanikawa Villa. The main portion of the house is a rectilinear block in reinforced concrete, on top of which Shinohara affixed a barrel-vaulted child's room with a lightweight steel-frame structure. The two structural methods used render these blocks formally disparate from one another. The principal living space on the first floor is dominated by massive structural beams that protrude through the floor and obstruct the space – evidencing a clash between the systems of structure and everyday living at play in the house. This structural system can also be read explicitly on the house's exterior, which addresses its urban environment without resolving its contradictions. The awkwardness, even violence, of these arrangements evidences the architect's concept of the 'savage machine', a process of generating or provoking meaning through the forceful unification of naked elements.

Location: Shibuya, Tokyo
Total floor area: 157.48 m^2

1 Exterior
2 Exterior, viewed from street
3 Second-floor children's bedroom
4 Detail of structure
5 First-floor living room, with central column

2

3

4

5

Kazuo Shinohara
House under High-Voltage Lines, 1981

1

Kazuo Shinohara's notorious 1962 declaration that 'a house is a work of art' indicated a separation of the house from the disorder of the industrial metropolis. At House in Uehara, however, the 'savagery' with which he placed various elements and systems in conflict with one another evidences a growing affinity with the chaotic urban fabric of Tokyo. House under High-Voltage Lines marks a definitive shift towards engagement with the city. The house occupies a typically cramped site, above which run high voltage power lines of the kind that criss-cross Tokyo streets. Planning regulations proscribed building within a cylindrical area around each of these lines, and the house's distinctive truncated roof precisely corresponds to the arc of these areas. This form is continued throughout the building's interior. Shinohara thus materializes the invisible boundaries and spaces which are as much a feature of the city as its physical structures. The structure appears as if mutilated by these regulations, but also gives the sense of resisting them, expressing a contradictory relationship – both antagonistic and accepting – between house and city. This exploration of the way architectural form is produced through conflicting forces is indicative of Shinohara's Tokyo Chaos theory, a belief in the value of the 'progressive anarchy' evident in Tokyo's disorderly architectural character.

Location: Setagaya, Tokyo
Total floor area: 259.46 m²

1   Second-floor bedroom
2   Exterior, with living / dining room on ground floor
3   Detail of transition between first-floor corridor and second-floor bedroom, with spiral staircase on left
4   Exterior with adjacent power lines

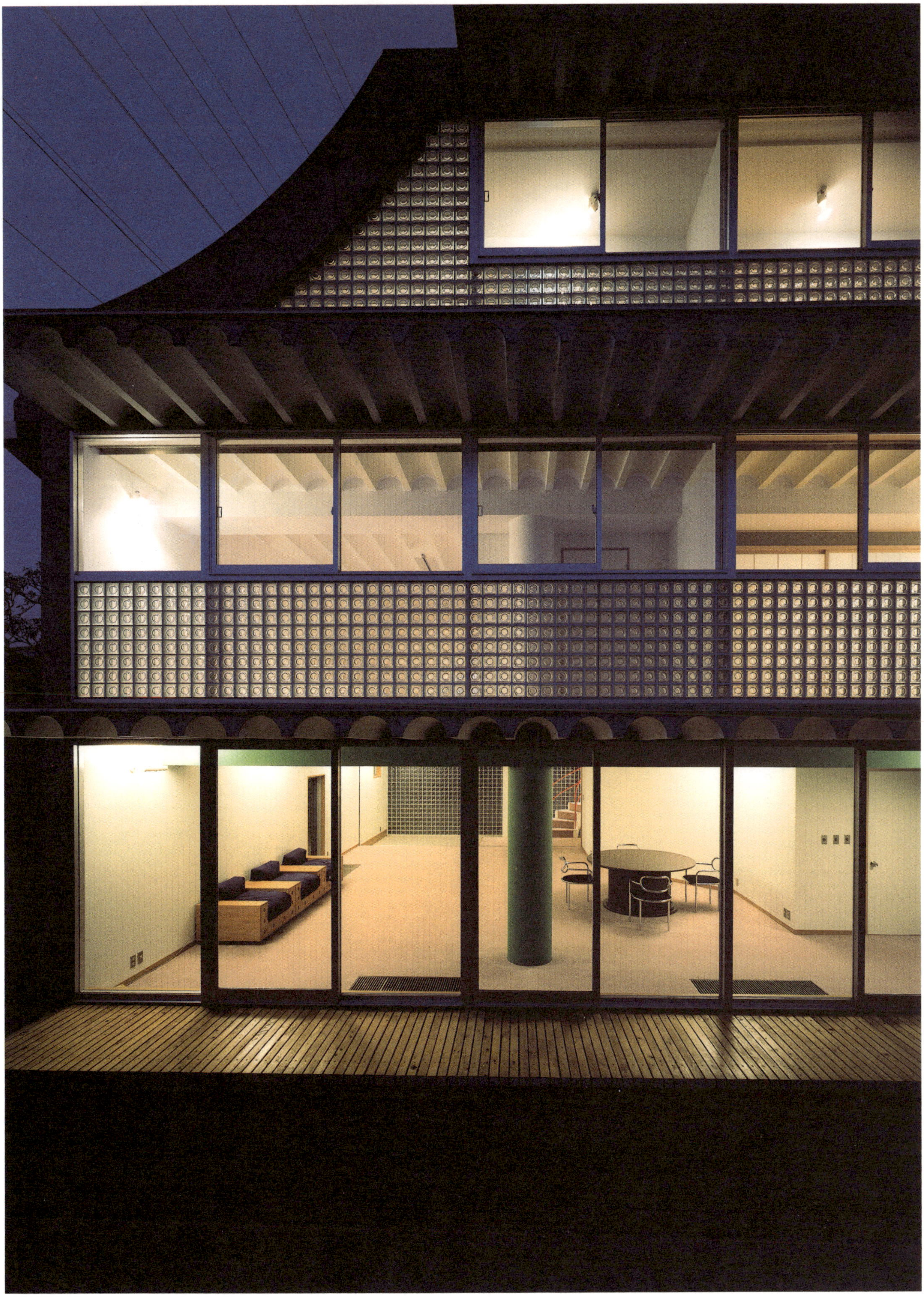

2

3

4

Closed to Open

A period of rapid industrial and economic growth in Japan in the 1960s brought increased air pollution and urban overcrowding, and in the early 1970s the circumstances for creating residential works steadily worsened. Toyo Ito and Kazunari Sakamoto, two architects of the same generation, critically responded to this urban and social context. In a series of houses in the 1970s and 1980s, they used domestic architecture to establish a space of critique, carrying on a close and productive dialogue between their projects. Although their practices seem idiosyncratic, they were engaged in open and logical investigations that were supported by a strong body of critical writing published in contemporary journals, ensuring that their debate remained open to their peers.

   Two of the architects' early houses (Ito's Aluminium House and Sakamoto's Machiya in Minase) set themselves apart from the typically open houses of Japan in that their walled-in interiors have a limited number of openings and minimal partitioning. The houses' facades are direct translations of the self-contained one-room spaces within. By severing the internal space from the external context, the spatial qualities and architectural composition of floor, walls, and windows are emphasized. However, this emphasis does not solely articulate the abstract autonomy of the architecture, which, on the contrary, is constantly set in contrast with the contingent *act of living*.

   Recognizing that the search for an autonomous internal space puts a great strain on the residents, Sakamoto and Ito began to pursue alternative strategies. Elsewhere, the modernist, functionalist approach to architecture was being criticized by postmodern thinkers such as Robert Venturi and Denise Scott-Brown, Aldo Rossi, and James Stirling, who advocated the continuing value of symbolism in architecture. Ito and Sakamoto's architecture developed in similar directions. In Ito's House in Koganei and Sakamoto's House in Sakatayamatsuke, both architects segmented the interior spaces, making them closer to living, but weakening their form in the process.
All extraneous elements were removed from the facades, so that they iconographically resemble a simple warehouse in Ito's case, and a 'house-form' in Sakamoto's. For Ito, the external form of the House in Koganei acts as a pastiche of International Style modernism, while for Sakamoto the gable-roofed form of his house symbolically conveys ordinariness and domesticity.
A contrast was therefore established between the interior, which forms the space for living, and the facade, which acts as the expression of cultural memory. Both architects subsequently became uncomfortable with the completeness of these facades, suspecting that these symbolic forms had become mere simulacra in an increasingly commodified Japan. In Ito's

House in Hanakoganei and Sakamoto's House in Soshigaya, this iconic form is weakened and the houses take on the character of conglomerations of mannerist fragments.

In the 1980s, under the influence of philosopher and critic Koji Taki, Ito and Sakamoto criticized both the symbolic and mannerist approaches. Ito's Silver Hut and Sakamoto's House F present architecture that has been decomposed into its constituent elements – roofs, walls, columns, and so on – and then reintegrated into a form that bears little resemblance to the traditional image of a house. This separation of architecture into its elements is paralleled by the High-Tech style trending in Europe at the time in the work of architects such as Richard Rogers and Renzo Piano. The development of entirely new structural configurations unhinged the conventional use of the various elements, which had been fixed over time. The results were a kind of primitive hut, free of convention and tradition. The brick-paved ground surfaces and roof frames that straddle both the courtyards and interior rooms have the effect of inspiring behaviours that similarly straddle inside and outside, marking a definitive break from Ito and Sakamoto's early houses, which had remained closed against external conditions.

Through their continued explorations, both Ito and Sakamoto scrutinized one of the central principles of architectural space, which is the fundamental separation between inside and outside.

Kazunari Sakamoto
Machiya in Minase, 1970

1

Machiya in Minase is an exploration of the concept of the 'closed box', the central concern of Kazunari Sakamoto in the early years of his career, during which he aimed to establish a contained world sequestered from the contradictory conditions of contemporary society. The philosopher and critic Koji Taki has stated that Sakamoto 'thought to produce something outside of daily life in the interior space, while preserving a form of daily life'.* The reinforced concrete facade lacks a noticeable entrance (the doorway is set inside the garage), and all the windows are set above the height of passing pedestrians. The interior consists primarily of a double-height living space, and individual rooms are enclosed within additional boxes nested inside the principal closed box. Originally a small, high-walled courtyard behind the house provided an exterior space that nonetheless remained enclosed. The house's defensive appearance is austere, but the handling of space is surprisingly rich and playful – a series of internal openings creates an intimate relationship between rooms, and there is even an unexpected drawbridge. The reinforced concrete structure is exposed throughout, but the material is painted white on the inside and silver on the outside. The painted walls establish an interplay between materiality and abstraction, simultaneously emphasizing and defamiliarizing the concrete.

Location: Hachioji, Tokyo
Total floor area: 102 m^2

1 Exterior
2 Entrance viewed from first-floor landing
3 Skylight viewed from first-floor landing
4 Garage, detail of painted concrete wall
5 Model, painted card

* Koji Taki, 'Pursuing Composition', *Kazunari Sakamoto: House: Poetics in the Ordinary*, trans. John Montag (Tokyo: TOTO Publishing, 2001), 13.

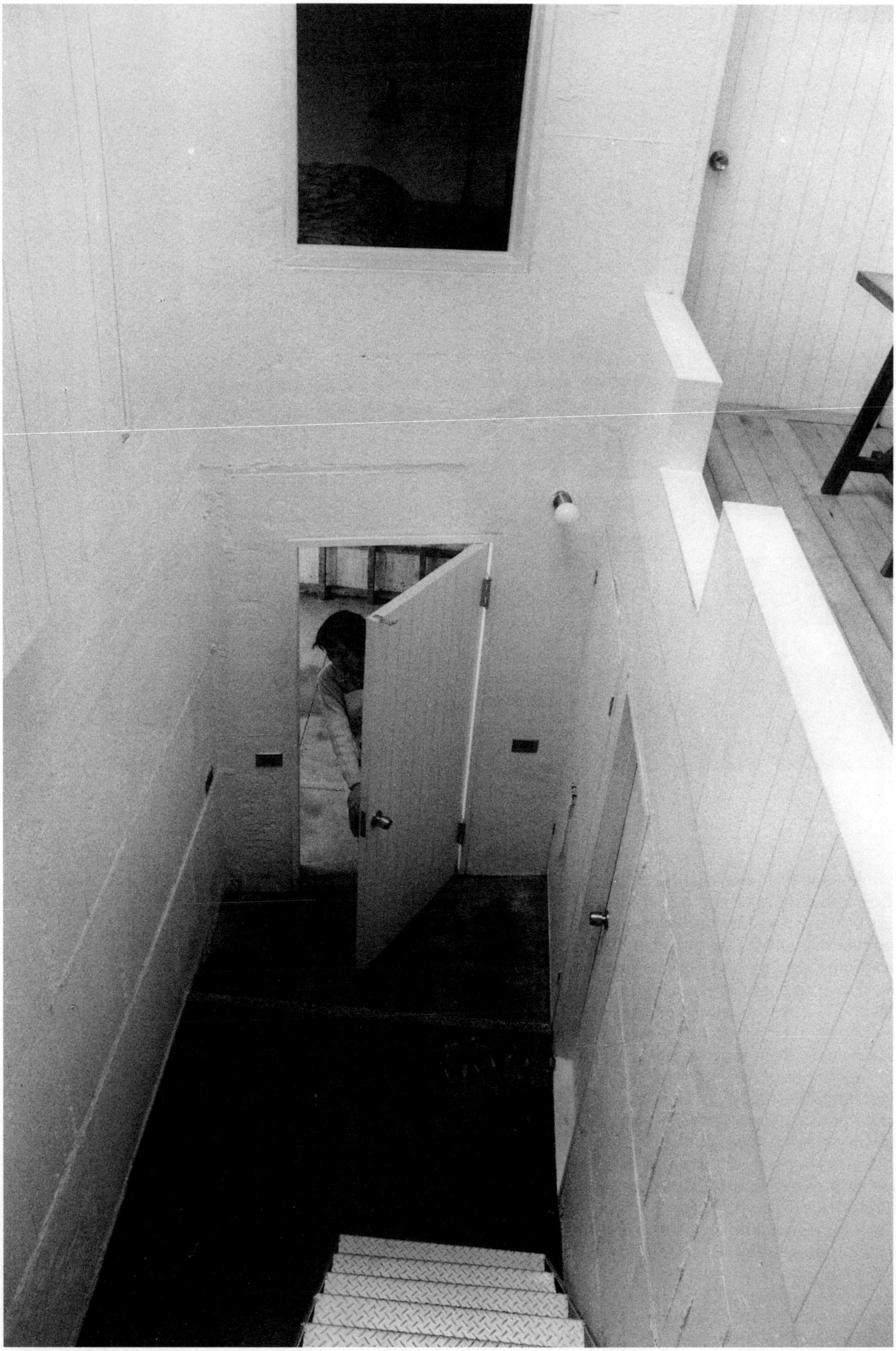

2

3

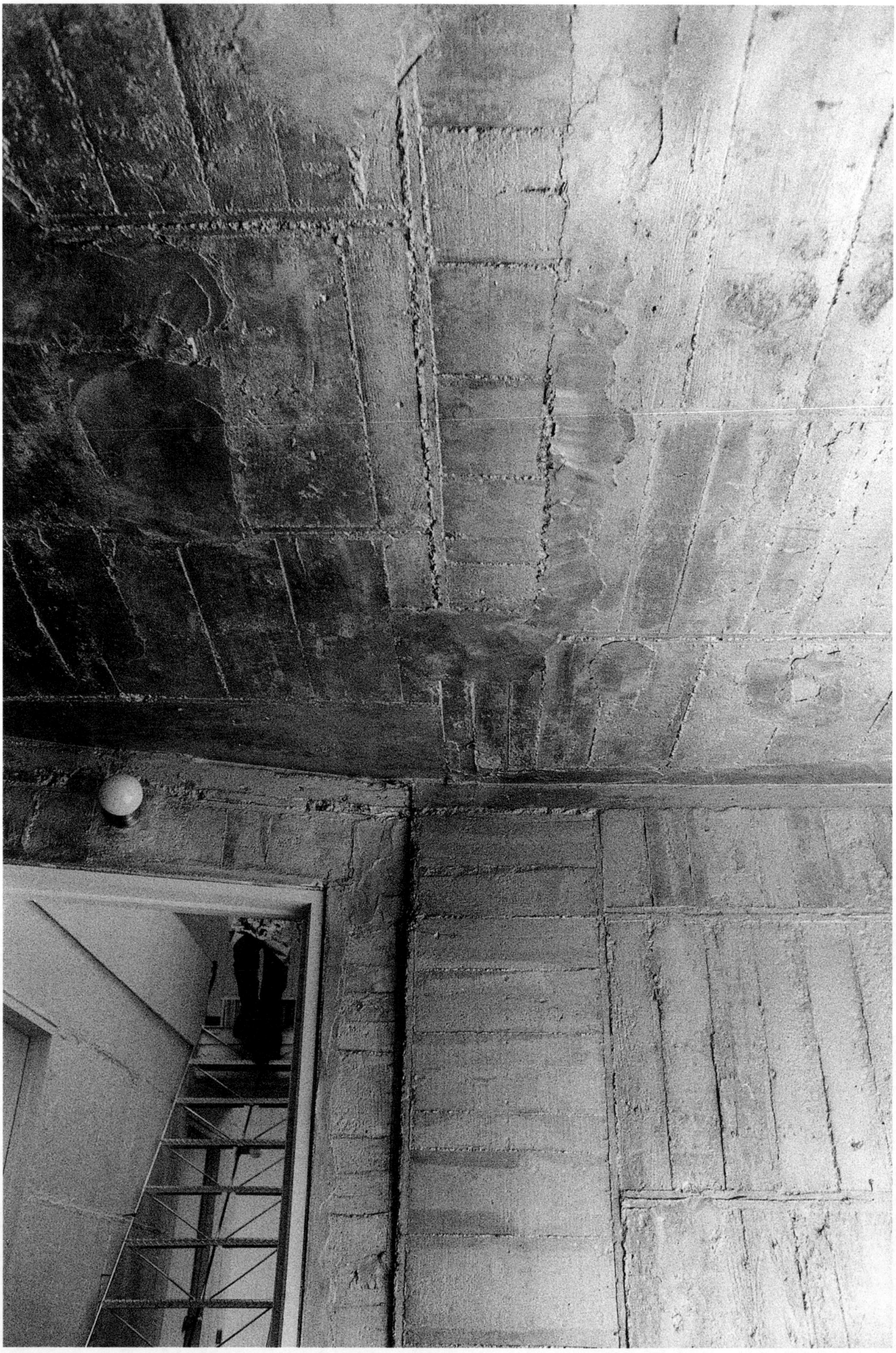

4

5

Toyo Ito
Aluminium House, 1971

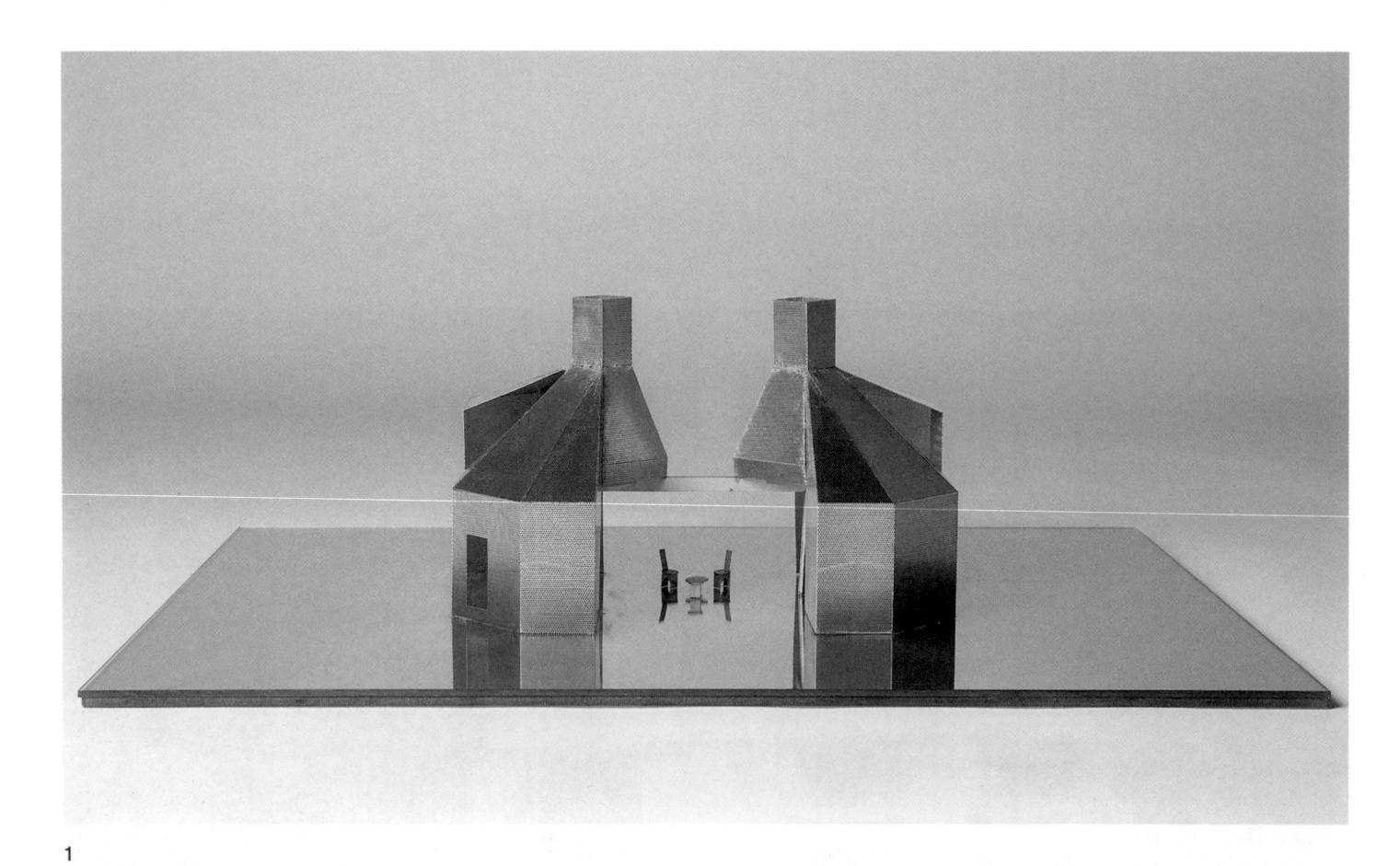

1

Toyo Ito's first building, designed when his office was operating as URBAN ROBOT, was the product of a set of contradictions. Situated in a coastal suburb, the house was commissioned by a family who wished to live by the sea, despite the fact that the area had become so built up that it had lost its seaside atmosphere. Ito exacerbated this condition by grafting elements of the shingle-style vernacular of California onto his design, embracing the illogical and disjointed nature of this imperfect translation. The house was clad in aluminium, its dull reflective quality and industrial associations expressing the architect's frustration at the state of society and the polluted, over-industrialized city. He stubbornly resisted a functionalist approach and the needs of the client, creating an almost entirely open-plan, irregularly shaped interior space that restricted privacy and resisted conventional divisions of functions. This difficult quality was an attempt to prompt the building's users into an active relationship with the architecture, forcing them to confront the space in order to make it functional. This strategy was wrapped up in Ito's exploration of the potential of uselessness, discomfort, and incoherence in architecture – a project explicitly placed in contrast to the technological utopias of the Metabolist group, including Ito's former employer Kiyonori Kikutake. The architect has likened Aluminium House to a failed Metabolist capsule, detached from its mega-structure and fallen discarded to the ground.

Location: Fujisawa, Kanagawa
Total floor area: 110.16 m^2

1   Model, glass, Plexiglas, and aluminium
2   Exterior
3   Studies for lightwells
4, 5   Axonometric drawings
6   Ground-floor living space

2

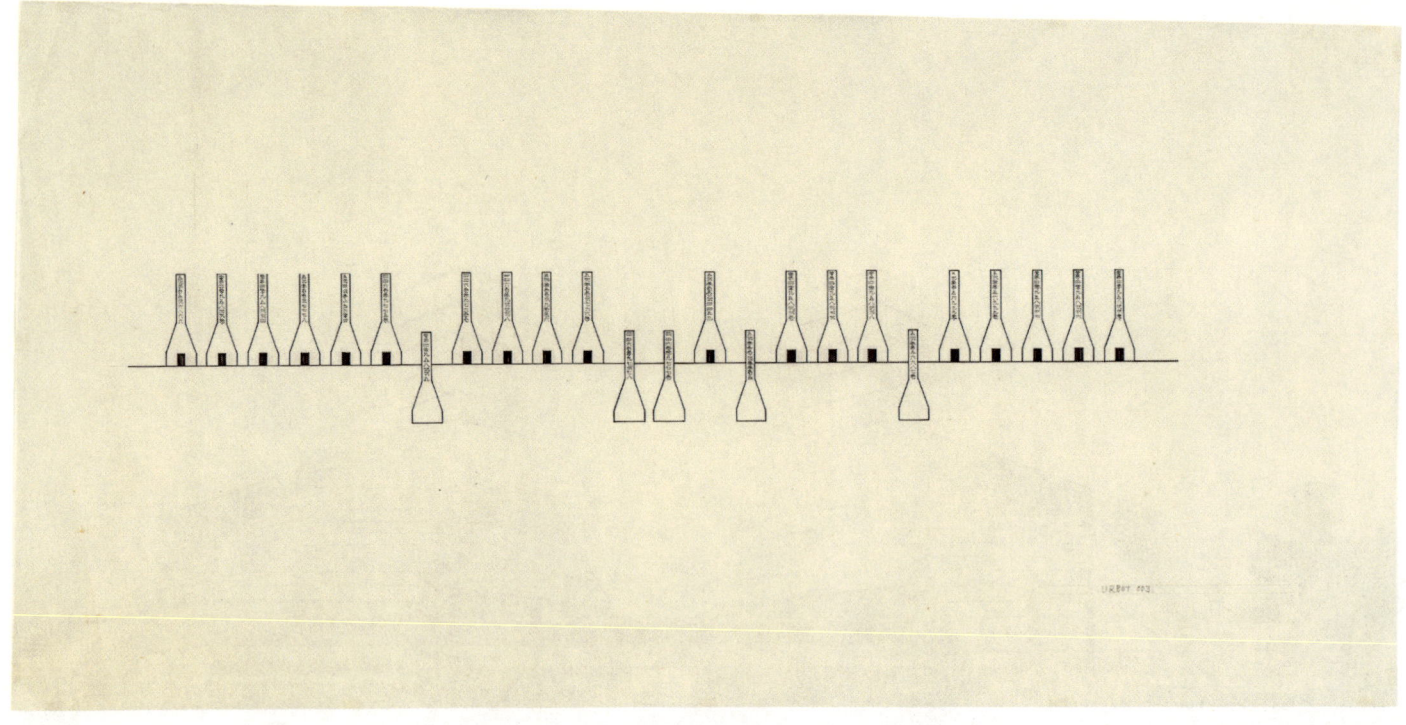

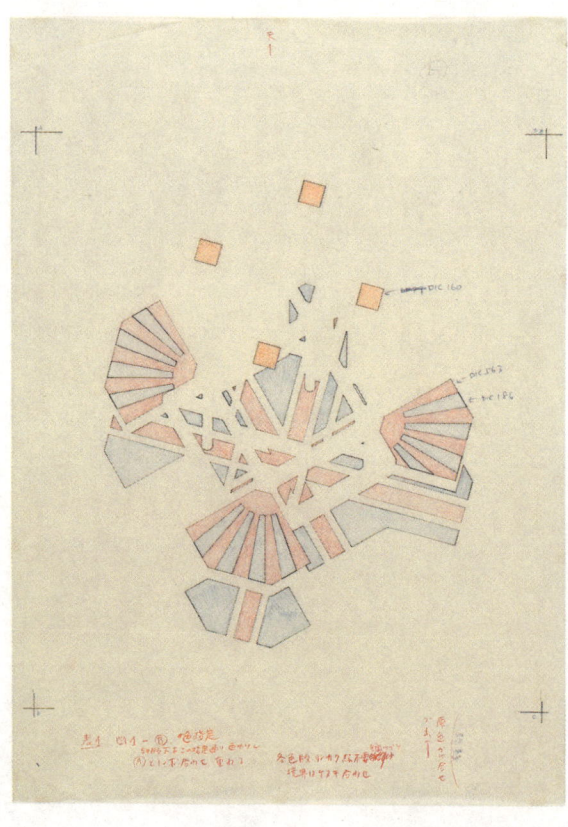

3

4

5

148

6

Kazunari Sakamoto
House in Sakatayamatsuke, 1978

1

In the 1970s, Sakamoto began a rigorous exploration of the 'house-type', a theoretical form expressing the fundamental character of the ordinary house, the absolute commonness of the everyday, when stripped of superfluous meaning. This strategy countered the excessive signification of consumer society. His strongest visual expression of this form was the gabled structure evident in his houses of this period. As is often the case in Sakamoto's architecture, however, what at first appears mundane is charged with a subtle tension. During this period the architect began to consider the facade and the internal structure as autonomous elements – the arrangement of windows does not correspond to the building's structural logic, as is apparent by the exposure of structural columns through the windows on the house's long side. The image of the house-type is somewhat compromised by the building's strange scale – while it appears to be two storeys, it is in fact closer to one and a half. Individual rooms are located on the ground floor, while the large main space sits within the eaves in the manner of an attic. These particularities speak to Sakamoto's attempt to achieve a conceptual ordinariness that does not collapse into kitsch domesticity.

Location: Oiso, Kanagawa
Total floor area: 107.58 m^2

1 Exterior
2 Section

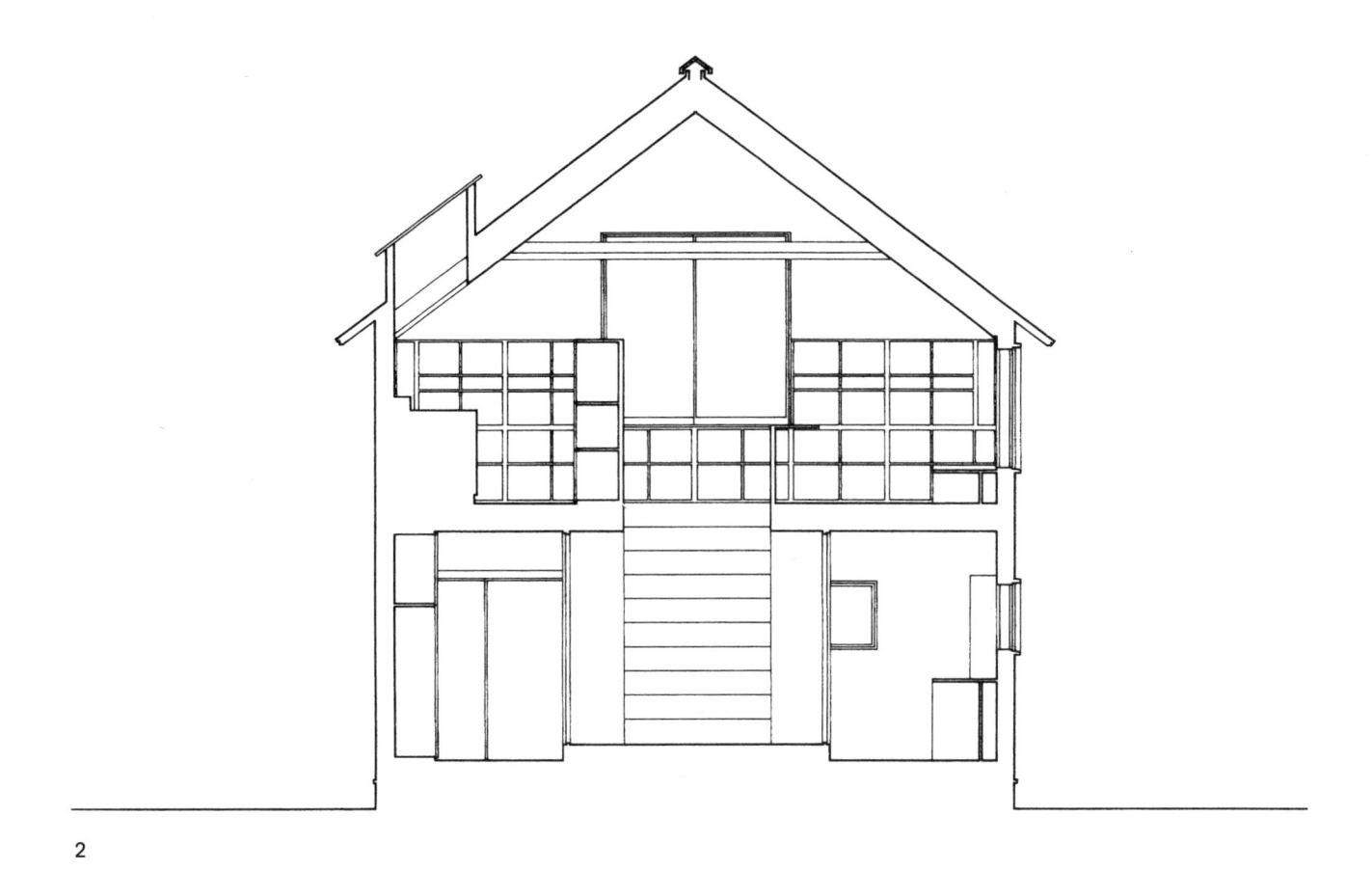

2

Toyo Ito
House in Koganei, 1979

1

House in Koganei was built for a family of four with a budget of only ten million yen, and Ito had been instructed to avoid any extraneous finishing. Accordingly he used cheap, prefabricated elements associated with industrial rather than domestic architecture and wrapped the house in a facade of thin concrete panels. The house was Ito's first use of a steel-frame structure, which subsequently played an important role in his architecture. Adapting the lessons of Le Corbusier's Dom-Ino House, the modernist architect's influential argument for the potential of such structures, Ito designed the facade and interior as autonomous elements. The horizontal strip windows (one of Le Corbusier's signature devices) are arranged in a way that corresponds not to the placement of interior rooms or the structural framework, but solely to the proportions of the rectangular facade. Ito recalls the aesthetics of International Style modernism in a way that divorces the style from its functionalist principles. The house is a key instance in Ito's turn towards concepts of collage, surface, and stereotyped form, prompted by the heterogeneous nature of the Tokyo streetscape.

Location: Koganei, Tokyo
Total floor area: 93.91 m²

1   First floor, with furniture by Teruaki Ohashi
2   Exterior

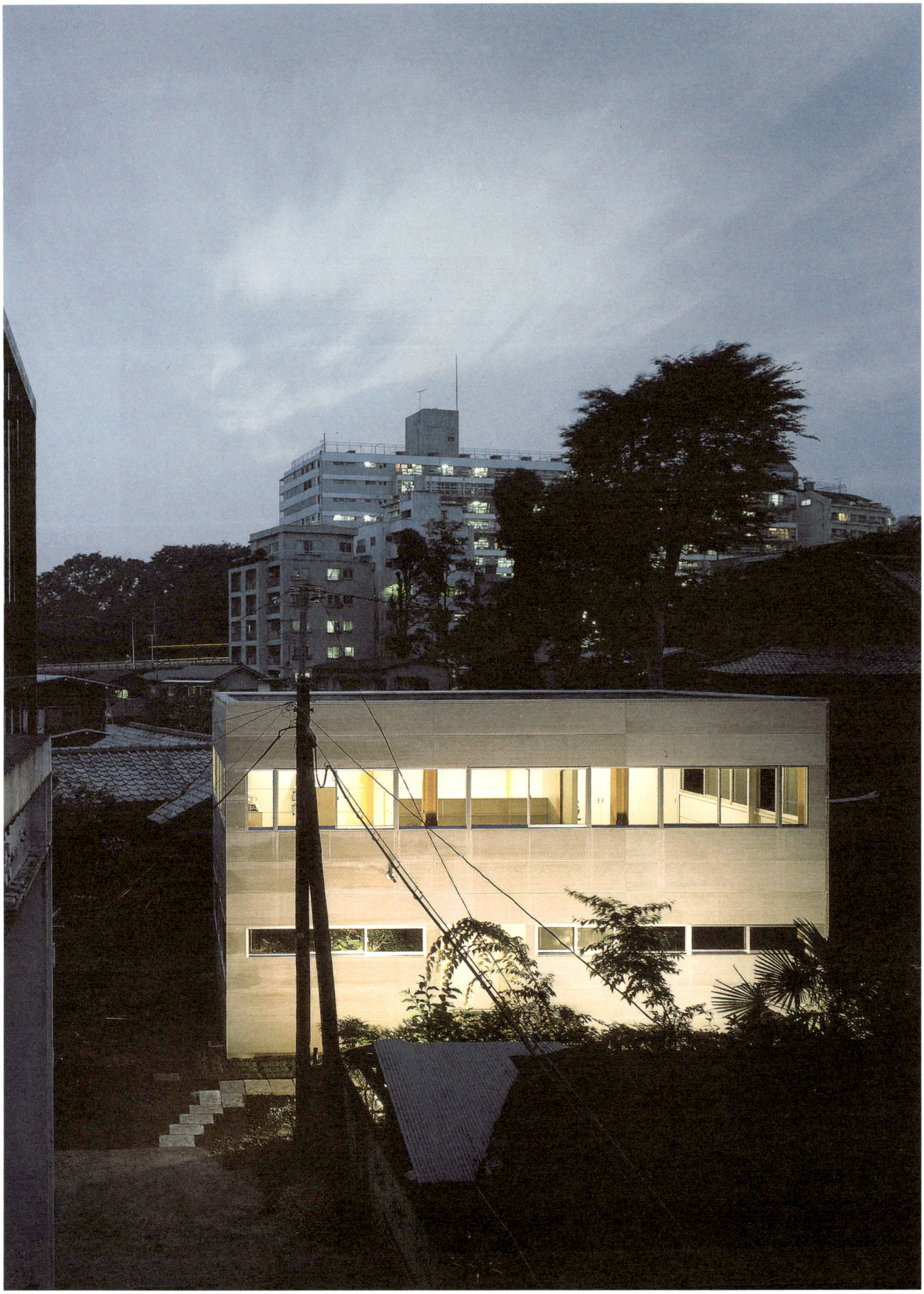

2

Kazunari Sakamoto
House in Soshigaya, 1981

1

The L-shaped plan of House in Soshigaya was determined not by the unified form of the 'house-type', but by the linear configuration of adjacent rooms. The architect's characteristic gabled roof appears on the exterior, but it is broken in half and juxtaposed with two half barrel vaults. This juxtaposition gives the house a shattered, fragmented appearance that indicates a weakening of the strong external form present in his previous houses. The interior consists of a number of aligned, individual rooms but the architect applied the same ornamental treatment throughout, with black wood below waist level and white above, in order to establish some sense of a unified whole. Sakamoto posed this playfully mannerist approach to geometry, form, and facade in opposition to the technological rationalism of the twentieth century, declaring that 'all sense of clarity is inclined to discard aspects of the pre-modern, thus rendering the "profundity" inherent in ambiguity as merely tenuous'.*

Location: Setagaya, Tokyo
Total floor area: 149.71 m²

1   Exterior
2   Ground-floor corridor
3   Side elevation

*   Quoted in Kazunari Sakamoto and Yimin Guo, *Anti-Climax Poetry: Sakamoto's Architecture* (Shanghai: Tongji University Press, 2015), 75.

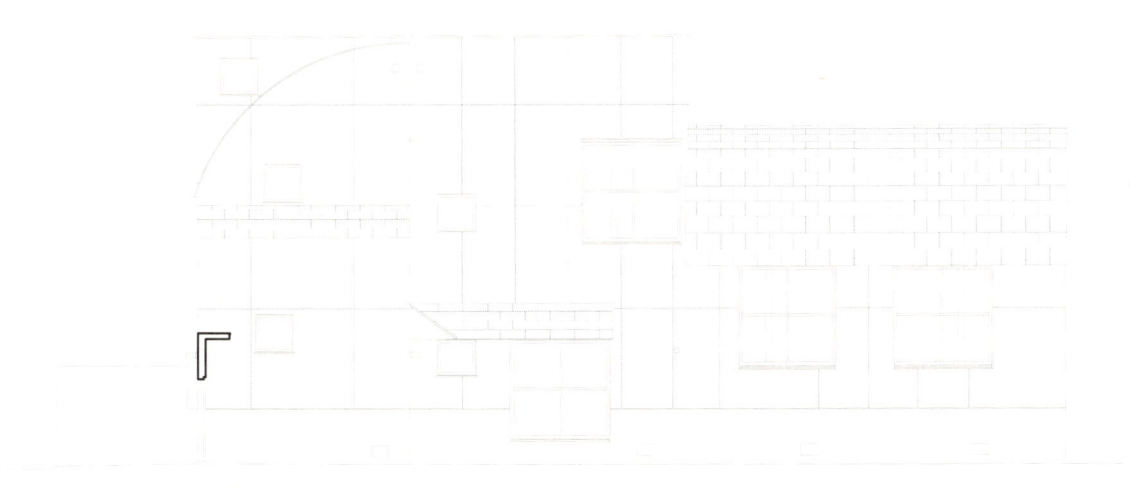

2

3

Toyo Ito
House in Hanakoganei, 1983

1

In House in Hanakoganei, Ito continued exploring the potential of more open spaces than those found in his uncompromising early houses. As with House in Koganei, the house is a closed box, but in this instance Ito included an open roofed structure on top. It is divided into two main blocks, and this division can be clearly read in the form of the facade, which is formed by the juxtaposition of barrel-vaulted and gable-roofed blocks. On the north side is a raised, enclosed space, while the south side is a light-filled space partly open to the outside. This semi-exterior space corresponds to the *doma*, a traditional feature of the Japanese house situated within the entrance of the home and historically floored with compacted earth. The bisected form of the plan makes visible the house's nature as a transitional project in Ito's career, between the enclosed spaces of the 1970s and the radically open, lightweight structures that followed. The architect has declared that 'when Hanakoganei was completed, I felt I'd become slightly more positive in my attitude toward society'.*

Location: Koganei, Tokyo
Total floor area: 152.2 m²

1   First-floor, interior
2   Exterior, viewed from the south
3   Exploded view

*   Toyo Ito, *Toyo Ito 1: 1971–2001* (Tokyo: TOTO Publishing, 2013), 87.

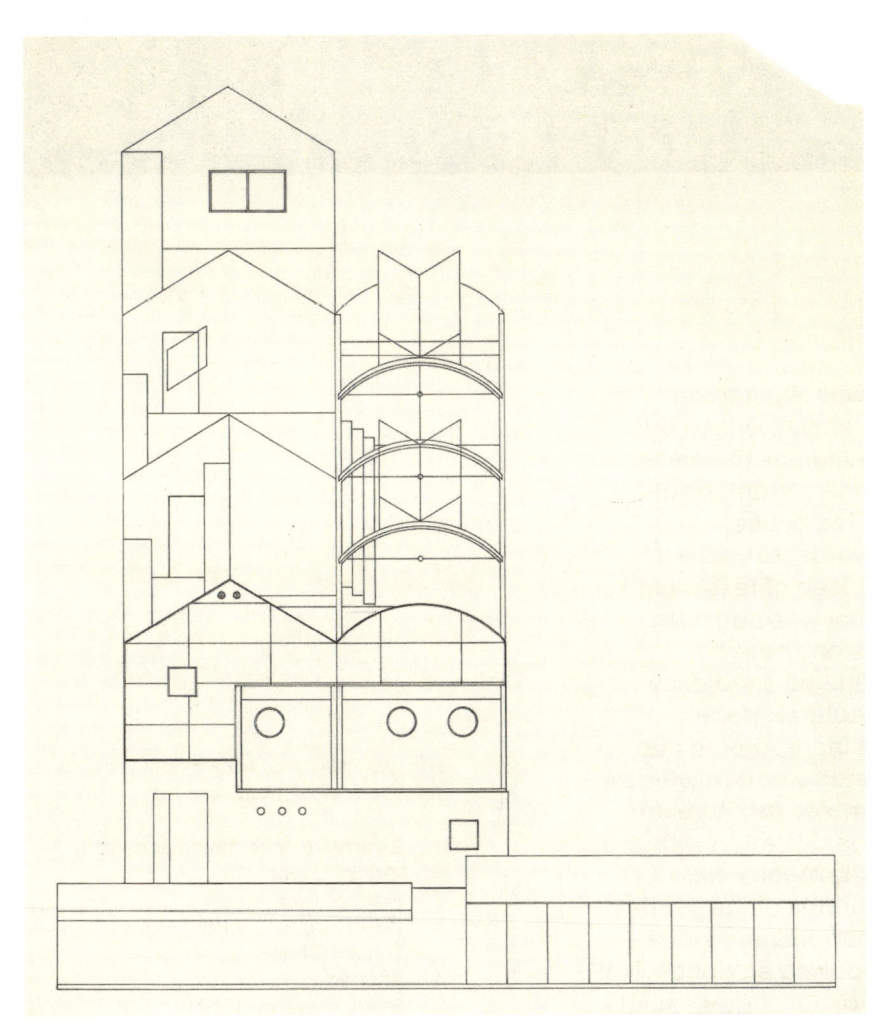

2

3

Toyo Ito
Silver Hut, 1984

1

Silver Hut, built as the architect's own home, was situated on the plot adjacent to his 1976 White U, a house characterized by a startling sense of interiority and enclosure. Whereas the earlier house had adopted a position of retreat from the conditions of urban life, Silver Hut marked a definitive shift. The house was formed of several individual rooms and courtyards, all vaulted with a lightweight steel-frame structure comprised of tessellated triangular frames. This structure, with a form that was both tent-like and industrial, broke down assumed divisions between a private inside and an urban outside and instigated a radically fluid approach to both domesticity and architectural space. The disjointed, chaotic context of the city was incorporated into the material of the architecture – Ito incorporated wooden window frames from his previous residence and assembled furniture and details from old car parts. This spoke to Ito's identification with Tokyo's 'urban nomads', the young, increasingly mobile class of consumers who arose during the economic bubble of the 1980s. With its bright, primary colours and makeshift appearance, Silver Hut exemplifies a kind of pop primitivism, proposing an ephemeral structure constructed from the found detritus of consumer society.

Location: Nakano, Tokyo (later moved)
Total floor area: 138.81 m^2

1 Courtyard, with dining and living rooms at rear
2 Exterior from above
3 Courtyard, with furniture by Teruaki Ohashi
4 Kitchen
5 Study drawing, 1982

2

3

4

5

Kazunari Sakamoto
House F, 1988

1

In the 1980s, Sakamoto continued to resist the commodification of residential architecture, which for him privileged the house as object and image over the house as a space for dwelling. In a series of unbuilt projects, of which House F was the only realized building, he shifted away from the 'house-type' towards a looser, more open configuration of architecture as environment. In House F, the composition is established by the overlap of three independently articulated elements – roof, walls, and floor. The configuration was not arbitrary, but was instead the result of a practical minimalism in which walls were only erected as needed, and the cover of the roof structure only extended as much as was required. The interaction of the autonomous layers creates a number of spaces, both exterior and interior, without forming a coherent architectural whole.

Location: Shinagawa, Tokyo
Total floor area: 172.01 m²

1   Exterior
2   Main room

2

Inhabiting the Experimental

From the end of the war until the 1960s, architects of residential buildings focused on the reinterpretation of tradition, the standardization of technique and production, and the achievement of new solutions to Japanese housing and lifestyles – their work employed shared architectural languages and through debate they aimed to reach consensus.

Throughout the 1960s and 1970s, however, attitudes among the architectural community, and the wider society in general, underwent a shift. The 1960 renewal of the Security Treaty between the United States and Japan – which meant the continuing presence of US Military bases on Japanese soil – had instigated widespread protest, establishing a tendency towards political dissent that culminated in the student protests of 1968. The global oil crisis and subsequent economic recessions of the early 1970s further undermined the public's faith in the myth of progress, while for architects the evaporation of public funds led to a necessary tendency towards experimental small-scale buildings rather than large-scale public projects.

For architects, this disenchantment with the preceding generation coalesced around the reception of two major design events at either end of the 1960s – Senri New Town and Expo '70. Senri New Town, established in 1961, was conceived as the largest planned community in Japanese history, with a projected population of 150,000 people and a land area of 1,160 hectares. It was imagined as the pinnacle of post-war housing developments. Once realized, however, it was beset with problems, including inadequate public facilities and a general lack of interest from potential residents. In 1975 the population peaked at 129,000, and subsequently entered a downward trend. For architects who had invested in the realization of urban master plans and ambitious public spaces, the disappointments of Senri New Town represented a considerable blow to the concept of a public architecture.

Expo '70, the 1970 world's fair staged in Osaka, was intended as an ambitious vehicle for the most pioneering elements of Japanese design. Vaunting the lofty theme of 'Progress and Harmony for Humankind', the festival featured contributions by Kenzo Tange and Arata Isozaki as well as Metabolist architects Kiyonori Kikutake and Kisho Kurokawa. It was the most complete realization to date of the technocratic utopianism of Metabolism, but in the eyes of a younger generation of architects these utopian ambitions were found to be hollow. The radical propositions of 1960s architecture were placed in the service of entertainment spaces and corporate pavilions, recast in the process as mere spectacle.

Expo '70 constituted a turning point in Japanese architecture, away from the public, social ambitions of architects such as

Tange and Kikutake towards a rejection of sociality. During the 1970s, many architects strove for a renewed autonomy by utilizing forms of playful, idiosyncratic, and sometimes esoteric design strategies. Architecture, they suggested, might not be a mere tool of a technocratic society, but instead a space for individual experimentation, expression, and play. The decade was marked by the sudden proliferation of diverse and irreverent architectural collectives, each promoting its own eccentric philosophies, often through the medium of little magazines and small built projects. The short-lived ArchiteXt group – formed by Takefumi Aida, Takamitsu Azuma, Mayumi Miyawaki, Makoto Masuzawa, and Minoru Takeyama – was characteristic. They refused to form a coherent manifesto, instead foregrounding a resolutely pluralistic, even anarchic, approach based on each individual's preferences and philosophies. Houses produced during this period promoted criticality and formal experimentation rather than social function or new forms of living. For architects such as Aida, Kiko Mozuna, and Hiromi Fujii, the house acted as a medium with which to make architecture as free as possible.

Amidst the quest for architectural autonomy, houses became increasingly divorced from society. In the first decades of the twenty-first century, a number of architects have revisited the playful strategies of the 1970s, seeking to build on this tradition while insisting on the need for architecture to connect to the wider world. Sou Fujimoto, Yuusuke Karasawa, and Junya Ishigami all employ unusual theoretical and design methodologies pulled from fields outside of architecture. Their work explores the way in which architecture overlaps and interplays with human behaviour, weather conditions, or the networked space of the information age. Their architecture incorporates a form of play that does not privilege the individual or the collective, but attempts to bridge the divide between the two.

Hiromi Fujii
Project House A, 1968

1

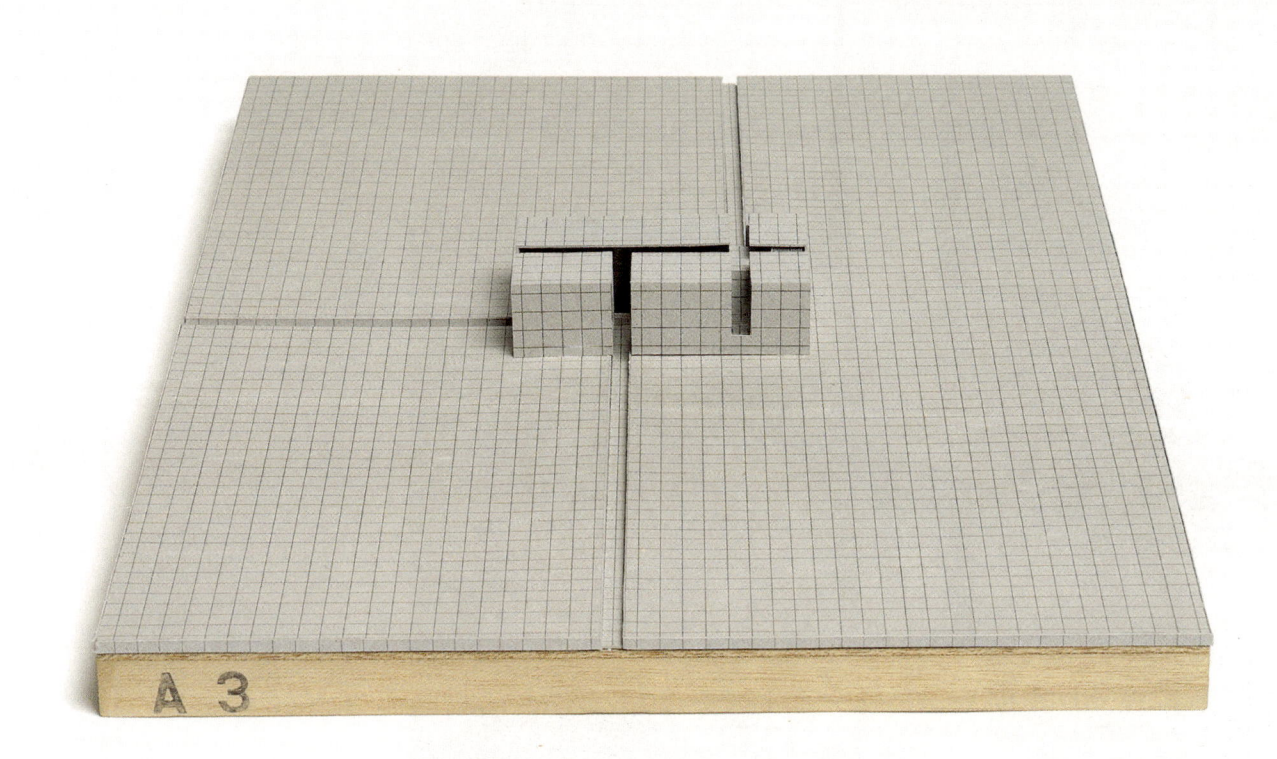

House A marks Hiromi Fujii's initial engagement with the grid, which has remained the central concern of his practice for almost five decades. The model proposes a cuboid form, without visible doors or windows – deep slits sliced into the structure's monolithic exterior provide the only variation in the neutral form.
The regular grid encompasses both structure and site, giving the impression that the house emerges only through the manipulation of a pre-existing matrix. House A is contemporaneous with the equivalent grids by Italian practice Superstudio, including their radical *Continuous Monument*, which hypothesized an infinite gridded structure enveloping the globe. Whereas Superstudio's grid was an act of cultural iconoclasm, however, Fujii's was concerned with the psychological and phenomenological experience of the individual. Emphasizing the grid's blank neutrality, Fujii aimed to utilize it to negate the preconceived meanings of architecture in order to prompt the user to actively produce new relationships with his or her environment. Addressing the emptiness of contemporary society, Fujii claimed that 'we are witness to the self-fulfilling prophecy of a sterile age determined to be sterile. The re-evaluation of architecture in this context is designed to induce an act of self-transformation on the part of man'.* The desired endpoint of this theoretical gambit was to activate the subjectivity of the user.

1   Study model, card, paper and wood, 1968

*   Hiromi Fujii, 'Existential Architecture and the Role of Geometry', *Architecture of Hiromi Fujii*, ed. Kenneth Frampton (New York: Rizzoli, 1987), 33.

Hiromi Fujii
Miyajima Residence, 1973

1

The Miyajima Residence was an early instance of Fujii's grid put into practice in a realized building. The client, a clarinettist, demanded that the architect should maximize the sunlight flowing into the interior, aware of the fact that the crowded Shinjuku neighbourhood in which it stood restricted the use of expansive windows. Fujii's solution was to create an imposing, closed structure containing deep, wide glass-covered grooves that formed light shafts. Further light was brought into the interior through an abundance of skylights. On the surface of the concrete structure, Fujii applied a regular stucco and metal grid on the exterior and painted plywood panels on the interior. Built-in furniture allowed for the further application of the grid and the establishment of a total environment, while practically maximizing interior space. Despite the seemingly closed nature of the house, the architect's comprehensive use of the grid was motivated by the desire to open the space by removing the distinction between interior and exterior – the grid is continuous throughout, negating any hierarchy between spaces.

Location: Shinjuku, Tokyo
Total floor area: 154 m^2

1 Exterior, detail
2 Exterior, detail of entrance
3 Exterior from above
4 First-floor bedroom with built-in furniture

2

3

4

Kiko Mozuna
Anti-Dwelling Box, 1972

1

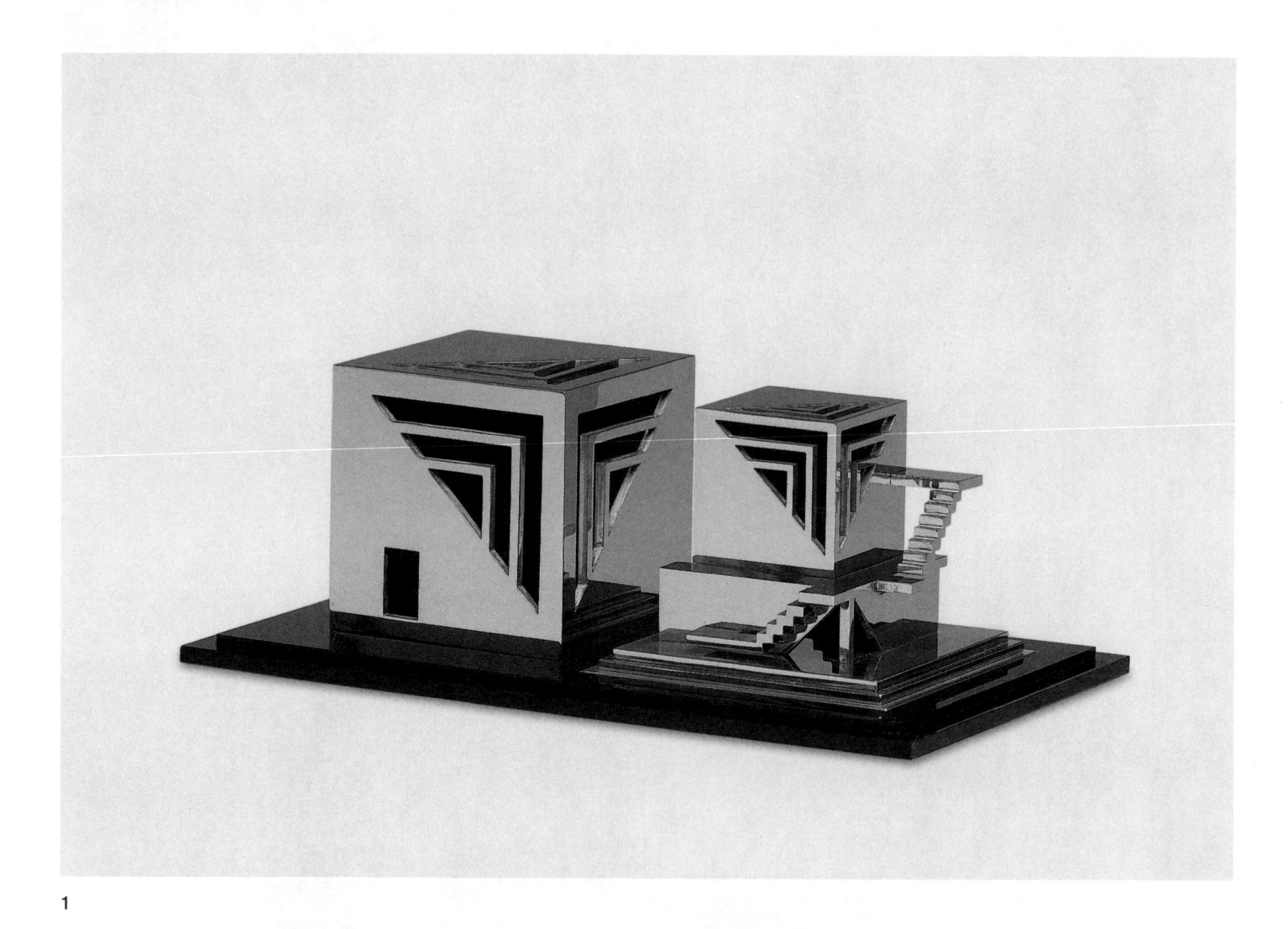

Anti-Dwelling Box embodies Kiko Mozuna's intention to produce a cosmological architecture that projects an image of the universe. A simple cube is articulated with large triangular openings, providing views into the interior in which a smaller cube is nested. The interior cube forms a mirror image of the exterior structure, an effect compounded by the use of triangular and circular openings throughout the structure, which perform as screens that both conceal and reveal the adjacent spaces and overarching system of the architecture. In this way Mozuna establishes an infinite regress of forms within the walls of the house. This configuration suggests the complex pictorial systems of mandalas, indicating the architect's indebtedness to the symbolism of esoteric traditions within Buddhism and Shinto. The strategy of doubling and reflection, which governs the design, evokes the architect's understanding of the cosmos – in a 1978 manifesto he declared that his cosmological space 'consists of various mirrored or double-mirrored images. The space can be regarded as a four dimensional space-model of the "elliptic universe" or the "nested universe".'*

Location: Kushiro, Hokkaido
Total floor area: 104.84 m²

1 Model with separate external and internal cubes, brass
2 Exterior
3 First-floor dining room, inner cube
4 Exterior

* Kiko Mozuna, 'Theory of the Cosmic Architecture', *A New Wave of Japanese Architecture*, ed. Kenneth Frampton (New York: Institute for Architecture and Urban Studies, 1978), 82.

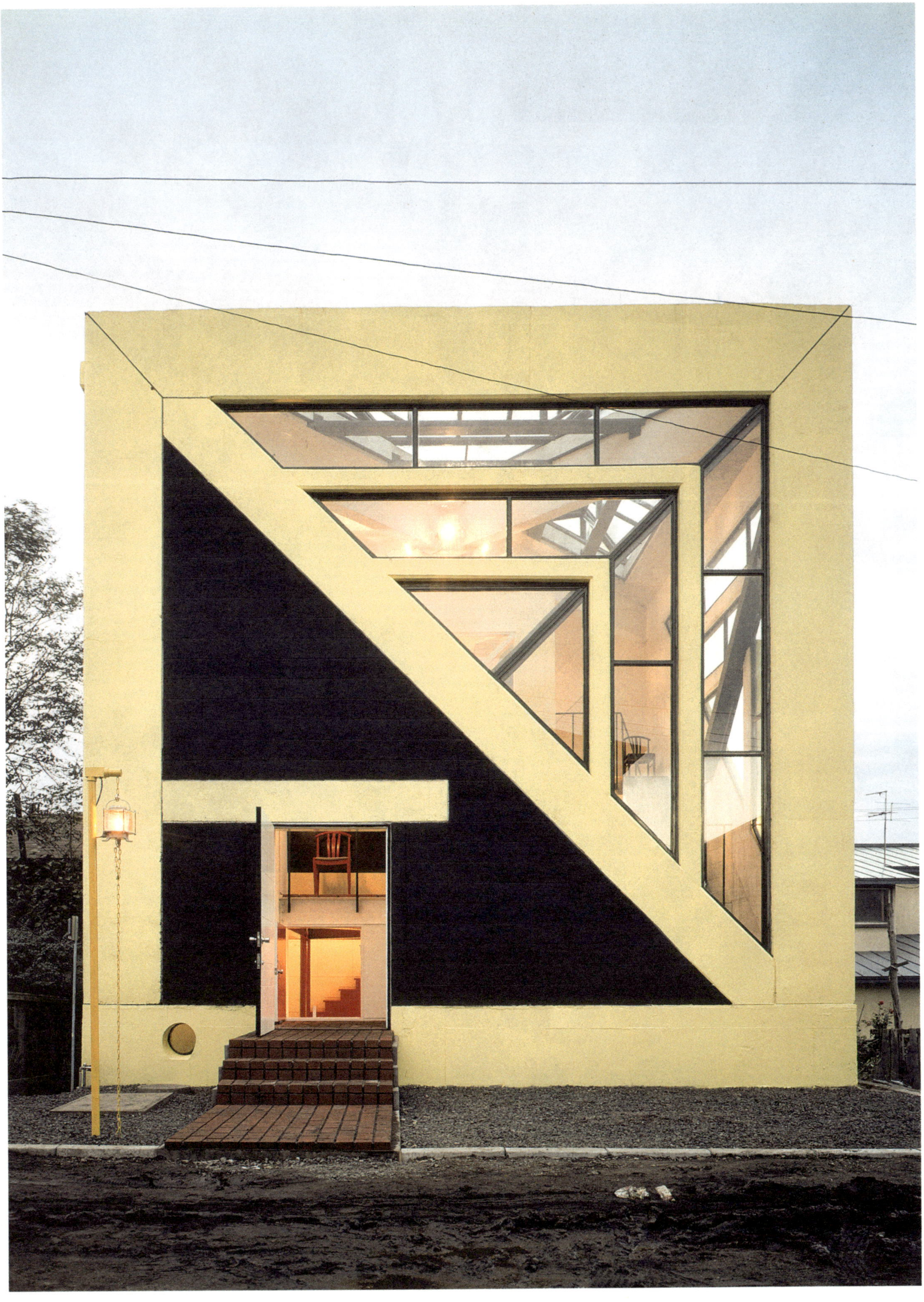

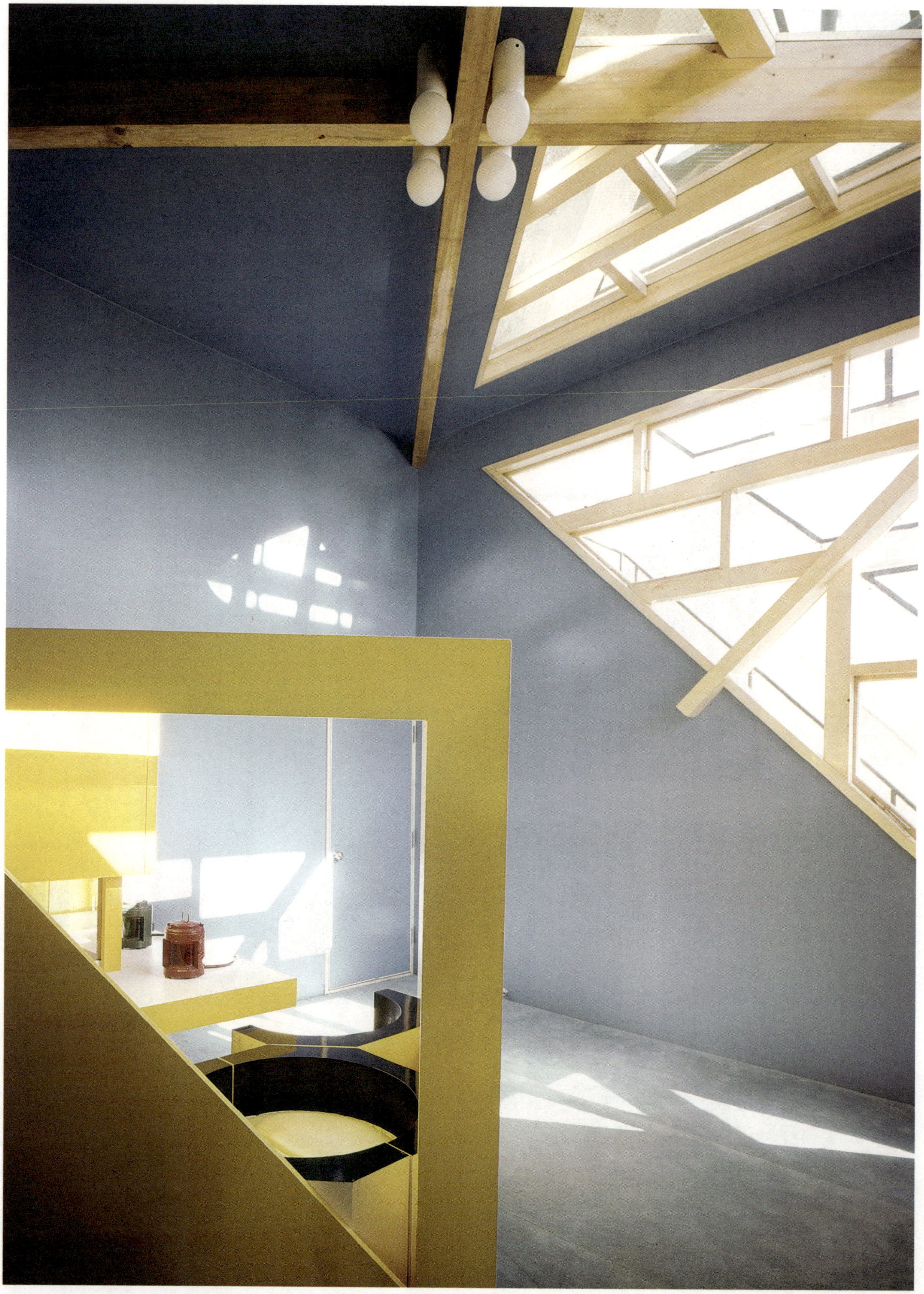

3

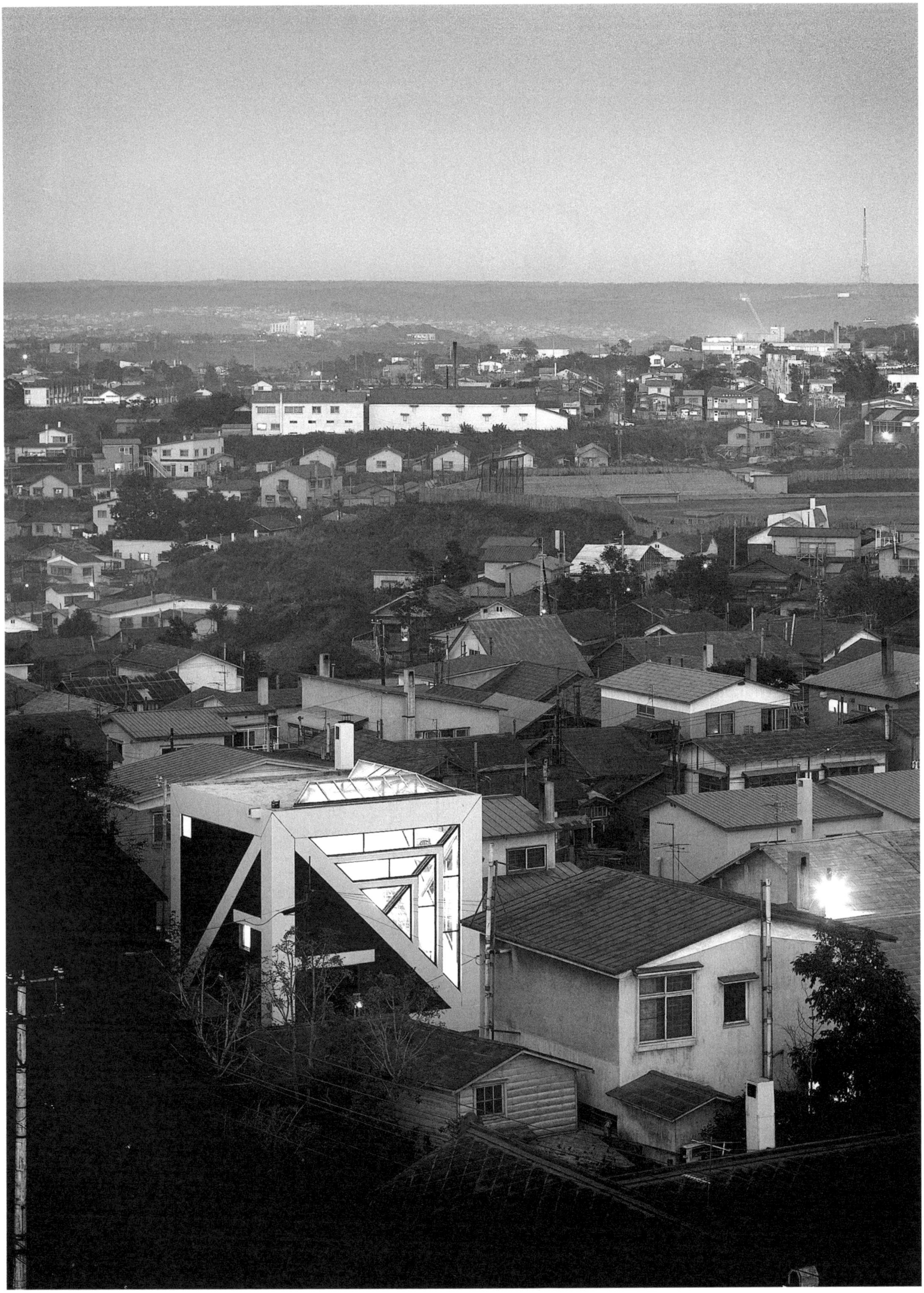

4

Kazumasa Yamashita
Face House, 1974

1

In one of the most controversial publications of twentieth-century architecture, *Learning from Las Vegas* (1972), Robert Venturi, Denise Scott Brown, and Steven Izenour offered an apologia for the oft-derided landscapes of consumer society, particularly the abundance of ornament, explicit signage, and quirky, unserious structures. Their promotion of communication to the level of function found fertile ground in Japanese cities, which had long been saturated in signs and images. Face House, located on a bland Kyoto street, is an explicit example of what Venturi and Scott Brown affectionately called a 'decorated shed' – a building in which a symbolic, communicative facade is applied to a utilitarian structure. The three-storey house is a simple concrete box with domestic spaces on the first and second floors and a graphic design studio on the ground floor. The domestic spaces are accessed by a staircase at the rear of the building, while the studio is accessed from the street. On the street-facing elevation, the architect arranged the windows and included a protruding light shaft in order to form a cartoon-like face – a visual pun on the nature of the facade as the public 'face' of the private house. Yamashita's architectural joke offered a literal attempt to humanize the city through the simple manipulation of external articulation.

Location: Kyoto, Kyoto
Total floor area: 151.98 m^2

1 Exterior

Takefumi Aida
Toy Block Houses, 1978–1984

1

Takefumi Aida, like many of the architects who emerged in the 1970s, developed his architectural thought in reaction to the dominant discourse of Metabolism. In Aida's case, the introduction of play into the design process provided a tool with which to counteract the technological determinism of modernist architecture. This interest culminated in the Toy Block House series, the first of which was built in Tokyo in 1978. Over thirteen years it came to include nine realized houses, two mass-produced toys, and a dollhouse produced for a competition run by British journal *Architectural Design* in 1983. Each house appears as if it was formed through the arrangement of basic geometric solids – cylinders, triangular prisms, and cuboids abound – and the autonomy of these elements is emphasized through the use of distinct, bold colours. As the series developed, Aida multiplied the geometric components and introduced illusionistic effects, rendering the formal simplicity of the early houses complex and ultimately positing the dissolution of the system. These apparently childlike compositions undermine modernism's supposedly rationalist handling of geometry and structure, while stressing the value of individual imagination and whimsy in architectural production. For Aida, in a playful perversion of one of modernism's central tenets, 'form follows fiction'.*

1   Toy Block House I, 1978, exterior
2   Toy Block House IX, 1983, model
3   Detail of ornamental scroll showing axonometric study of Toy Block House IX, a doll's house designed for a competition held in *Architectural Design*, 1983

*   Takefumi Aida, 'On Playfulness and Toy Blocks', *JA* (September, 1985), 43.

2

3

Sou Fujimoto
Primitive Future House, 2003

1

The 'primitive hut' has been a central trope in architectural theory since the eighteenth century, when architects and thinkers began to imagine architecture's archetypal point of origin. The image of the primitive hut has taken many forms, but it has consistently worked on functionalist assumptions – that humans first created architecture to respond to their needs for shelter, security, and warmth. Much of Sou Fujimoto's architectural project has been concerned with conceiving a new kind of primitive hut.
The hypothetical Primitive Future House is based on the idea that the cave rather than the hut marks the birth of architecture – in other words, a pre-existing natural space to which the user is forced to adapt rather than a manmade structure adapted to the user. Architecture is therefore distilled to a pre-functional relationship between body and space. In proposing the necessity of adaptation on the part of the user, the architect hopes for a more active and open engagement with our environment, unshackled by the conventions of architectural tradition. While looking back to a tradition of visionary architects that includes Giovanni Piranesi, Claude Nicolas Ledoux, and Mies van der Rohe, Fujimoto imagines a new concept of architecture to fit the changing landscapes of the contemporary world.

1   Concept model, Plexiglas

Sou Fujimoto
House N, 2008

1

House N, in Fujimoto's own words, 'is a home for two plus a dog'. It was built in Oita in 2008 as an evolution of a preliminary version dating back to 2003. The older version provides an interesting clue to understanding the final project because of the owner's original request for a 'renovation / extension' of the existing, rather anonymous, house. Fujimoto's original proposal was a shell around the old house that expanded the living spaces and created a progression from the street to the inner home and from the exterior to the interior, giving the house a completely new presence in the city. Most of these features were preserved when the owner altered his commission and asked the architect for a new house, which was built as a sequence of three concrete cells in diminishing sizes 'nested one inside the other'. Apart from the dramatization afforded by a few signature elements – complete white, the generic outer box, the artificial order of the openings – the design beautifully exploits the idea of progressive in-between spaces from the street to the house, from the exterior to interior common spaces and the private rooms. As in many of Fujimoto's works, we can easily trace his recurring elements: the mix of light and opacity typical of the forest, the metaphor of the tree, and the creation of multiple gradating spaces between public and private.

Location: Oita, Oita
Total floor area: 85.51 m^2

1   Exterior

Yuusuke Karasawa
s-house, 2013

1

Born in 1976, Yuusuke Karasawa is part of the first generation of architects for whom computer-aided design dominated from education onwards. Unlike many of his peers, however, he approaches the computer not as one tool among many, but as a factor that fundamentally alters the character of architecture itself. His practice revolves around an attempt to establish a new kind of space formed through the reconciliation of the literal space of architecture with the abstract 'network space' of information systems. He is primarily influenced not by the physical structures of architectural history but by the 'small-world networks' proposed by Duncan Watts and Steven Strogatz in 1998. Built for a philosopher specialized in network theory, s-house materializes the interests of both client and architect. Inside a glass cuboid exterior, the architect produced a multi-layered structure that was achieved through the use of an algorithm. Within the transparent form float a number of interwoven door-less and wall-less spaces connected by over a dozen staircases. The complexity of the spatial arrangements found in the house express the architect's critique of the flatness and homogeneity of modern society, and his desire to establish new kinds of social and spatial networks and relationships.

Location: Omiya, Saitama
Total floor area: 103.76 m²

1 Exterior
2 Interior

2

Junya Ishigami
House and Restaurant, 2013–

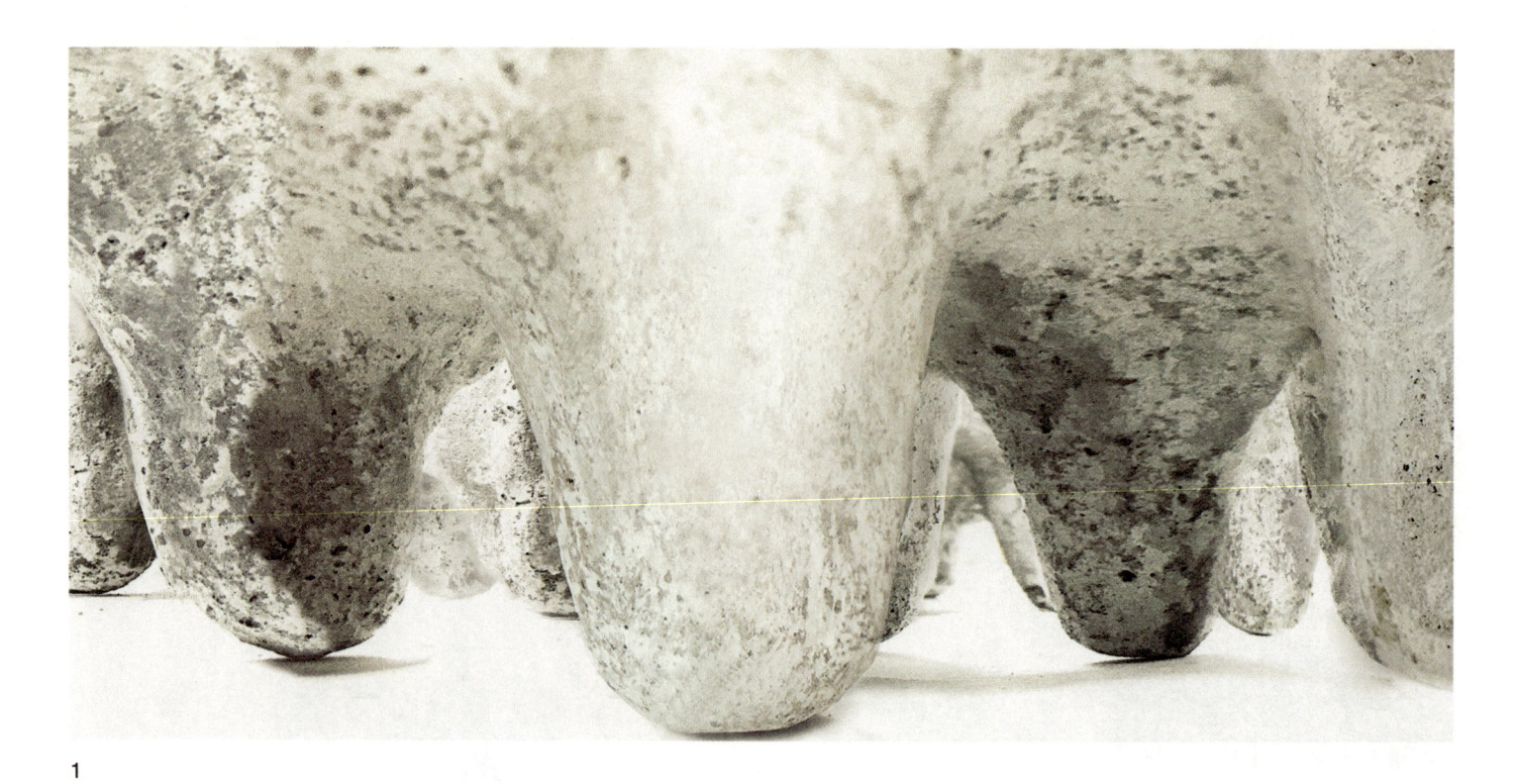

1

Junya Ishigami's design for a combined restaurant and house, currently under construction, continues his exploration of the limits of architecture. A series of holes, asymmetrically arranged, will be dug across the site and subsequently filled in with concrete. The surrounding soil will then be excavated in order to reveal a flat-roofed concrete structure, which on its underside resembles a cave. Glass walls inserted into the structure will establish a loose delineation of individual rooms, but overall the design enacts an ambiguous inversion of public and private, interior and exterior, negative and positive space. Known for ethereal, abstract creations that often verge on the immaterial, Ishigami here engages with a sculptural process of design that embraces the contingency of material. He proposes an architecture that is not only radically open to the natural world, but even mimics the dynamic forces through which nature shapes our environment.

Location: Yamaguchi

1   Detail of study model
2   Study model, positive cast
3   Study model, negative cast

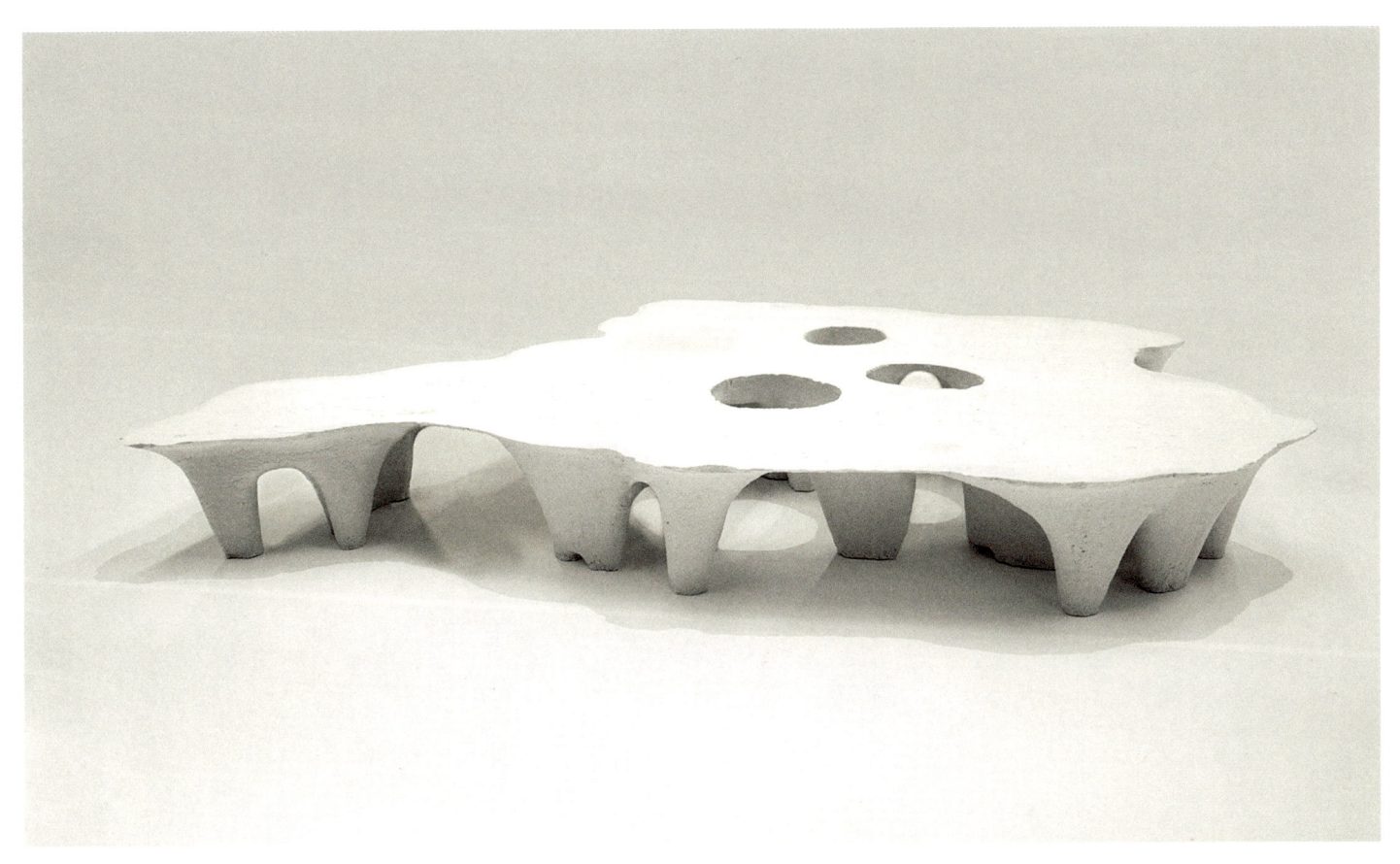

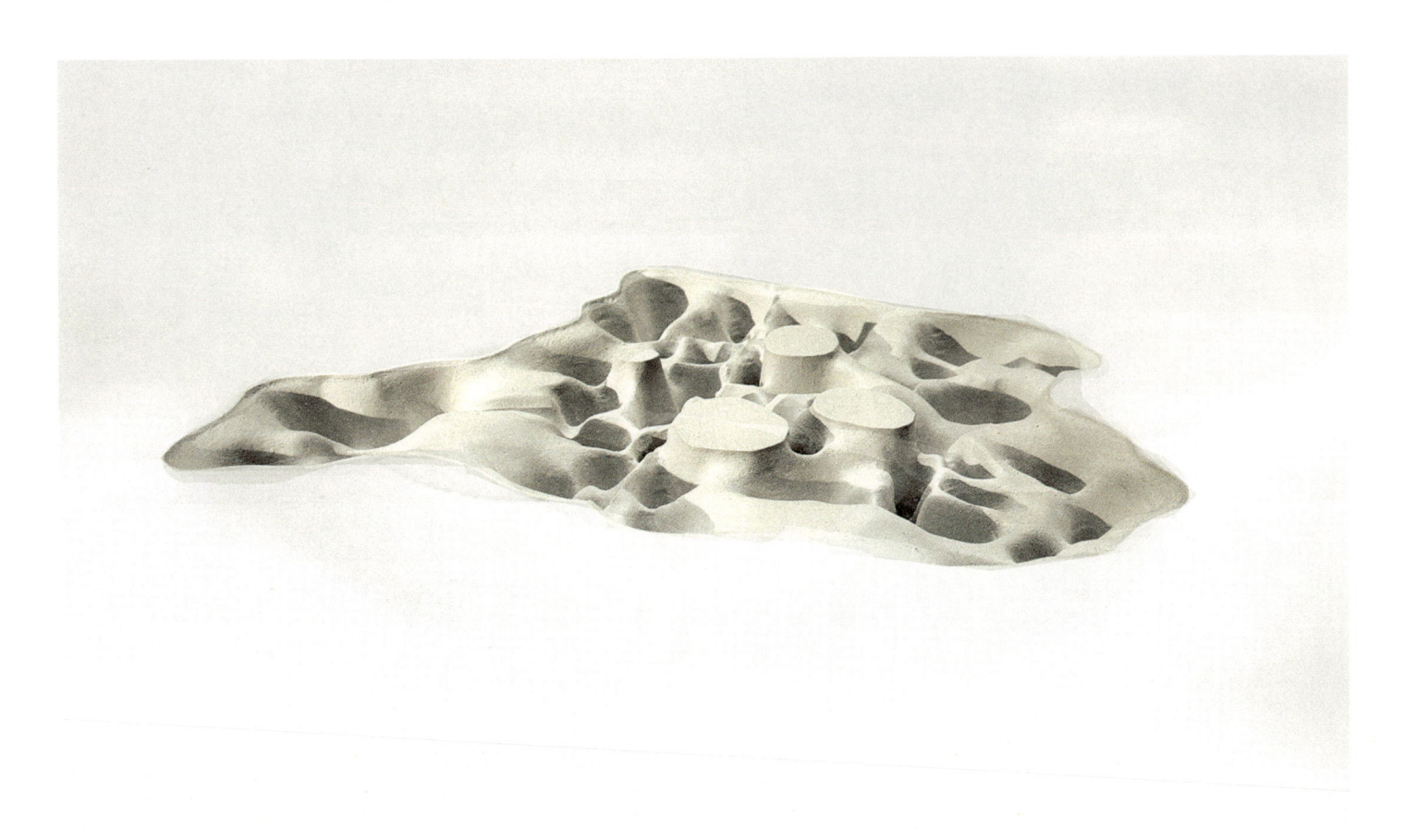

2

3

185

Sensorial

The house is not always a functional, rational machine. Rather, it can act as a space of alternative reality, an autonomous space protected from the pressures of the external world. The desire to create a separate interior reality is rooted in the social conditions of Japan in the post-war period, when the country underwent rapid economic growth and industrialization, inevitably accompanied by an explosion in urbanization. As the 1960s drew to a close, there was an increasing awareness of the downsides of this untrammelled growth, identified most worryingly with dangerous levels of pollution and the bloated, chaotic nature of the urban environment. Architects responded by designing houses as a defence against the encroaching transformations of the twentieth century. In a 1973 essay titled 'Urban Guerilla Housing', Tadao Ando wrote: 'By abstracting the facade as a gesture of "aversion" and "rejection" of the external environment, and trying to enrich the internal space [the aim is to] reveal a microcosmos and pursue a new reality in the space.'[1] Ando explored this idea in a series of enclosed, concrete houses that express an oppositional attitude between the individual and the city. Other architects, however, have taken a rather less confrontational approach, seeking instead to provide a protected interior that nevertheless seeks to gently maintain intimate relationships between one individual and another, and between individuals and the city. In these pure spaces with their emphasis on abstraction, a heightened sensitivity, which we term 'the sensorial', is activated. This quality is made manifest in the concentration of light and the choice of colour, which give an acute awareness of human presence. With their blurred interior divisions, they foster closeness between family members, insisting on the continued value of human relationships in the face of the relentless changes of the outside world.

   An important precedent for these architects can be found in the work of Kazuo Shinohara, in particular his symbolic handling of white, with its claim to immateriality, transcendence, and abstraction. In his seminal House in White (1966), his use of white throughout the interior foregrounds the abstraction of the architecture, reducing the emphasis on function and structure in favour of a geometric purity. Its uniform whiteness completely eliminates the disordered demands of the exterior environment. The use of white to achieve a kind of abstraction became a crucial device for the younger architects who were influenced by Shinohara's work, including Itsuko Hasegawa (who worked for him for a number of years) and Toyo Ito. During the 1970s, Hasegawa, who had a background in both abstract painting and mathematics, produced a series of small houses that engaged with complex spatial compositions. In her House in Yaizu (1972), a plain black exterior (typical of local buildings) contains a dramatic interior in which alternating black and white walls are starkly juxtaposed. The resulting interior space is one that seems to simultaneously reject and embrace the surrounding urban context. Toyo Ito's House in Sakurajosuin (1975) similarly produces a white interior that has been apparently penetrated by the black of the exterior – the architect has explicitly described this composition as representing the intrusion of the outside into the protected internal space. In his seminal White U (1974), he conceived of a space in which a pronounced sense of abstraction formed a gentle buffer between a grieving family and the outside world. The house's whiteness centres on a courtyard, floored in black soil, which meets the client's desire to be close to the earth. The house attempts to give form to a space that responds to the most subtle changes in atmosphere, whether physical or emotional – the white walls act to magnify changes in light and movement. What emerges is an exemplar of a 'sensorial' space – non-uniform, fluid, and irrational.

During the 1980s and 1990s, this kind of enclosed, sensorial space became less common in Japanese architecture, as architects explored a very different concept of open, diffuse, or fragmented space. Over the last twenty years, however, architects have begun to return to the sensorial space. As people seek once again to occupy the densely populated urban centres, the need to create an emotionally fulfilling interior space that offers some respite from the chaos of the city. Many of these architects have worked directly under Toyo Ito. The architecture of Kazuyo Sejima, for example, demonstrates what Arata Isozaki calls a 'conciliatory, interfusing attitude',[2] creating spaces that are simultaneously introverted and extroverted, virtual and physical. She employs effects such as reflection and translucency as well as unusual spatial devices in order to explore new kinds of spaces that are neither closed nor open to the outside world. Her work, which has itself been immensely influential on an emerging generation of architects, suggests the way the abstraction of the 1970s has been adapted to the expectations of an advanced information society. The complex internal spaces that have emerged in recent years reflect an increased awareness of networks and communication, and an emphasis on new forms of connection rather than separation. If spatial relations presuppose social relations, the sensorial space might be seen to suggest new ways for the individual and the family to relate to the wider society.

---

1   Tadao Ando, 'Toshi Gerira Jukyo' (Urban Guerilla Housing), *Toshi Jukatu*, no. 7307 (July, 1975), 18-19
2   Arata Isozaki, 'Sei Shonagon, or Ariadne – Architecture in the Metropolis', *JA*, 99 (Autumn, 2015), 10.

Itsuko Hasegawa
House at Yaizu 1, 1972

1

House at Yaizu was Itsuko Hasegawa's first independent building, designed for a relative on a low budget. At this stage of her career, Hasegawa expressed the desire to focus on small autonomous spaces rather than the large-scale urban projects of Metabolist architects such as Kiyonori Kikutake, her former employer. House in Yaizu is a simple wooden structure enclosing a long internal space that loops back on itself. The space is an early instance of Hasegawa's configuration of the concept of *garando* – a void or 'expanding emptiness' – which formed the principal motivation of her residential projects, conveying the idea of an empty interior space that could facilitate a flexible programme of everyday and non-everyday activities and relations. In this house, the sense of a void is reinforced through the abstract treatment of the wall surfaces, which are painted alternately black and white. This exaggerates the thinness of the structure, reducing its material presence and establishing a distinct and independent interiority.

Location: Yaizu, Shizuoka
Total floor area: 78.65 m²

1 Exterior
2 Ground-floor dining room and entrance
3 Study drawings, showing circulation and composition for House at Yaizu and hypothetical houses

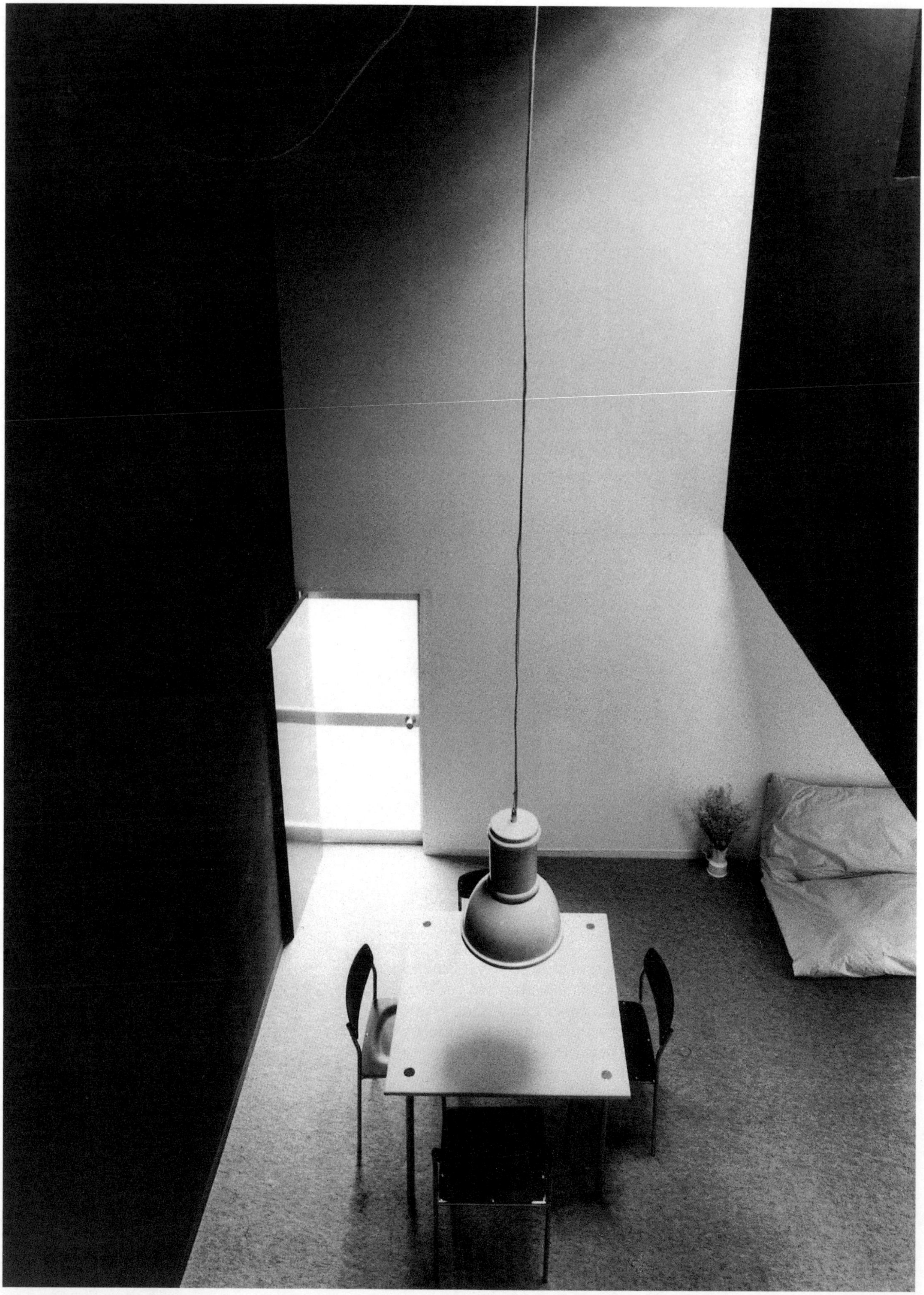

2

Length and Void

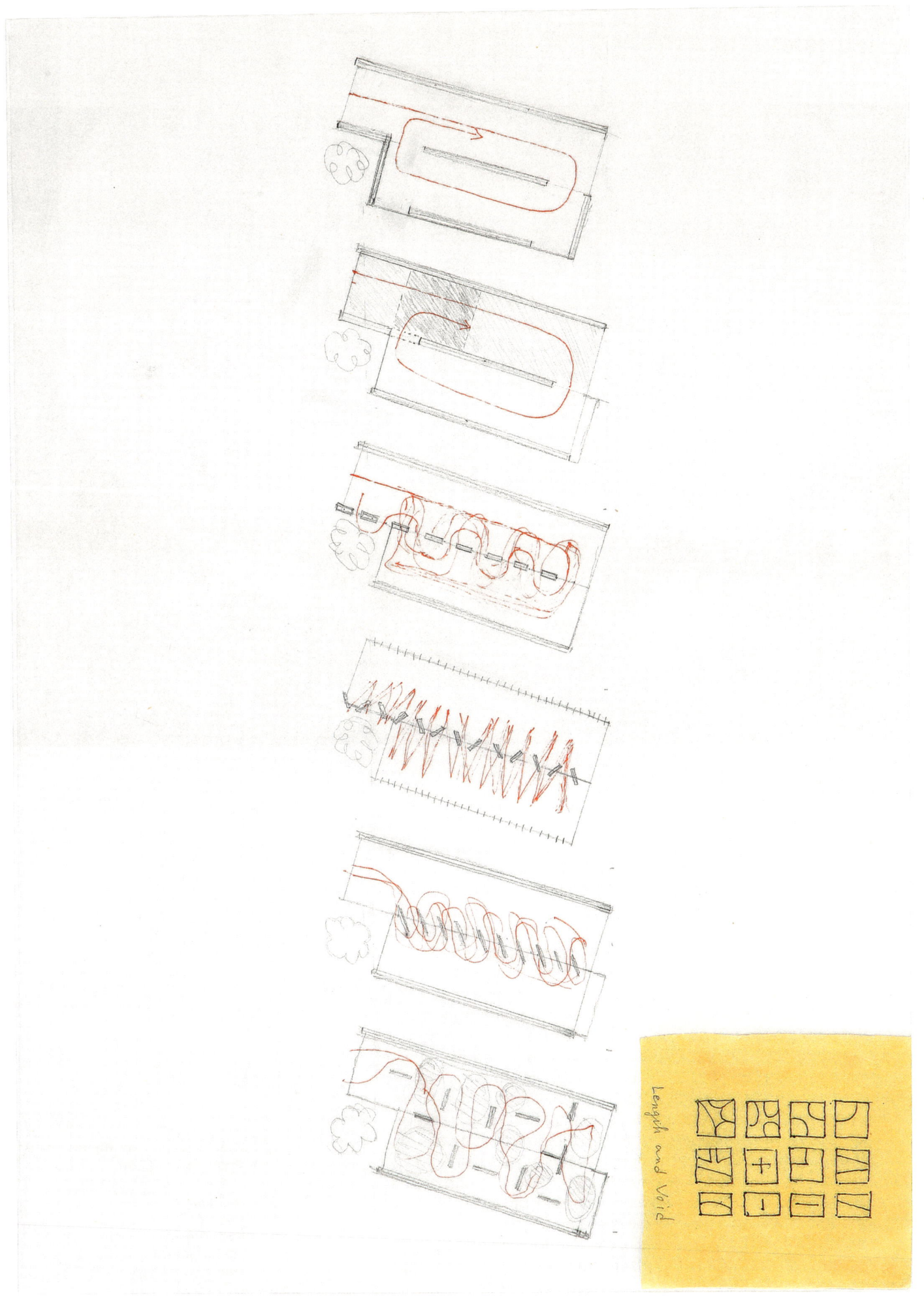

Toyo Ito
White U, 1976

1

White U was built for the architect's sister, a musicologist with two children whose husband had recently died. Both client and architect were willing to forego certain conventional domestic conveniences in order to produce a space of abstract beauty, which would necessarily be closed to the disorderly surrounding environment (the house was located in a busy central Tokyo neighbourhood a short journey away from the chaos of Shinjuku). The client had been living in an eighth-floor apartment, and expressed the desire to live close to the earth. Accordingly, the core of the house was a soil-floored courtyard, around which was wrapped a tubular space. The house lacked a facade, presenting an unarticulated, curved concrete wall to the street. Light is introduced into the interior through skylights and a glass sliding door leading to the courtyard, allowing for the elimination of street-facing windows. Private rooms were arranged on the straight edge of the plan, but the curved section forms one continuous internal space. The borders between walls and ceiling were plastered in order to create a continuous curved surface throughout, conveying a sense of immateriality and even infinity. The smooth, immersive whiteness of the interior is varied through striking shadows created by the placement of industrial spotlights at various points.

Location: Nakano, Tokyo (demolished)
Total floor area: 148.25 m²

1,2 Central courtyard
3 Exterior from above
4 Study drawing, floor plan
5 Interior, with spotlight and chair by C R Mackintosh
6 Interior

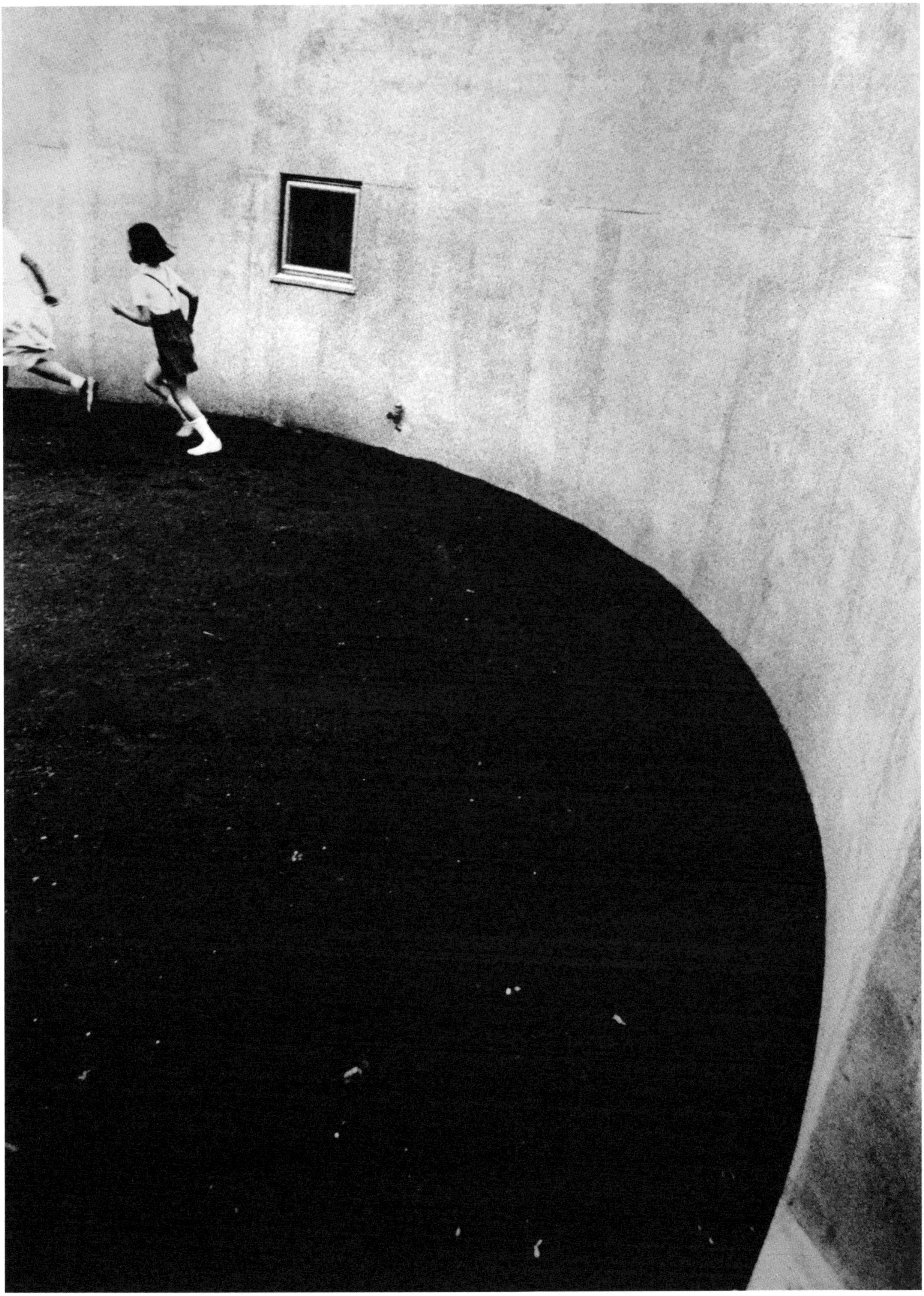

2

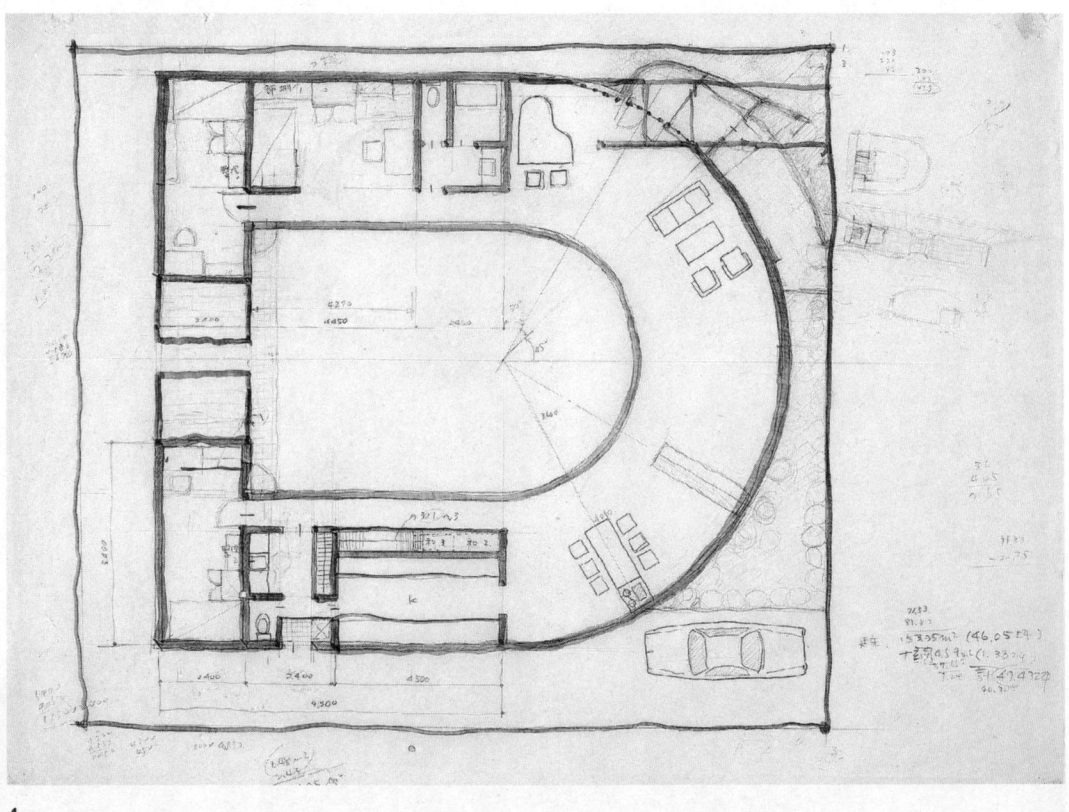

3

4

5

6

Kazuyo Sejima
House in a Plum Grove, 2003

1

House in a Plum Grove was built for a three-generation family of five. The site is small, and space was constrained even further by the decision to push the structure back in order to preserve the cluster of plum trees growing on the plot. The clients had requested an open-plan house, but the architect recognized that the differing preferences of each family member, the clutter of personal possessions, and the area of the site made a wholly open plan unsatisfactory. Her solution was to establish a series of small, nested spaces. Each space is independent, but without a clear division of rooms – internal openings establish a sense of continuity throughout the interior. Kazuyo Sejima intended the spaces to have the scale of furniture, and one such space is only large enough to precisely fit a bed, for example. To achieve this profusion of spaces within a constrained site, the architect employed steel walls only 16 mm thick, which give the house a remarkable sense of lightness. The gentle, soft divisions between spaces suggest a different kind of family life predicated on altered configurations of intimacy and privacy.

Location: Setagaya, Tokyo
Total floor area: 77.68 m^2

1 Exterior, seven years after completion
2 Bedroom
3 Rooftop terrace
4 Bedroom
5 Ground-floor plan

2

3

4

5

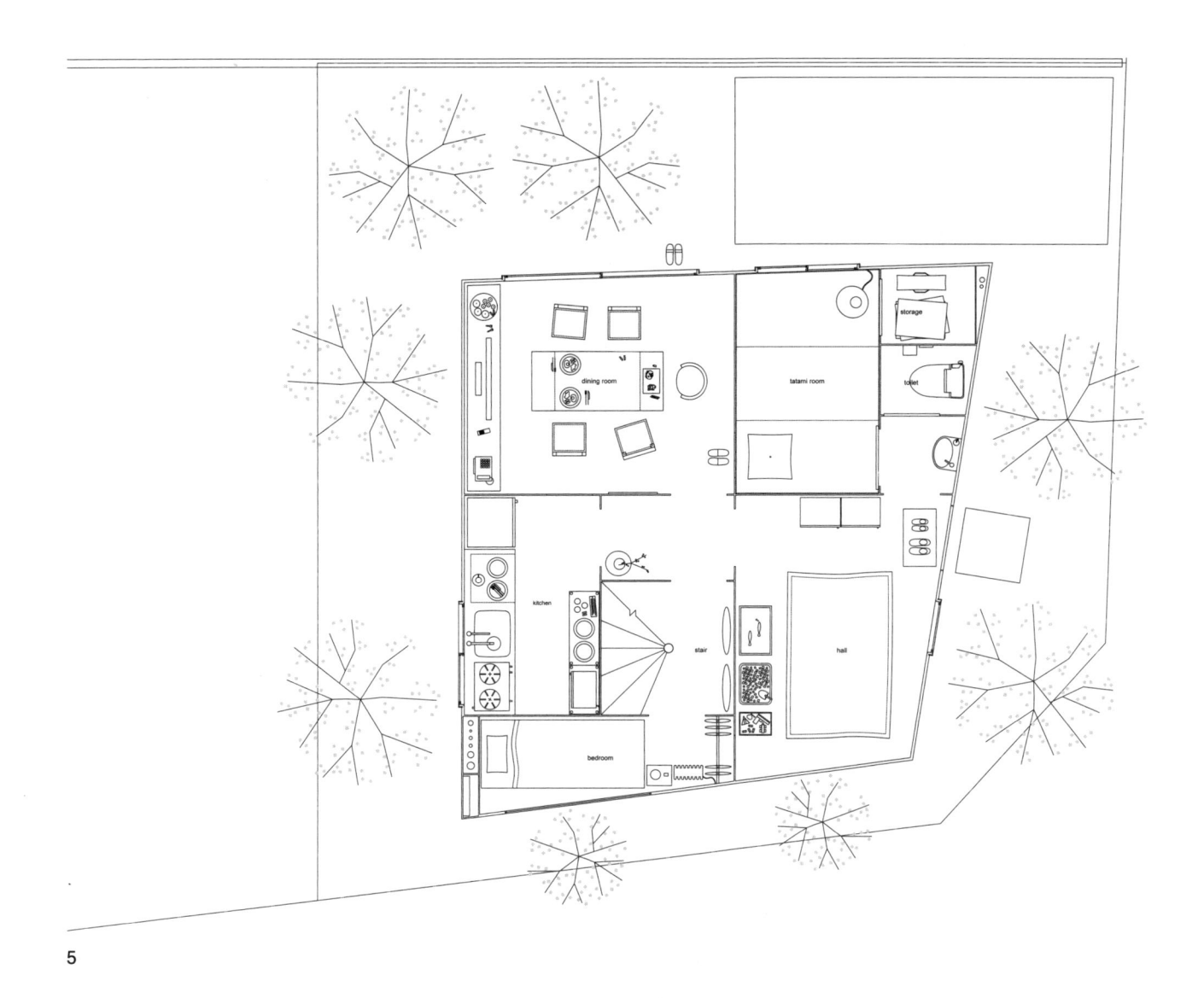

Jun Aoki
G, 2004

1

Well known for his Aomori Museum, a series of Louis Vuitton Stores, and a number of successful public and commercial buildings, Jun Aoki designed G in 2004. Built for a family in a very generic urban context in Tokyo, the house aims at performing a dialogue between determinism and incertitude. The design, in fact, investigates the friction generated by the juxtaposition of 'ordinary' forms and materials and a contemporary approach to the design of living spaces. G actually consists of a 'house-like' volume entirely built in wood, sitting on top of a square, concrete base. The roof is a mono-material box enveloping the bedrooms, while the concrete podium hosts the living, dining, and cooking area. As in many contemporary Japanese houses, the outer shells do not exactly correspond to the inner space: the large upper volume is bigger than the rooms and creates a large in-between double-height area inhabited by light; the 80 cm difference between the base and the house offers another specific access to the light, defining the architecture of the living space. G is the first of a series of Aoki's residential projects – especially A and N – that insist on investigating the co-existence of vernacular and modern elements.

Location: Meguro, Tokyo
Total floor area: 154.98 m^2

1   Stairwell, viewed from first floor

Sou Fujimoto
T House, 2005

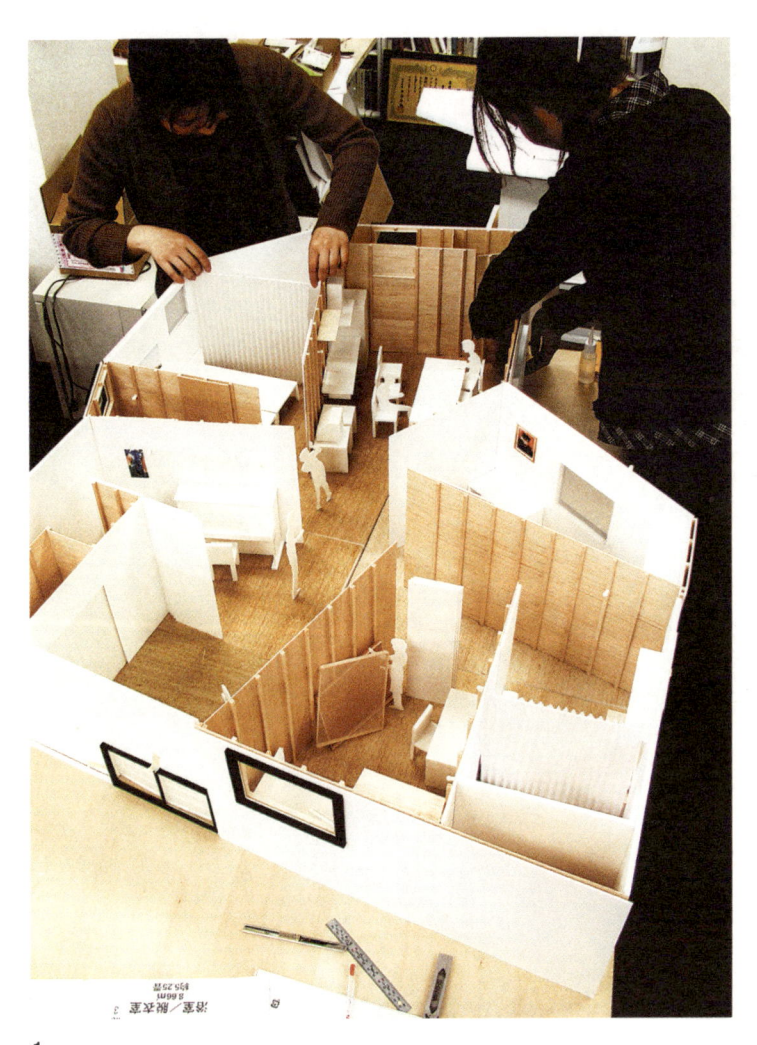

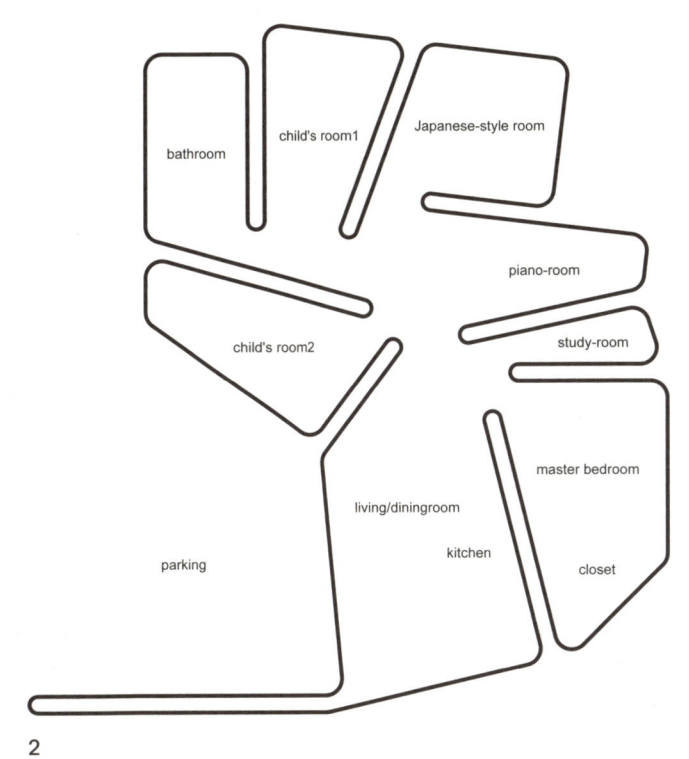

1

2

T House, built for a family of four, is essentially one large space that is neither open plan nor subdivided into distinct, closed rooms. Divisions are established between spaces by means of thin wooden partitions that radiate inwards from the perimeter wall, which has very few openings onto the street. These spaces thus take on the character of corners, nooks, or crannies within a single continuous space that appears as if it has been bent or warped into a more complex form. The house advances Sou Fujimoto's belief that 'at its most basic, a house is a place of separation and connection, and the vast field of interrelationships within'.*
The spatial arrangement indicates that Fujimoto views 'separation' and 'connection' on a modulated spectrum rather than distinct or opposing concepts. As the residents move through the space of the house, the architect's intention is that they will gradually establish their position in relation to the space and to one another.

Location: Maebashi, Gunma
Total floor area: 90.82 m²

1   Sou Fujimoto Architects staff working on model
2   Concept drawing, plan

*   Sou Fujimoto, *Sou Fujimoto: Architecture Works 1995–2015* (Tokyo: TOTO Publishing, 2015), 42.

Hideyuki Nakayama
O House, 2009

1

Hideyuki Nakayama's buildings begin life as a series of childlike sketches that propose a certain narrative or spatial relation. Through the design process, these concepts – initially impressionistic and fragmentary – cohere into functional structures that retain something of the whimsical, fantastical quality of Nakayama's initial imaginings. Occupying a deep, narrow site in Kyoto, O House consists of a curved, gabled, two-storey central block flanked by two 'lean-tos'. These adjacent structures, through which the house is entered, contain the bulk of the everyday functions, including kitchen, dining, and bathroom facilities. The bedrooms, on the other hand, are located on the first floor of the main block, but are accessed directly from the garden by means of an external staircase. This arrangement leads to a proliferation of routes through the building, and prompts a kind of ambulatory movement weaving in and out of the different spaces. The relegation of domestic functions to the secondary rooms also establishes the ground floor space of the main house as distinct from the mundane. Its pronounced verticality and entirely glazed front emphasize its unusual atmospheric quality, and a theatrical element is introduced by the translucent curtain that hangs from floor to ceiling, designed by Akane Moriyama. This speaks to the architect's desire to establish a structure within which the family can change the meaning of everyday life.

Location: Kyoto, Kyoto
Total floor area: 59.71 m²

1 Exterior
2 Concept drawings

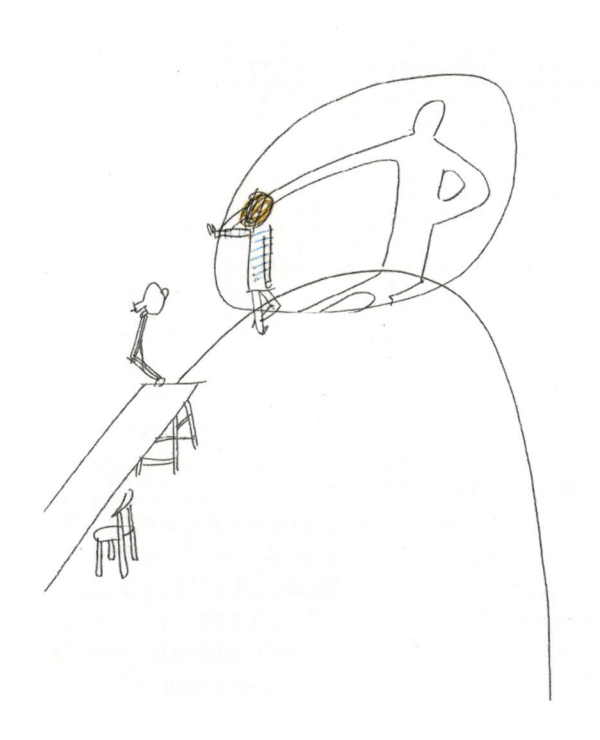

2

203

onishimaki + hyakudayuki architects
Double Helix House, 2011

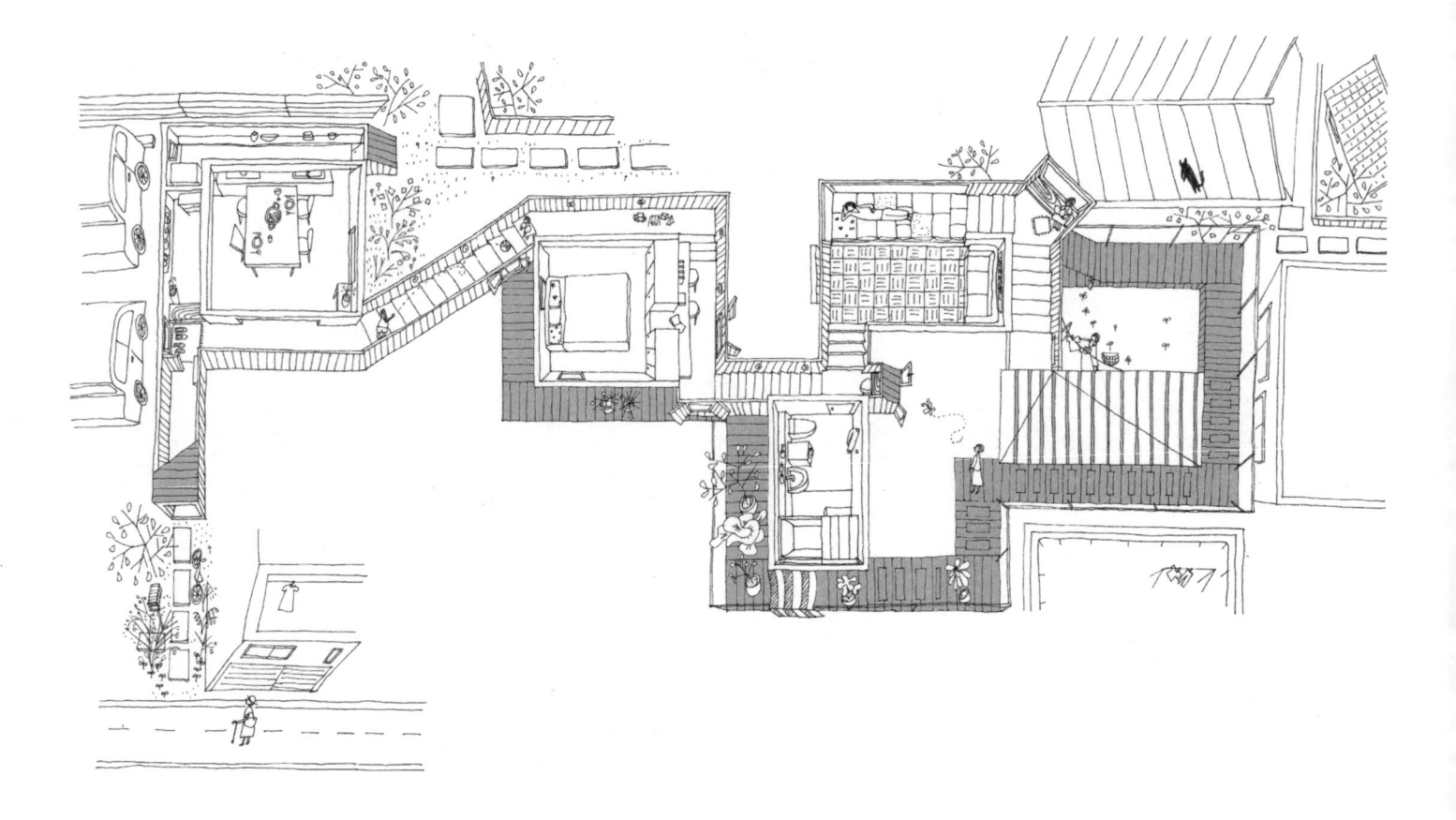

1

Double Helix House is located in Shitamachi, a neighbourhood that survived the fire-bombings of World War II relatively unscathed and is characterized by a profusion of old wooden houses, historical temples, and very narrow alleyways. Desiring to incorporate this atmosphere into the design of the house, the architects assimilated the concept of the alleyway into the vertically oriented structure. The house consists of two distinct yet interwoven spaces. The principal, everyday spaces are contained within a white concrete core. Around this is wrapped an 'alley' in the form of a dark wood-panelled corridor, which provides circulation but also houses a library and study area. The negative space formed by the relationship of core and corridor was also utilized by the architects to establish a series of external terrace spaces and staircases. The double helix of the house's title refers to this woven arrangement of interior and exterior space. Maki Onishi has compared the spiralling composition to the experience of memory as a chain of fragmented images, calling it 'a house that faithfully reproduces the way spaces appear in our memory – arrayed in a chain extending from the street to the hall to the living room to the stairs to the bedroom'.*

Location: Taito, Tokyo
Total floor area: 91.22 m²

1   Concept drawings
2   Exterior

*   onishimaki + hyakudayuki architects, *8 stories* (Tokyo: LIXIL, 2014), 21.

2

Beyond Family

Prior to the 1950s, Japanese families lived in very different conditions to those in the Western homes that were popularized in post-war Japan. People commonly lived in two *tatami*-floored rooms with non-specific functions – they dined by bringing out a table, which was then stowed away and replaced with a *futon* on which the entire family slept *zakone* style (that is, all together side-by-side). During the post-war democratic reforms, prompted by the Allied Occupation, this flexible style of living was criticized and revised. The change was primarily driven by the hope that by separating places for eating and sleeping, and also by separating the sleeping places of family members of different ages and genders, housework would be streamlined, women would be empowered, and quality of life would generally be improved. Underlying this was a deep sense of remorse for having condoned a highly patriarchal and even feudalist domestic environment that had served to bolster the monarchical state and dragged the nation into a disastrous, failed war.

    The reality for housing reformers in post-war Japan was harsh, however. An estimated three million units were required to resolve the housing shortage caused by the destruction of Japanese cities during World War II, and the construction industry was beset by scarcity of construction materials and economic inflation. It was not until the Nihon Jutaku Kodan (Japan Housing Corporation) was established in 1955 that the state was finally able to tackle the housing shortage problem through collective housing. The claims for democracy in the home were assiduously applied to the planning of this collective housing. The so-called '2DK' floor plan configuration comprised a dining / kitchen area intended to be used with Western-style furniture, two independent *tatami*-floored rooms accessible separately from the dining / kitchen area, and a bathroom area. It was a more comfortable alternative to the collective housing supplied by municipalities, and it became particularly popular among middle-class 'salaryman' families. From this point on, houses began to be described using a combination of letters (L, D, K) and a number (n), where the former denotes rooms with a specific function and the latter rooms with no predefined purpose.
As the economy developed, people came to believe that n should correspond to the number of members in a family. The idea that all family members should have their own private rooms in order to guarantee their rights as individuals (which was already assumed in the West) had taken root in Japanese society.

    As the industrialization of housing was further advanced during the period of rapid economic growth and mass-produced houses entered the market, the image of the family became standardized. These standardized assumptions were then materialized in the physical environment, with the effect of fixing the relationships and lifestyles of the people who lived on a particular site. As the process was repeated, the assumption that there should be one house per family and that places of living and working should be zoned into distinct areas solidified into unquestioned dogma.

In contrast to these mass-produced houses and the assumptions they bring, architects have used houses to emphasize the specificity of individual families, and question the preconceived images of the family. In the 1970s, for example, architect and Marxist theorist Takashi Kurosawa launched a critique of domestic space and the gendered divisions it imposes on the family, arguing for a departure from the master bedroom towards a house formed of private spaces for each individual. He argued that in proposing the individual rather than the nuclear family as the basic social unit, individuals (especially women) would become more empowered to participate in society.
A decade later, Toyo Ito's hypothetical Pao: A Dwelling for Tokyo Nomad Women presented a scenario in which the family had entirely dissolved, and the individual was now housed in a structure defined only by a thin membrane, like a jellyfish floating in the sea of consumption.

In this century, the social and urban landscape has undergone considerable changes as the result of the decline of suburban residential developments, the growing number of single-person households, the increasingly aged population and the growth of the information society. These changes have offered architects new opportunities to rethink the family, and many houses have exhibited an openness to the idea of accepting non-family members into the domestic space, blurring the boundaries between the public and private. This is expressed most clearly in the trend towards combining living and working spaces, or in shared living arrangements. Questioning the assumption of 'one house per family', these houses propose a shift from the nuclear family towards the expanded family.

Takashi Kurosawa
Hoshikawa Cubicles, 1977

1

In 1968, Takashi Kurosawa published an important thesis on domestic* spaces in the inaugural issue of the magazine *Toshi jutaku* (Urban Housing). Kurosawa declared that the traditional enclosure of women within the domestic space was anachronistic in the contemporary situation, where increasingly empowered women were joining the labour force in great numbers. As an alternative, he suggested that husband and wife should occupy individual rooms, allowing them to connect to the community independently. This structure, which stressed the autonomy of the individual over the nuclear family, recalls the *phalanstères* proposed by early nineteenth-century utopian socialist Charles Fourier, co-operative communities founded on the liberation of the individual. Kurosawa saw that Fourier's proposal was already becoming a reality due to the onward march of capitalism, and his 'individual room dwellings' formed his response. In the Hoshikawa Cubicles he put these ideas into action – the first storey consists of rental accommodation, while the second storey houses the residence of the owner, a unit of only 20 m². Appliances such as washing machine, dryer, and refrigerator are located in a shared common area on the ground floor.

Location: Ichikawa, Chiba
Total floor area: 57 m²

1 Exterior showing separate entrances for individual cubicles

* Takashi Kurosawa, 'Historical Perspective of Σ Individual Room Dwellings', *Toshi jukatu*, no. 1 (May, 1968), 67–72.

Toyo Ito
Pao: A Dwelling for Tokyo Nomad Women, 1985

1

Influenced by both the writing of Gilles Deleuze and Félix Guattari and his own bar-crawling Tokyo lifestyle, Toyo Ito's work of the 1980s engaged with the urban 'nomad' – a creature of late capitalism, most at home wandering the hypertrophied, information-saturated urban landscapes of Bubble-era Japan. Ito posited that since the city could respond to all of the needs formerly met by the home, the house might become defunct. When the architect was asked to participate in an exhibition on 'what happens when an architect designs a kitchen' for the Seibu department store in Shibuya, he took the opportunity to propose a new form of home suitable for the future nomad – here explicitly associated with the fashionable young women who spent their leisure time in Shinjuku and Shibuya. A fabric tent contained three components referred to as 'pre-furniture', each responding to a different need or desire – 'Intelligence', 'Styling', and 'Snack'. These lightweight, portable structures would form platforms onto which the woman could temporarily alight during her voyages through what Ito called the 'sea of consumption'.*
The Pao suggested a future in which architecture as we know it might dissolve in the increasingly virtual space of an information society.

1–3 Kazuyo Sejima, an employee of Ito's at the time, demonstrating use of the three 'Pre-Furniture' components, for Intelligence, Styling, and Snack
4 Concept drawing

* Toyo Ito, 'Architecture is Possible Only in the Sea of Consumption', *From Postwar to Postmodern, Art in Japan:1945–1989*, ed. Doryun Chong (New York: Museum of Modern Art, 2012), 360.

2

3

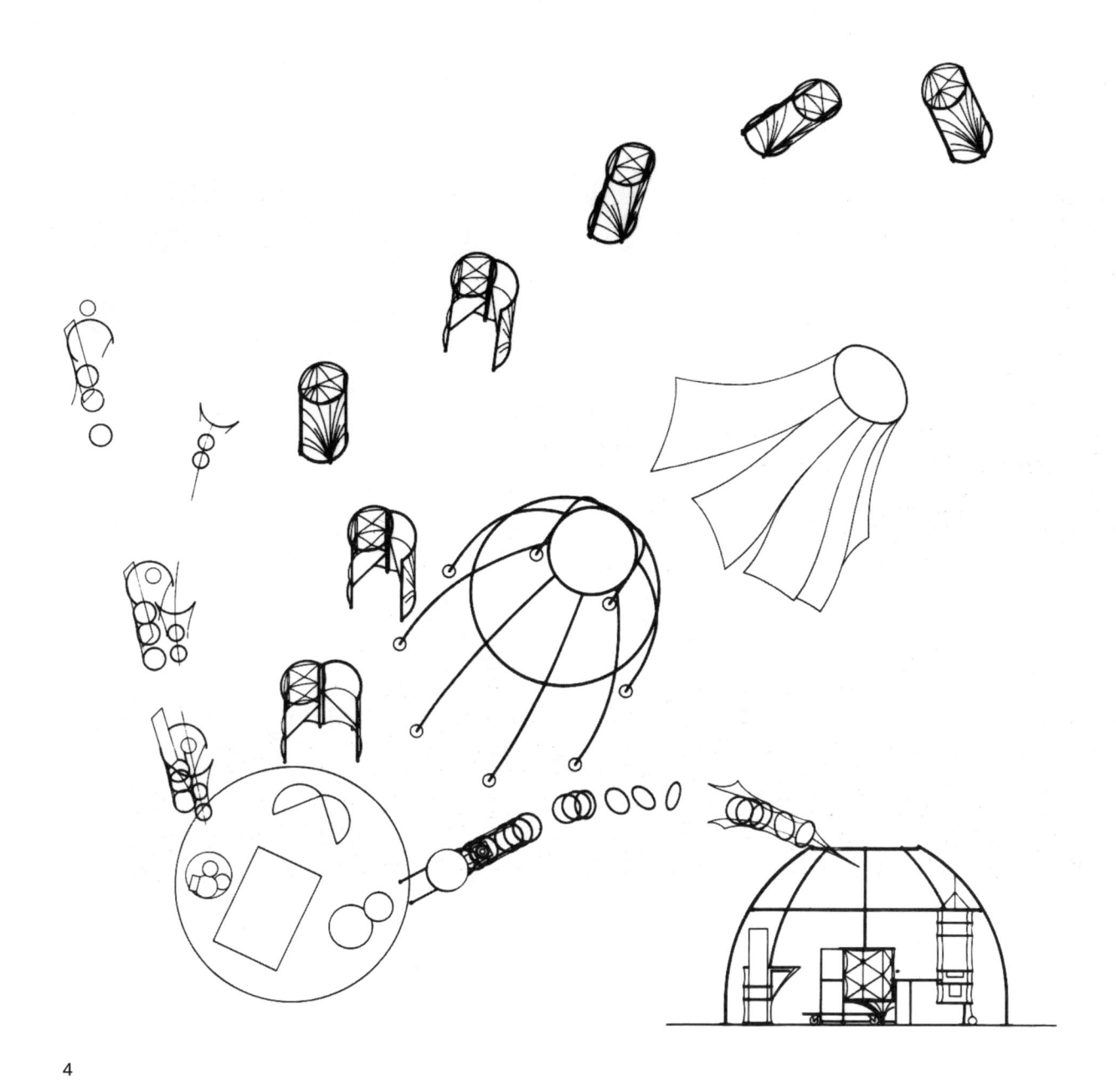

4

Riken Yamamoto
House in Okayama, 1992

1

For Riken Yamamoto, space is a social device that shapes the boundaries between communities. In the House in Okayama, built for a couple and their daughter, he attempts to reposition the family in relation to the community by reconfiguring the spatial layout of the house. The structure is enclosed within a tall perimeter fence, but within this boundary the architect deconstructed the house into three separate units containing private rooms, a kitchen / dining room, and a bathroom, and divided by a large earth courtyard. The three private rooms are pushed to the front of the plan, directly facing the entrance and forming a transition between the public space outside the compound and the 'family' space beyond. This emphasis on transitional space stresses Yamamoto's belief that the family and the home are not distinct and autonomous things but are structurally dependent on what is outside it. As the architect argues, 'If the house is a spatial apparatus for controlling the interface between one community and the community in which it is subsumed, then that spatial apparatus is controlling the interface where those two communities are connected or separated; that is, it is controlling the relationship of one community to what lies outside it'.*

Location: Okayama, Okayama
Total floor area: 166.37 m²

1 Kitchen / dining unit viewed from across internal courtyard, with bedrooms to the right and bathroom to the left

* Riken Yamamoto, 'Community within a Community', in *Riken Yamamoto* (Tokyo: TOTO Publishing, 2012), 47.

Osamu Ishiyama
Light Coffin, 1995

1

Light Coffin was built for a gay couple in a rural village. According to the architect, one of the clients had been bullied as a child and the only place he had felt safe was inside a treasure chest in his parents' home. Their principal request, therefore, was for a house that was like a box. They additionally specified that the house should have no ornament or unnecessary architectural features. Osamu Ishiyama's design takes the form of a distorted box that, with its industrial, utilitarian materials and lack of windows, resembles an agricultural shed or a hangar. Inside the closed structure, the space is entirely open – there are no doors to separate rooms, not even to the bathroom. A narrow skylight running the length of the building produces a shaft of light that animates an otherwise austere space. The house, entirely shuttered from society while maintaining a total openness on the interior, conveys a sense of family as a bulwark against the pressures of orthodox society. It was controversial at the time for its resemblance to the headquarters of the notorious Aum Shinrikyo cult, who in the same year released sarin gas into the Tokyo subway system, killing twelve people.

Location: Chosei, Chiba
Total floor area: 101.87 m^2

1   Exterior, with clients on drawbridge
2   Exterior
3   Interior
4   Interior, with plastic tent used as living room and recycled barber's chair (one of the clients was a hairdresser)
5   Bathroom / toilet

2

3

4

5

Osamu Ishiyama
Setagaya Village, 1997–

1

Setagaya Village is the architect's own home and workspace. The Ishiyama family owned a house on the same plot which was, at fifty years old, nearing the end of its lifespan. Desiring to maintain the old house for as long as possible, Ishiyama erected the new building on four tall steel masts so that it was suspended above the plot. Thanks to this suspension technique, there was no need for structural walls and within the structure the architect established a completely open space. The construction was an exercise in bypassing the conventional system of contractors – the structure was built by an associate of the architect who was trained as a shipbuilder, and Ishiyama himself took on as much of the rest of the production as possible. Throughout his career, Ishiyama has incorporated technologies and materials foreign to architecture into his designs, and his own house has become a laboratory for experimentation – the bright orange colour comes from an industrial rust paint, while the architect has utilized wetsuits to cover interior walls. The house is a testament to Ishiyama's on-going advocacy of 'Open Technology', a belief that unconventional technologies can be used to establish an alternative to the commodification of the building industry. The house, with a busy studio integrated within, promotes an experimental lifestyle where living and working are one and the same.

Location: Setagaya, Tokyo
Total floor area: 499.93 m^2

1 Exterior, with former Ishiyama house visible beneath the structure
2 Employees of the architect working in the first-floor studio space
3 Kitchen
4 Balcony
5 Steel staircase
6 Double-height interior with bedroom in background
7 Double sink unit in bathroom

2

3

4

5

6

7

Atelier Bow-Wow
House and Atelier Bow-Wow, 2005

1

In the early twenty-first century, Atelier Bow-Wow identified a trend by which Tokyo houses, with their lifespan of less than thirty years, could be divided into three 'generations' since the 1920s, and that each of these generations coexisted in the city. They determined that the development of these generations entailed a 'spiral of intolerance', in which the removal of exterior spaces such as porches and gardens, the reduction of window scale and the separation of living spaces and public working spaces such as shops and studios had caused houses to become introverted, asocial places that severed the nuclear family from the wider community. For the architects, this inwardness exacerbates social problems including the isolation of the elderly and domestic violence. Their own house and office establishes a new direction for the 'fourth generation' house, which is characterized as a more public-facing, generous building type open to non-family members. The thin partition walls make efficient use of space in a cramped site, while also softening the distinction between building and street and between the domestic and office spaces within. The domestic spaces occupy the upper levels and are accessible only through the principal staircase also used by staff members.

Location: Shinjuku, Tokyo
Total floor area: 218.67 m²

1   Exterior viewed from the street
2   'Graphic anatomy', section drawing

屋上テラス
roof top terrace

寝室
bed room

踊場 4
landing floor 4

リビング・ダイニング
living・dining room

踊場 3
landing floor 3

事務所 2
office 2

エントランス
entrance

事務所 1
office 1

機械室
machine room

2

223

Osamu Nishida + Erika Nakagawa
Yokohama Apartments, 2009

1

Yokohama Apartments take a further interesting step in the dialogue on the concept of urban living space between Japanese architects and society. Located in an area with little access to transportation and with an aging population, the Yokohama Apartments are designed as an important means of social transformation. The building is basically composed of four 'suspended' units looking into – and accessible through – a very public 'open space'. The wooden units sitting on the four pilasters are rental homes for younger people. On the one hand the large, 5 m-high central space offers the tenants a large common living room; on the other hand its thin transparent separation from the city – afforded only by a vinyl curtain – makes it a 'semi-outdoor' space. The city's activities can easily expand into the common space, and, at the same time, the residents' regularly organized events are themselves open to the city. In architectural terms, Yokohama Apartments emphasize once again the intention of merging traditional and contemporary elements for the sake of the quality of life. The absolute white contributes to creating a decisive contrast with the banality of the urban context, and the uncanny sectional view of the building once again emphasizes the co-existence of architecture and life in the house.

Location: Yokohama, Kanagawa
Total floor area: 152.05 m²

1 Section drawing
2 Ground-floor common area, viewed from top of staircase of one apartment unit

2

Ikimono Architects
Atelier Tenjinyama, 2011

1

Atelier Tenjinyama houses the architects' studio workspace as well as the home of its founder Takashi Fujino. The divisions between living and working space are minimal, an expression of the fundamental openness that characterizes the design. Despite the building's rather unpromising urban site, bordered by a busy road, the architects were determined to create a house like a garden. To do so, the reinforced concrete walls were stretched upward in order to allow for tall windows that flood the space with light. The roof is also entirely glazed, while the floor is earth. The introduction of sunlight and soil into the interior of the space allows for the planting of trees and shrubs directly into the floor, so that the building's users are placed into active engagement with nature. The transparent ceiling, meanwhile, acts as a screen onto which are projected the shifting clouds and changing seasons. On completion of the project, the architects produced a poem that conveys the role of the natural world in the building: 'In spring, smell of flowers covers the office, / In summer, shade of tree is dropped, / In autumn, the leaf falls in the bed of awaking, / In winter, the Sunshine pours into the ground'.

Location: Takasaki, Gunma
Total floor area: 61.93 m²

1   Studio space, showing young trees planted into the floor shortly after construction
2, 3 Concept drawings
4   Bird's eye view of model
5   Exterior

2

227

3

4

5

The Machiya

The House that Shapes the City

Today, the single family detached house is Japan's most common form of housing. Its use, however, does not have a long history – introduced through suburban residential development in the 1920s, it was popularized during the reconstruction efforts of the post-war period. Prior to this, various types of indigenous housing were adapted over centuries to regional climates, available resources, and the lifestyles of residents. The *machiya* (townhouse) is a notable example. First developed during the Edo period (1603–1868), the *machiya* is a wooden-structured urban dwelling intended to be built on deep, narrow lots. Although the building type varies from region to region, there are a number of shared characteristics. They typically incorporate a shop or workplace (*mise*) at the front side, facing the street from behind lattice doors, and living spaces at the back, indicative of a culture in which living and working were not yet segregated. Rows of *machiya* standing side by side along the length of roads formed the rich, mixed-use streetscapes of traditional Japanese cities. In order to combat the humidity prevalent in this densely populated urban context, their plans combine interior and exterior spaces – including a yard that provides circulation along the length of the house (*tooriniwa*) and a small garden (*tsuboniwa*).

The *machiya* intelligently responds to a wide range of conditions and constraints, but in the twentieth century it was disparaged for being cold and dark and for having no parking facilities. Modern urban planning, aiming to redevelop Japan's cities according to fireproofing standards and twentieth-century expectations for living, put constant pressure on the house type. Despite having survived the war, a great many *machiya* were supplanted by multi-storey apartment blocks and detached houses during the mid-century economic growth period.
The result is the disorderly streetscapes of contemporary Japanese cities. The *machiya* and the detached house differ not only in their architectural form, but also in their social contexts. Their differences reflect a trajectory in which the organic relationship between social behaviours, housing typologies, and the urban landscape have unravelled, and every element of daily life – from furniture to homes and land – has been transformed under the conditions of industrial society into consumer goods. This process has weakened the bonds of the communities of *machiya* residents, and reversed centuries of traditional architectural and social knowledge.

To reinterpret *machiya* is to propose a lifestyle antithetical to those promoted by industrial society. This critical practice is spurred by an effort to utilize the architectural intelligence that dwells within the *machiya* rather than merely drawing on its forms. Through attempts to incorporate this intelligence within a response to present-day circumstances and modern technologies, a new generation of *machiya* has emerged. Japan's period of rapid economic growth saw the replacement of traditional *machiya* with detached houses and back yards, and the consequent subdivision of land into ever smaller plots with each new generation. The present era may yet be a period in which the properties of the detached house will be fragmented and replaced by *machiya* once again.

Tadao Ando
Row House in Sumiyoshi, 1976

1

Row House in Sumiyoshi is inserted into a crowded street of terraced houses sharing structural walls (*nagaya*). Faced with a narrow plot, Tadao Ando wrapped the entire site within a perimeter wall, formed from concrete cast *in situ*. The concrete's silken surfaces, achieved by coating the plywood formwork with urethane paint, give the material a delicate textural quality that has become a distinctive characteristic of the architect's practice. Within the austere, unarticulated boundary walls, Ando employed the divided plan of the town house (*machiya*), arranging two interior blocks separated by a small, stone-paved courtyard. This uncovered courtyard provides the only access from one block to another, so that the resident has to walk outside to access the bedrooms. For Ando, this exposed courtyard is a means of confronting the house's inhabitants with nature, expressed not as a domesticated garden but in the more elemental forms of wind, rain, sunlight, and snow. The traditional use of open spaces in the *machiya* becomes a conceptual tool for exploring the place of the natural world in the industrialized urban landscape.

Location: Sumiyoshi, Osaka
Total floor area: 64.72 m^2

1   Exterior
2   Exterior viewed from above, with courtyard in centre
3   Exterior viewed from street
4   Central courtyard

2

3

4

Kazunari Sakamoto
House in Daita, 1976

1

House in Daita represents a shift in Kazunari Sakamoto's practice, which prior to 1976 had employed the compositional and conceptual device of enclosed, nested boxes. In this house, the aligned plan of the *machiya* typology facilitated a partial opening of this closed system. Initially intended as a concrete structure, the house was built in wood for budgetary reasons, a decision that ultimately defined its distinctive gabled facade. A garage on the ground floor partially opens onto a central courtyard, which in turn is accessed by the double-height living space at the back of the house. This arrangement establishes a visual and spatial continuity from the street through to the rear, an effect reinforced by the use of polished marble paving to floor both the courtyard and the ground floor interiors. The exterior is clad in titanium zinc panelling. Characteristically, the architect paid close attention to the subtle relationships between rooms – carefully placed apertures open out from the first floor private spaces onto the courtyard and main room, creating a balance between privacy and openness throughout.

Location: Setagaya, Tokyo
Total floor area: 127.88 m²

1 Exterior
2 Ground-floor living room viewed from courtyard

2

Waro Kishi
House in Nipponbashi, 1992

1

For some time in the Western world of architecture, Waro Kishi's House in Nipponbashi embodied the typical minimalistic charm of twentieth-century Japanese design. Stalwartly urban, built in an improbably small plot (13 × 2.5 m) in downtown Osaka, and constructed from an extremely limited set of architectural elements such as steel, glass, and minimum horizontal components, the house presents all the successful features associated with Japanese architecture of the 1990s. However, Kishi's project, which received much attention from Western architecture media, is also an investigation into the translation of the vernacular type of the *machiya* into the peculiar constraints of our times.
This main narrative becomes obviously clear in the section which demonstrates how vertical generosity compensates for narrowness in space. Paying tribute to urban congestion, the most public space of the house – the dining room – is elevated to the 6 m-high fourth floor, on top of three very low 'private' levels. For similar reasons, the typical role of the garden in the traditional *machiya* – here made impossible because of the size of the plot – is transferred to a terrace on the third floor, connecting the city to the generous height of the dining room.

Location: Naniwa, Osaka
Total floor area: 112.6 m²

1   Exterior

Atelier Bow-Wow
Split Machiya, 2010

1

Located in busy Shinjuku, Split Machiya is an exercise in adapting the *machiya* typology to the demands of contemporary urban living. Like much of Atelier Bow-Wow's residential design, it is the result of a creative response to the increasingly restricted plots that are a prominent feature of contemporary Tokyo. The house consists of two small gable-roofed buildings slotted into a deep, narrow site and separated by a small garden courtyard, or *tsuboniwa*. The earth-floored passageway (*tooriniwa*) connecting the front and rear of the *machiya* is employed here as a compositional device. A direct circulation route runs through the length of the ground floor, with a wide wooden bench in the courtyard serving the dual purpose of providing both a place for rest and a passage between the two interiors. Additionally, a series of aligned windows on each of the house's gables allows for a direct sightline from back of the plot right through to the street, mirroring the linear arrangement of the *machiya*. The relationship of windows and courtyard establishes a natural ambience and a sense of openness that is surprising in such a densely populated central Tokyo neighbourhood.

Location: Shinjuku, Tokyo
Total floor area: 54.62 m²

1 Exterior
2 'Graphic Anatomy', section drawing
3 Section model
4 Study viewed from courtyard

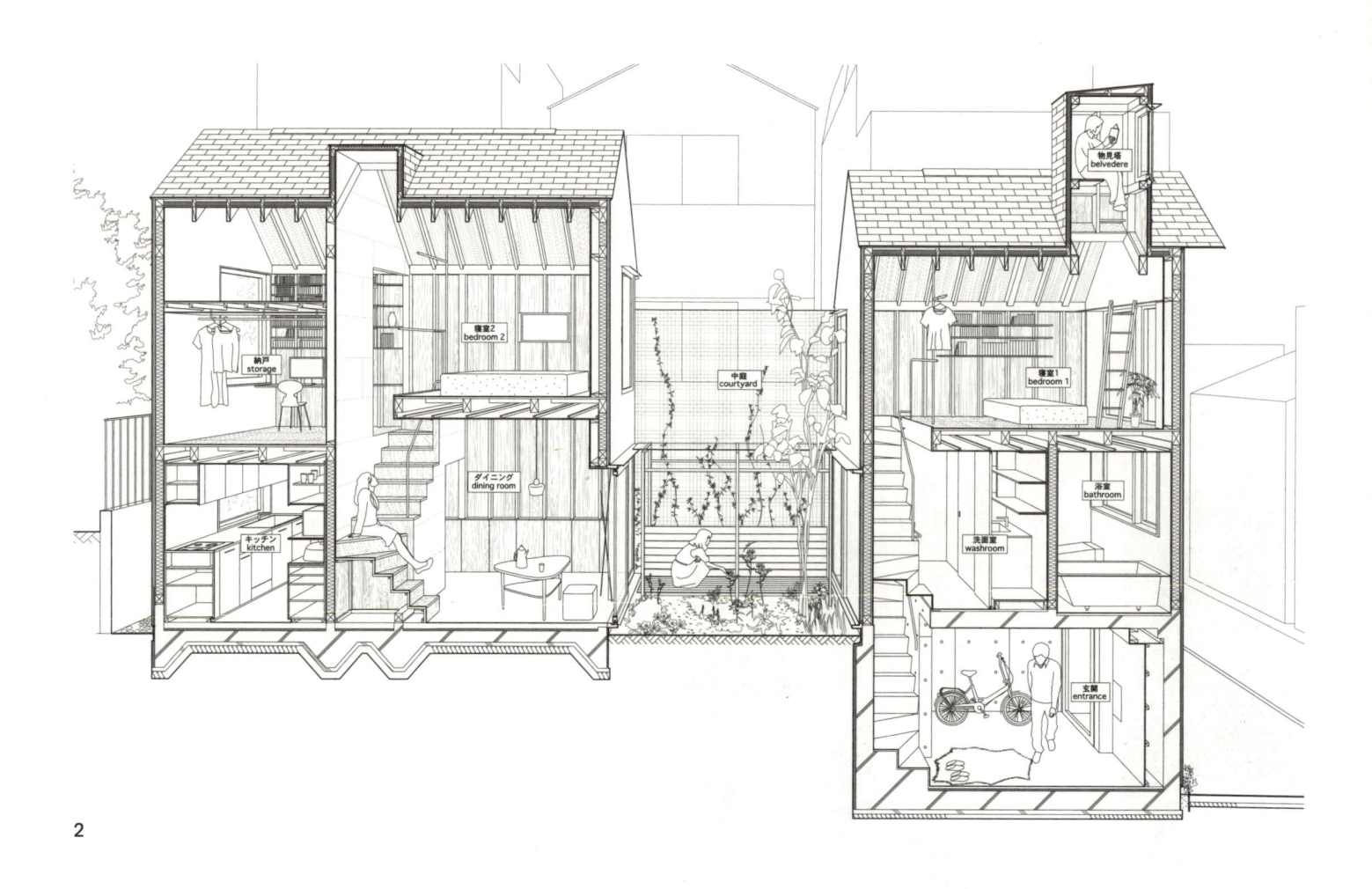

2

3

241

Redefining the Gap

In the wake of the Industrial Revolution, Western European societies of the nineteenth century were beset by social problems caused by overpopulation in industrialized urban centres. Ebenezer Howard, in his influential *The Garden Cities of To-morrow* (1902), argued for a new type of urban development in which city and countryside were blended in environments rich with greenery, a concept that was to eventually develop into the suburb. Howard's garden cities, however, were more politically radical than the contemporary image of the suburb – his proposals included collectively owned real estate that would be leased rather than sold, preventing individual landlords from privately profiting from the appreciation of land values.

By the 1920s, suburban residential developments were being built in Japan, funded by private capital. In a departure from the original utopianism of the garden city, however, these suburbs were centred on the assumption that property should be privately owned, and workplace and home should be separated rather than integrated. Even as the nation was being rebuilt from the ashes of its defeat after World War II, a combination of economic hardship and the policies of the Allied Occupation prevented bold urban planning and large-scale collective housing. Instead, it was implemented through a 'do-it-yourself-if-you-can' approach – sporadically and through the building of privately owned detached houses. During both the rapid economic growth of 1954–1973 and the bubble economy of the late 1980s, detached houses with private yards remained the most desirable form of residence, and suburban residential developments expanded ever further.

Following the collapse of the bubble in the late 1990s, young people began to return to the urban centres. Some opted to live in standardized collective housing but many still preferred detached private homes – a continued preference that created a demand for increasingly small urban lots. The plots occupied by large (and by then expensive) first-generation suburban houses, now relatively close to the centre, were subdivided and populated with multiple ready-built houses with no gardens. As gardens were sacrificed in order to maximize interior space, the character of the urban landscape was altered. Where once there had been detached houses separated by external space there was now only an overcrowded streetscape formed of houses with only the narrowest of spaces between them. This density has brought with it a host of problems for both architect and resident – narrow spaces create unusable 'dead spaces' in the city, placement of windows is constricted by the proximity of neighbours, and facilities such as parking spaces reduce inhabitable space even further.

The late 1990s, however, also saw the emergence of a residential architecture that critiqued this situation. These houses work against the enclosure of urban space, exploiting and emphasizing the interspaces between and within private properties.

These interspaces, accidental by-products of unplanned urban development, are unwelcome for an urban society in which inflationary land prices have created the impulse to fill all available space with useful, profitable, structures. By imagining new uses for these leftover gaps, architects provide much-needed breathing spaces in an overcrowded city and, ultimately, reveal that the myriad problems associated with contemporary urban living are as much the result of conventional house design as they are of the small sites themselves.

Taira Nishizawa
House in Ota, 1998

1

Taira Nishizawa's design focuses on the investigation of architecture as an element of mediation between the body and the city. Houses are therefore the most effective subject of his projects, which are rigorously fashioned in accordance with his clients' lifestyles. In the case of House in Ota, this approach is made evident in two main aspects. The first is the choice to push the simple volume of the house completely onto one edge of the plot, leaving an open 'public' space as a meeting area for the private lives of the inhabitants and the diverse elements spilling in from the city. Nishizawa has described, semi-seriously, the house's garden as a nursery for the neighbourhood's abandoned plants. The second interesting aspect is the 'Japanized' version of the *raumplan* developed by the architect for the section: unusually for Japanese architecture, the lateral rooms of the house are 3.7 m high, forming a lower space for life and a higher one for architecture. Windows are large and very high, affording a clear view of the sky. Near the central vertical core of the house the floors, which were originally two, become four, facilitating circulation and access to services.

Location: Ota, Tokyo
Total floor area: 87.9 m²

1   Exterior

Atelier Bow-Wow
Mini House, 1998

1

The planned construction of a major road as well as new housing developments meant that the environment of Atelier Bow-Wow's Mini House was in flux before the house was even built. Resisting the temptation to entirely enclose the domestic space to shield it from this external chaos, the architects produced a design composed of two interlocking volumes – a main block that is partially sunk into the ground, and an elevated, cantilevered block that protrudes outwards from the first floor. This arrangement establishes a void between the house and its environment, which allows the building to remain independent from its surroundings while engaging with them. A lightweight, thin steel structure provided considerable freedom for the production of form and the placement of openings, combatting the significant constraints of the small site and unpredictable environment. The result is a house that lacks the frontality associated with the detached, single-family home, and is instead composed of several overlapping facades containing precisely placed windows. The structure, with its multiple viewpoints, appears as an object that is alert and sensitive to the changing environment. It is an early example of Atelier Bow-Wow's influential approach, which harnesses the complex, even chaotic, relationship of internal and external conditions.

Location: Nerima, Tokyo
Total floor area: 90.32 m^2

1   Exterior

Ryue Nishizawa
Moriyama House, 2005

1

Moriyama House is situated in a Tokyo neighbourhood characterized by a dense arrangement of houses, external alleys and gardens which relate somewhat chaotically to one another. Ryue Nishizawa's design incorporates this character while offering an alternative to the dense overcrowding of the Japanese city. The project was designed for a client who had made the unusual decision to stop working, and therefore wanted a portion of the house to be utilized as profit-making rental units. This initial brief led the architect to fragment the house into a number of distinct units separated by garden spaces, and this 'decomposition' became the determining principle of the design. The house is formed of ten units ranging from an architectural to a bodily scale – the largest three storeys high and the smallest housing only a shower. To go from one room to another, the residents must pass through an exterior space that is flush with the street. The house is thus intimately intertwined with the surrounding city, embodying the architect's belief that 'life can't be contained within a single lot. People's sense of living expands beyond it, effectively erasing all borders.'*

Location: Tokyo
Total floor area: 263.32 m²

1 Exterior of one-storey unit with roof terrace
2 Exterior viewed from street
3 Concept drawing showing decomposition of units
4 Ground-floor plan
5 Exterior, photocollage

* Ryue Nishizawa, *Tokyo Metabolizing*, ed. Koh Kitayama (Tokyo: TOTO Publishing, 2010), 98.

2

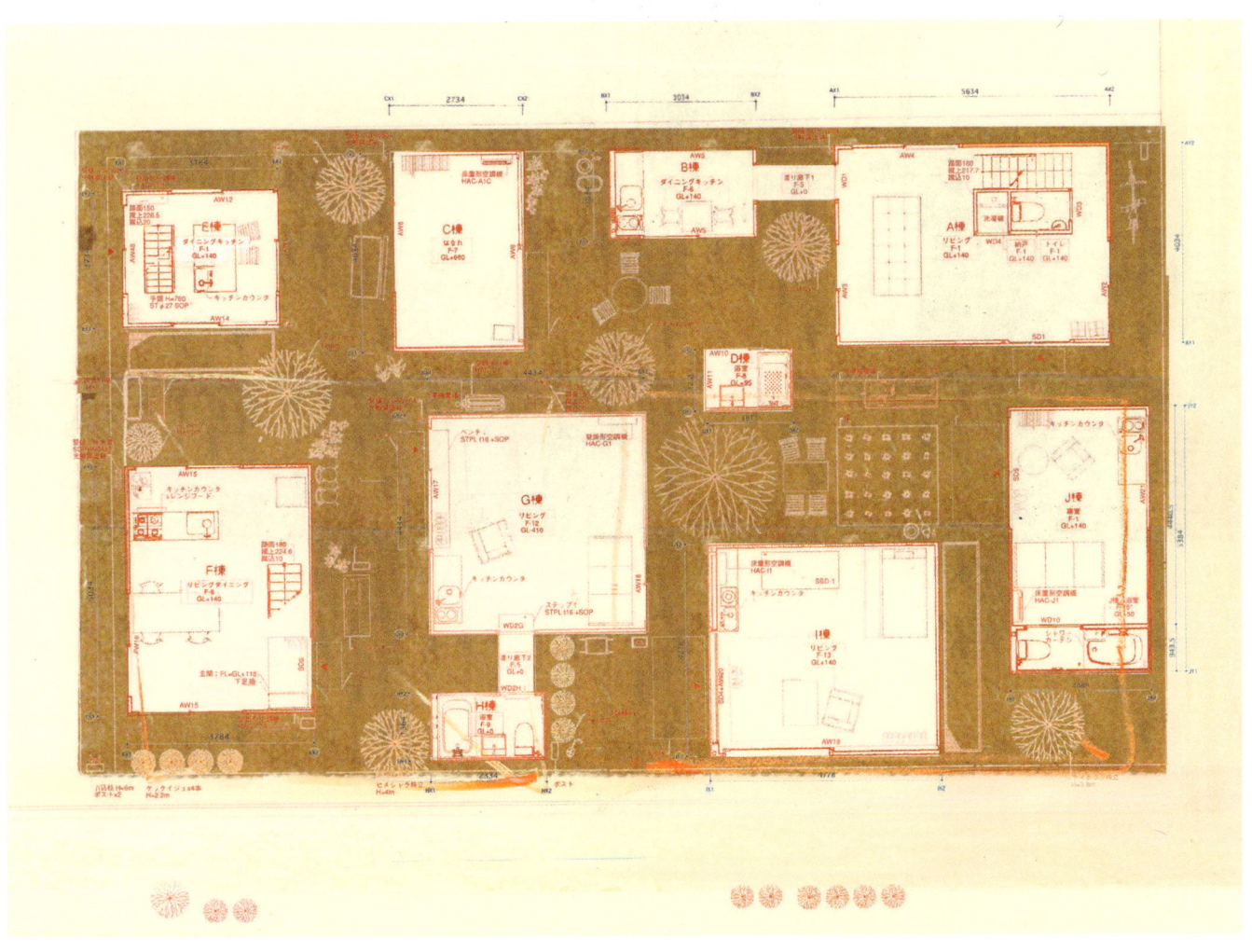

3

4

249

5

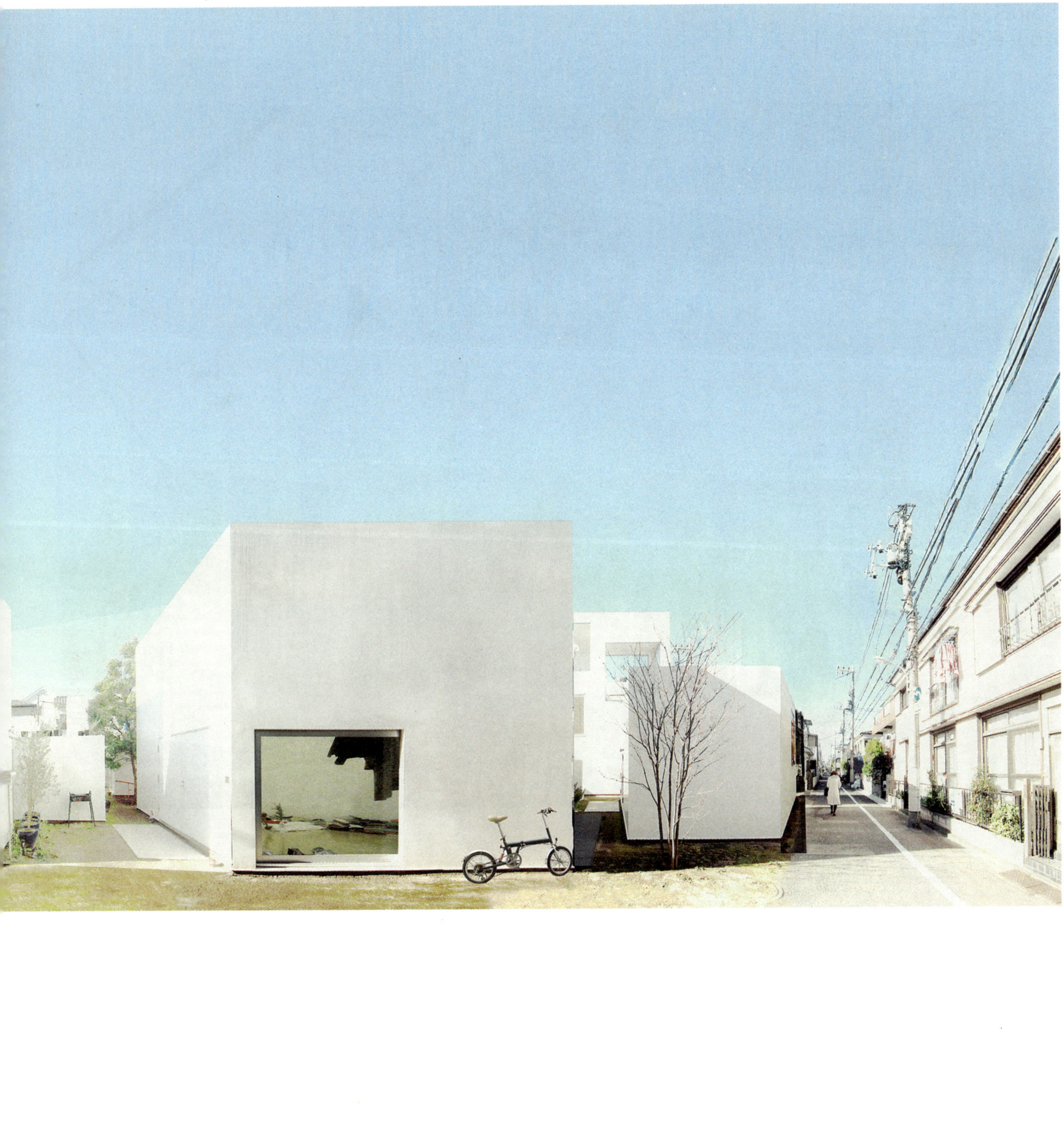

Sou Fujimoto
House NA, 2011

1

Rejecting standard spatial units such as rooms and storeys, House NA is formed of a series of small, irregularly layered platforms. This stratified arrangement produces a complex interior space which is neither one open-plan room nor many individual rooms, but is instead a hybrid of both. The change from one furniture-scaled space to another is suggested by a minor difference in height, which allows for a highly flexible engagement with the structure. The floor of one platform, for example, can be used as a table or chair for an adjacent, lower platform, the function being produced by the user rather than dictated by the architecture. The stacked form of the house reflects an idea of the city as a conglomeration of countless small objects. The house thus bridges the scale of the body with that of the metropolis. House NA's intermediate nature, standing between resident and city, is underscored by its surprising openness – the house is entirely encased in glass and it has no internal walls. This transparency emphasizes the skeletal, tree-like quality of the structure (the architect has referred to the house as an 'artificial thicket'), and establishes the building as an airy lacuna within a closely packed streetscape.

Location: Tokyo
Total floor area: 73.76 m^2

1 Exterior, detail
2 Exterior

2

Lightness

Japan's greatest contribution to the global history of architecture has perhaps been the realization of 'lightness' as an architectural value of significant importance. To a certain extent, this tradition is rooted in the country's environment – the warm, humid climate and frequency of earthquakes are two factors that have resulted in a need for lightweight, open, airy structures. Whereas the European mason would produce heavy structures utilizing hard materials excavated from the ground, the Japanese carpenter would traditionally enclose a space with a wooden frame consisting of columns and beams, filling the gaps with earthen walls of bamboo lathing and mud, and fitting them with sliding doors (*fusuma*) and screens (*shoji*) made from slender wooden beams and Japanese paper (*washi*). However, lightness is not necessarily a quantifiable characteristic or property, but a quality that has taken on many guises and meanings, expressed in many different materials and architectural compositions.

Kenji Hirose's Steel House series, beginning with SH-1 (1953), form one archetype of lightness in Japanese architecture – adopting the industrial materials and techniques of light-gauge steel structures. These houses are the result of an effort to minimize the consumption of resources by literally reducing the amount of materials used. This technologically-oriented impulse towards thinness has motivated one strand of architectural experiment within Japan – consider, for example, the tent-like steel roof of Toyo Ito's Silver Hut (1984). In the 1980s designs by Itsuko Hasegawa, meanwhile, perforated aluminium panels form surfaces that allow for the penetration of light into the interior, conveying 'lightness' in terms of both weight and illumination. Hasegawa's translucent and reflective surfaces filter and manipulate the flow of light, creating layers of differing visual sensations that give the materials the appearance of weightlessness. Lightness may also be associated with the quality of floating, and the impression is accentuated when things appear as if unfastened to the ground. In both Kiyonori Kikutake's Sky House (1958) and Ryue Nishizawa's Garden and House (2013), internal and external spaces are arranged on concrete platforms elevated on *piloti*, expressing the idea of a house that floats in the air.

Lightness, too, can be associated with a sense of unburdening and freedom. The simple wooden hut built by thirteenth-century poet Kamo-no-Chomei as his own retreat and residence (described in his important text of 1212, *Hojoki*, or 'Record of the Ten-Foot-Square Hut') was erected with few materials in a short period of time by only one person. Materially, socially, and economically, it is as light as can be. The 'retreat' or hut still forms a strong tradition within contemporary Japanese architecture as an expression of the desire to lay down one's load and escape the burdensome shackles of society – Kengo Kuma and Satoko Shinohara's Small Bathhouse in Izu (1988) is a characteristic example of the way material, aesthetic, and functional lightness and freedom are conflated within a single structure.

'Thinness', 'translucency', 'flotation' – these terms convey some of the various connotations which have attached themselves to 'lightness' over the last seventy years of Japanese architecture. If architecture is produced at the nexus of human lives, technologies, and natural resources, the lightness or heaviness of buildings might be read as a metaphor of its historical and social context. A grand and expansive construction process requires a dense, 'heavy' network of funders, architects, builders, resources, and stages of decision-making. In contrast, the 'lightness' of the individual house is perhaps what enables their performance as critical spaces, architectural experiments which might float above the constraints and ideologies of the wider social and economic landscape.

Kenji Hirose
SH-1, 1953

![Exterior photograph]

1

In the 1950s, Japanese buildings were built with either wooden structures, using the traditional techniques of Japanese carpentry, or the more recent import of reinforced concrete, prized for its durability and resistance to earthquakes. When Kenji Hirose designed his own house, neither material was adequate. For the architect, traditional wooden architecture was not sufficiently scientific, too dependent on the particularities of an organic material and the accidents and variations of the human hand. Concrete, on the other hand, was costly and produced buildings that looked heavy and intimidating. In response, he designed the first building in Japan to use light-gauge steel construction – a structure that retained many of the advantages of a wooden frame, but exponentially increased efficiency because its components could be prefabricated in a factory setting. The resulting lightweight structure was spare and economical in its use of material, allowing for an open, spacious quality that is surprising in a building of such constricted dimensions. The industrial aesthetic of the steel structure was offset by the inclusion of brick reinforcing walls, while Hirose playfully painted the interior in yellow, green, and blue, with custom-made furniture in white, grey, and red.

Location: Kamakura, Kanagawa (demolished)
Total floor area: 47.01 m^2

1 Exterior

Kiyonori Kikutake
Sky House, 1958

1

In 1947, the Allied Occupation redistributed land away from the traditional landlord class in an attempt to end Japan's quasi-feudal agricultural system. The Kikutake family were among those landowners who lost their land, an experience that was formative for the architect. As a principal figure of the Metabolist group, he built his reputation on a number of visionary urban proposals that sought to reclaim new territories suspended in air or floating on the sea. Many of these ideas germinated in his own house. The reinforced concrete house originally consisted of a single room raised above ground on four piers. Influenced by traditional Japanese homes, in which little was fixed or immovable and most fittings and partitions could be rearranged to adapt to the changing seasons, Kikutake aimed to establish a highly flexible space within the bold geometric structure. Kitchen and bath facilities were designed as portable 'movenettes' which could be easily replaced as technologies advanced – as was the children's bedroom which, limpet-like, was attached to the underside of the house. The architect expressed the unusual desire to create a house like a weed, explaining that 'weeds are wonderful things, for they are an expression of pure vitality. They don't try to put forth flowers or fruit; they simply thrust their roots into the ground and attempt to stay alive.'*

Location: Bunkyo, Tokyo
Total floor area: 98 m^2

1   Exterior
2   Exterior viewed from below
3   Concept drawing
4   Living room
5   Site plan

*   Kiyonori Kikutake, 'Sky House', in *Kiyonori Kikutake: Between Land and Sea*, ed. Ken Tadashi Oshima (New York: Lars Muller Publishers, 2012), 91.

2

Sky House

K. Kikutake
58/8/15

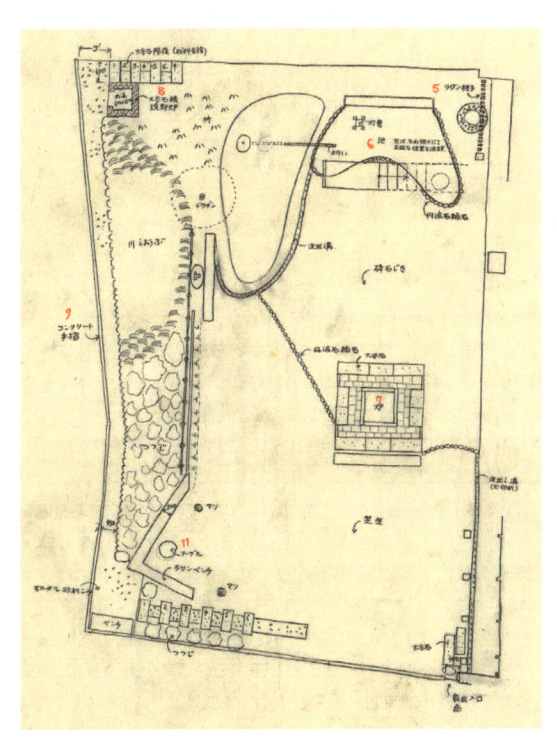

4

5

Itsuko Hasegawa
House in Kuwabara, Matsuyama, 1980

1

This house marks Itsuko Hasegawa's first use of perforated aluminium panels, which were to become a recurring motif. She was attracted to the material because of the way it introduced fine 'grains' of light into the space, recalling childhood memories of sunlight dancing on the surface of the sea. The client provided access to his company, which produced metal components, and Hasegawa went through a rigorous process of testing samples in order to achieve her desired effect, observing and measuring the changing shadows they cast throughout the day. The pattern she developed became an industry standard for Japanese architects. The aluminium provides an indistinct reflection of the surrounding atmosphere, while the perforated screens establish porous boundaries between interior and exterior, recalling the paper surfaces of *shoji* screens. The interior contains similarly 'pliable', membrane-like partitions, including fine steel meshes. The house is characteristic of Hasegawa's practice, which seeks to synthesize traditional architecture, organic form, and advanced technology.

Location: Matsuyama, Ehime
Total floor area: 415 m^2

1 *Engawa* viewed from garden
2 Interior with standing screens, hanging partitions and stone floor
3 Study drawing for elevation

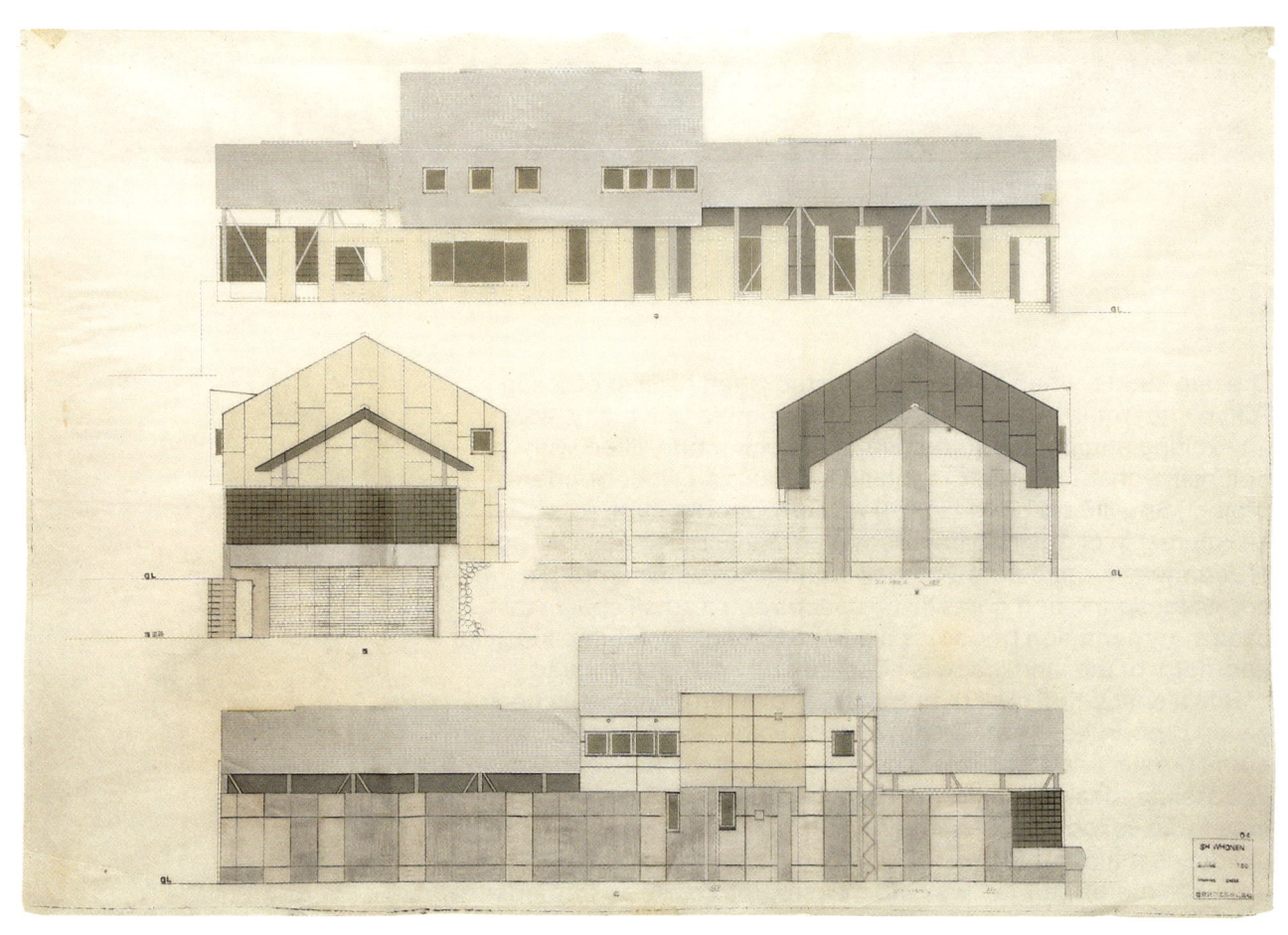

2

3

Kengo Kuma + Satoko Shinohara
A Small Bathhouse in Izu, 1988

1

The late 1980s, when Kengo Kuma established his first office in Tokyo after returning from his year at Columbia University, was an exciting and contradictory time for architecture, filled with optimism, chaos, and fragmentation. Kuma's first independent project, Small Bath House in Izu, was an opportunity to re-scale his interest in chaos and fragmentation within the specific scope of Japanese architecture. A Small Bathhouse is built around a hot-water spring and hosts living spaces and a small spa. In this case, fragmentation becomes a device through which the irregular geometry of the landscape is adapted and an opportunity to create a space that is both domestic and determined by its health-giving properties. As at Fallingwater by Frank Lloyd Wright – whom Kuma greatly admires – the irregular shape of the house makes it impossible to take in its form in a single glance and at the same time focuses the viewer's attention on individual elements: the building's materials (concrete, wood, glass) and vernacular details (roof, structure), and the way the main rooms create an immediate connection with the landscape. Unpretentious and not particularly refined, this early project anticipates many aspects that Kuma would develop in his later and more popular works.

Location: Kamo, Shizuoka
Total floor area: 93.23 m^2

1   Study model, corrugated cardboard
2   Exterior

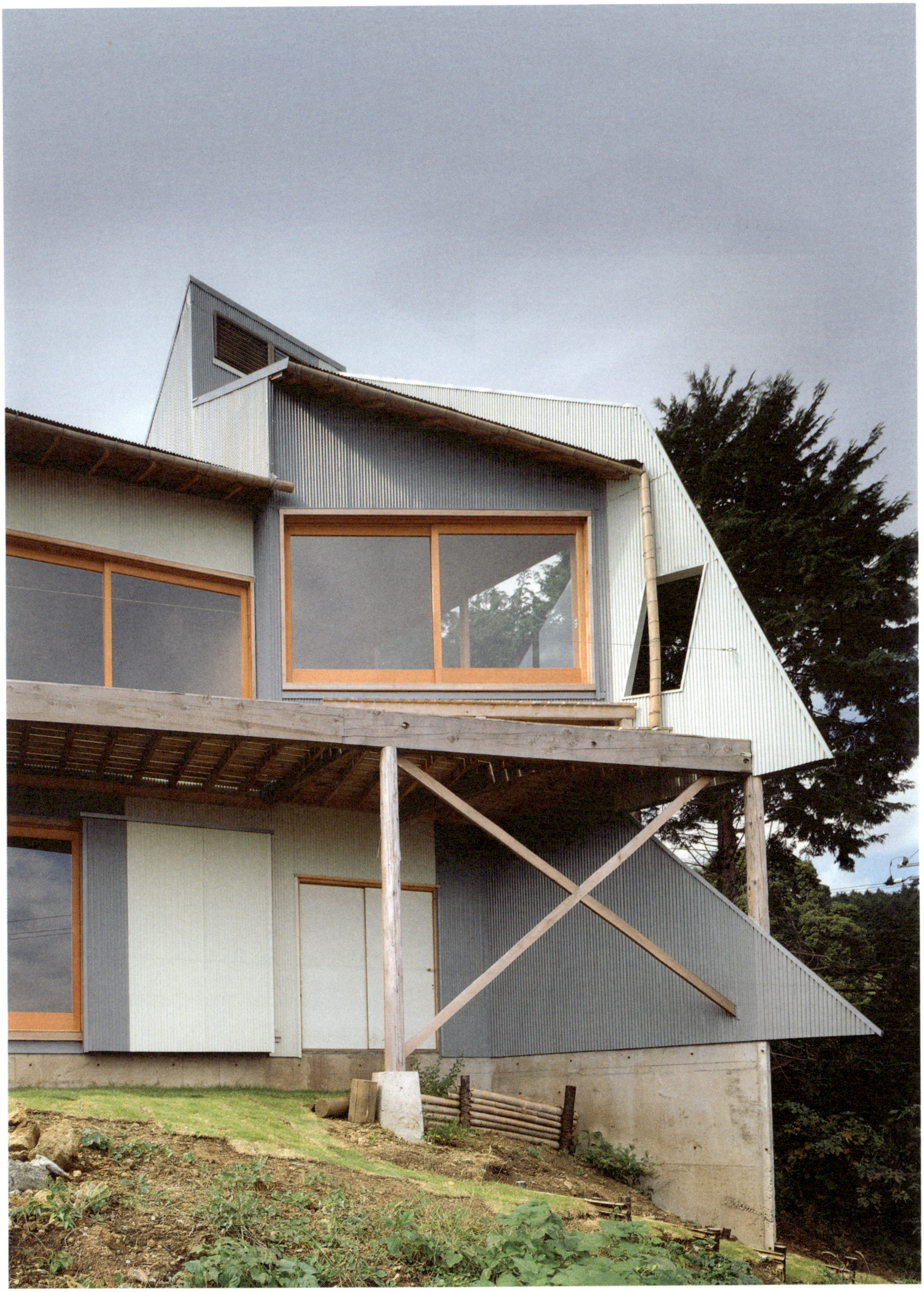

2

Go Hasegawa
House in Kyodo, 2011

1

House in Kyodo was built for two publishers, and the storage of their collection of books and mangas was a central concern. This priority ran the risk of overcrowding the small plan with objects, so Go Hasegawa divided the house into two clearly defined spaces connected by a small staircase. The ground floor, low-ceilinged and clad in wood, houses a bathroom and bed nestled within a library, with floor-to-ceiling shelving packed with books that take on the weighty, solid character of pilasters. The first floor, by contrast, is a light-filled, high-ceilinged space with an extremely light, reflective roof made of 6 cm-thick steel sandwich panels, which appears to hover over the house's walls. A portion of the space is devoted to an airy, semi-exterior terrace, while a series of sliding windows can be opened to give the entire floor a sense of openness. Within the small, simple form of the house, the architect has allowed for a generous contrast of intimacy and openness, shadow and light.

Location: Setagaya, Tokyo
Total floor area: 69.52 m²

1 Exterior
2 First-floor terrace

2

Yo Shimada
House in Rokko, 2011

1

House in Rokko is located midway up a mountain, with dramatic views over Kobe. Due to the site's location, heavy machinery could not be used, so most of the construction was undertaken manually. In response, the architect opted for a lightweight steel-frame structure, composed of small, thin components – only elements under 100 kg could be carried to the site. The ground floor is entirely walled in glass, creating a remarkable degree of continuity between the site and the interior and making the first floor appear to be floating above the city. A toilet is even contained within a free-standing wooden box so as not to restrict the openness of the space. The gable-roofed first floor, clad in corrugated steel plating, contains a bedroom and bathroom, and has access to a balcony that encircles the house. The balcony and eaves provide shade in summer for the transparent glass ground floor, while mountain breezes cool the interiors. Like much of Shimada's work, the bold design possesses a high degree of environmental sensitivity.

Location: Kobe, Hyogo
Total floor area: 94.5 m²

1 Exterior
2 Exterior with view of Kobe
3 First-floor landing viewed from bedroom

2

3

Ryue Nishizawa
Garden and House, 2013

1

Working with a narrow site, Ryue Nishizawa maximized space by producing a wall-less building. Four concrete slabs are supported on thin columns and wrapped in curved planes of glass. Each floor consists of a single room with an adjacent terrace (some of these terraces are earth-floored). The plants form a verdant counterpoint to the clean, abstract geometry of the structure, as well as providing an organic facade – the traditional function of the perimeter wall as delineating the house from the city is replaced here by a permeable, living border. Exterior and interior spaces interpenetrate, and as the visitor ascends the steep spiral staircase that rises through circular openings in each slab they pass through a number of environments in which the distinction between architecture and nature is subtly blurred. The house was designed for two colleagues rather than a traditional family, and Nishizawa aimed to achieve a new building form to parallel new forms of living. Influenced by the work of philosopher Catherine Malabou, he aimed to create architecture that encourages 'plasticity' – 'the courage to continue the process of destruction and creation, without compromising to the present situation'.*

Location: Tokyo
Total floor area: 66.03 m^2

1   Exterior from above
2   Residents on first-floor terrace
3   Third floor viewed from rooftop terrace
4   Exterior
5   Studies for floor plan

*   Ryue Nishizawa, *Ryue Nishizawa: Studies by the Office of Ryue Nishizawa* (Tokyo: INAX, 2009), 25.

2

3

4

5

274

275

The Vernacular

In the aftermath of the great 1923 earthquake, pioneering cultural anthropologist Wajiro Kon developed methods of research to observe, record, and describe the variety and creativity of improvised shelters that shaped Tokyo's post-disaster landscape. In the context of reconstruction and modernization, Kon witnessed the transformation of urban life using drawing as a privileged tool to record what he called *bunka seikatsu*, or the culture of daily life. 'I am further trying to develop an anthropological method in order to record and examine comparatively our contemporary material culture'.[1] His ground-breaking study *Modernologio* (1930)[2] epitomized Kon's mastery of fieldwork and on-site observation in search of exact measurement through notes, diagrams, and sketches. Wajiro Kon extended his practice to writing, photography, architecture, and interior design, observing material culture in the street as well as in domestic private homes.

Following the influential 'eccentric gaze' of Wajiro Kon, the Roadway Observation Society, or ROJO, was created in 1986 to take photographs of 'unusual objects that most people overlooked: a staircase leading to nowhere, a slide cut off in the middle, an exceptionally narrow building, a tree's shadow cast along a fence, a chicken hutch made from a broken television'.[3] Based on observation and collection, ROJO's photographs and drawings elevated Kon's 'archaeology of the present day' into a school of thought. ROJO's sensitivity was driven by makeshift structures, available materials, and amusing artefacts.

As an architectural historian and former member of ROJO, Terunobu Fujimori looks at the vernacular as a circular manifestation of time challenging the progressive march of the modernist trope: 'An "international vernacular" can be seen as a movement that turns its back on an international quality of the twentieth-century kind and aspires to the first internationalism of the Stone Age'.[4] Fujimori proposes an architecture that does not turn its back on modernity, but seeks to 'wrap technology in nature'. In the late 1990s, the activities of Atelier Bow-Wow developed methods of study for urban spatial research with an integrative approach combining sociology, biology, and anthropology. Their observation of strange buildings in their seminal book *Made in Tokyo*[5] offered a renewed conception of time and history through the interaction of the internal rhythms of individual buildings with the many layers formed by several generations of houses aggregating in the chaotic cityscape. Focusing their practice on small houses responding to individual needs, their practice resisted the capitalist needs that fuelled the 1960s Metabolists as well as the dominant institutionalized figure of the architect: 'Why is vernacular architecture so much more charming and seductive than the newest buildings designed by famous architects?'[6]

The social role of vernacular architecture inspired a younger generation of Japanese architects to take a humanist approach, with houses designed to improve the life of the community. Following the path of Atelier Bow-Wow, many architects have travelled across Japan and internationally, developing their own field studies and grammars of classification through editorial means. Often working in collective research groups, these architects pay just as much attention to marginal rural and urban spaces and structures as they do to the epicentres of hyper-modernity. The design of their houses reflects their sensibility towards people's lives, postures, and human activity: 'Architecture is not a creation that renews the world, but a method that enables me to discover new expressions of the world. By setting down pieces of architecture, I wish to seek out, as much as possible, the order quietly surrounding our daily lives,' writes Kumiko Inui.[7]

1   Jilly Traganou and Izumi Kuroishi, *Design and Disaster: Kon Wajiro's Modernologio*, catalogue for the *Design and Disaster: Kon Wajiro's Modernologio* exhibition (held at the Arnold and Sheila Aronson Galleries, Sheila C Johnson Design Center, Parsons The New School for Design, curated by Kuroishi and Traganou, March 13–March 27, 2014), 12.
2   Wajiro Kon, *Modernologio (Moderunorodio)* (Tokyo: Shunyo-do, 1930), reprinted in Wajiro Kon, *Introduction to Modernologio (Kogengaku Nyumon)* (Tokyo: Chikuma Shobo, 1987).
3   Terunobu Fujimori, 'The Origins of Atelier Bow-Wow's Gaze', in Atelier Bow-Wow, *Behaviorology* (New York: Rizzoli International Publications, 2010), 125.
4   Terunobu Fujimori, 'Toward an Architecture of Humankind', in *Fujimori Terunobu Architecture* (Tokyo: TOTO Publishing, 2007), 45.
5   Momoyo Kajima, Junzo Kuroda and Yoshiharu Tsukamoto, *Made in Tokyo* (Tokyo: Kaijima Institute Publishing, 2014).
6   Atelier Bow-Wow, *Behaviorology*, 8.
7   Kumiko Inui, Ryuji Fujimura, and Ryue Nishizawa, *Kumiko Inui: Episodes* (Tokyo: INAX, 2008), 11.

Terunobu Fujimori
Leek House, 1997

1

Leek House was built for the architect's close friend Genpei Akasegawa (1937–2014), a prominent conceptual artist known for his participation in Japan's Neo-Dada movement of the 1970s. Both men were formerly members of the Roadway Observation Society (ROJO), a collective dedicated to documenting the overlooked quirks of the urban landscape. Several members of this group were called upon to contribute to the construction of the house, for which Fujimori had designed crudely finished details which were better suited to amateur craftsmen than the precise techniques of highly skilled Japanese artisans. Leek House evidences a deep appreciation for natural materials such as wood, which appears as planks, blocks, branches, and logs. Fujimori embedded rows of *nira* (Chinese leeks) on the house's slanted roof, an early example of his strategy of 'greening architecture' by interweaving the natural and the manmade. The value placed on simple, natural materials and techniques is related to Fujimori and Akasegawa's interest in the principles of sixteenth-century tea master Sen no Rikyu, who promoted an aesthetics of simplicity, humility, and artlessness. Fujimori included a small barrel-vaulted tearoom protruding from one end of the house, simply stuccoed in crude white plaster and lit by dappled natural light.

Location: Machida, Tokyo
Total floor area: 172.62 m²

1   Exterior with Chinese leeks planted in roof, and teahouse unit to the right
2   Detail of window, plaster wall, and wood-block ceiling in teahouse
3   Model carved from a single log

280

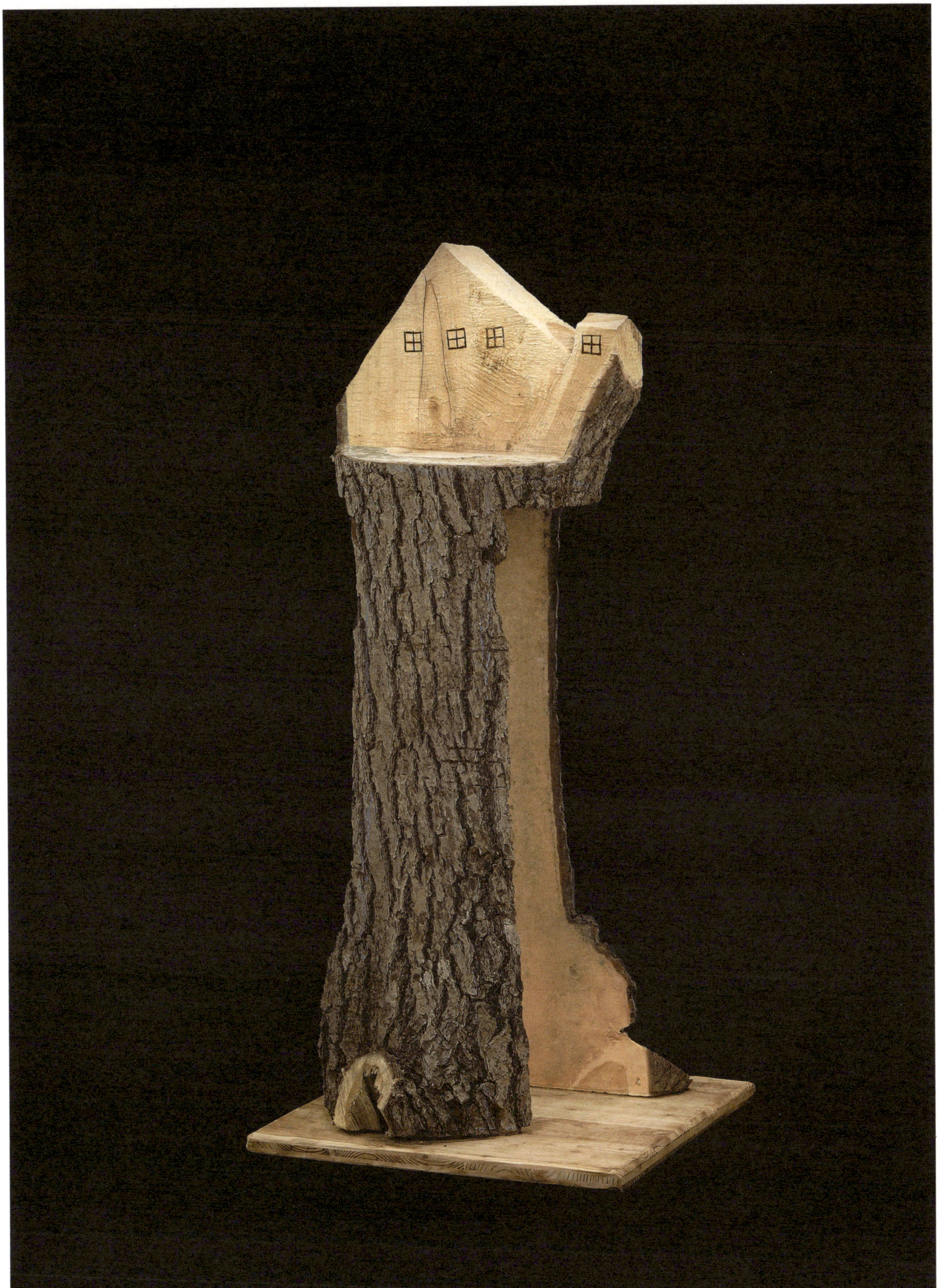

3

Tezuka Architects
Roof House, 2001

1

Roof House was built for a family with young children. The family had enjoyed spending time on the roof of their former home, and when they built a new house they requested that this unusual engagement with the architecture should form the basis of the design. The single-storey house is topped with a large roof, on which are placed a dining table, a stove, and even a shower. Skylights from each of the interior rooms lead directly to the roof by means of ladders, ensuring that it performs as the house's primary space. The roof's gentle slope is oriented towards Mt Kobo to the south, establishing the entire structure as a viewing platform. Projecting over the ground floor, it also provides an *engawa*-like zone beneath the eaves – unlike the roof platform, this semi-exterior space provides cool shade in the summer, as it did in the traditional Japanese dwelling. Like much of the architects' work, the house explores the ways users can imaginatively engage with the environment, suggesting a more open relationship with the natural world that resists society's demand for enclosed, climate controlled spaces.

Location: Hadano, Kanagawa
Total floor area: 95.86 m²

1   Exterior
2   Residents and friends eating a meal at rooftop dining table
3   Ground-floor living room

2

3

Jun Igarashi
Rectangle of Light, 2007

1

Rectangle of Light is located in the architect's native Hokkaido, Japan's northernmost prefecture. Significantly less populated than the country's busy southern areas, the largely rural island is known for its harsh winter climate. Local conditions call for a different kind of architecture than that found in much of Japan, and Igarashi's design often begins as a response to these factors. Rectangle of Light, a wooden barn-like structure closed to the outside, is typical of his practice. The house's hard, resilient exterior is contrasted with a soft, airy atmospheric quality inside. In the double-height living space the source of the reflected and diffused light is a tall bay window, which does not provide any direct views onto the suburban exterior, but is offset to one side of a wedge-shaped corridor on the south side. This space is one of two 'buffer zones', which form windbreakers that control air flow to protect the domestic interior, as well as soft transitions from public to private spaces.

Location: Sapporo, Hokkaido
Total floor area: 71.54 m^2

1   Exterior
2   'Buffer zone' leading into the double-height dining room

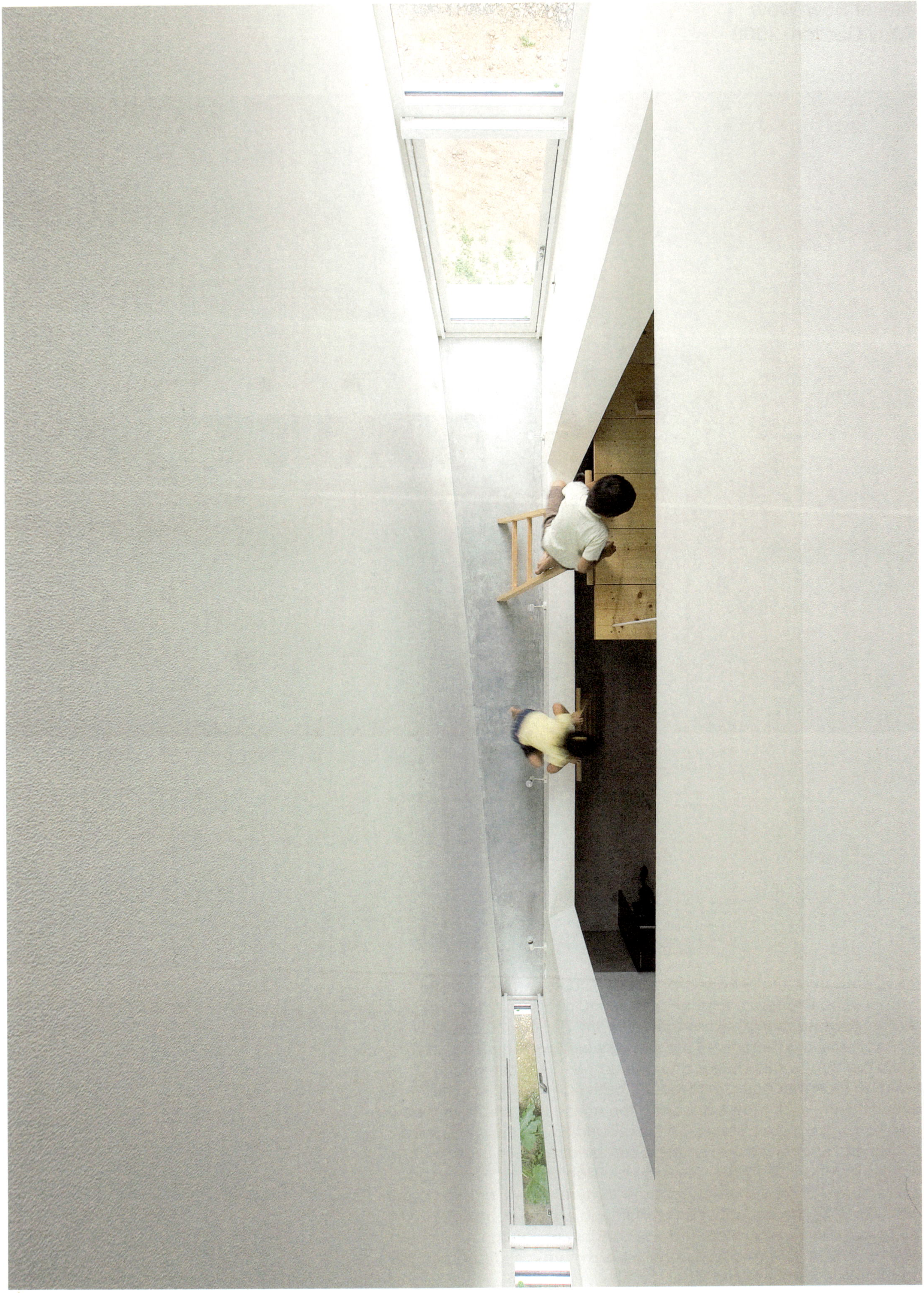

2

285

Atelier Bow-Wow
Pony Garden, 2008

1

Pony Garden is a rural house for a pony and its owner, a single woman who wanted to explore a new kind of living in her retirement. The design was dictated by the needs of the pony. Accordingly, the majority of the site was designated as a pasture, while the house was slotted into one corner. Searching for a building type that could incorporate both human and equine activities, the architects conceived the house as a stable that could also accommodate people. On the ground floor, which houses a dining and kitchen space, shutters can be opened in order to form a semi-exterior loggia that blurs the division between domestic and external zones. This spatial arrangement allows for a reciprocal intimacy bond overlap between human and animal behaviours. While a pet is usually relegated a secondary role in the household, Atelier Bow-Wow's design reverses this dynamic and approaches architecture from an animal perspective.

Location: Sagamihara, Kanagawa
Total floor area: 71.72 m²

1 Exterior

dot architects
No. 00, 2011

1

No. 00 was built for a ceramicist who lives with her mother and daughter. The ground floor is devoted to a ceramics school and studio, while private spaces are distributed on the first and second floors. The house's composite appearance is due to the use of different construction systems on each storey – reinforced concrete with steel *pilotis*, reinforced concrete and wood frame, and wood frame alone. The structure is topped by a hip-and-gable roof, or *irimoya-zukuri,* of the kind typically found in traditional *minka*. The architects privilege difference over stylistic coherence, and the various components of the building are allowed to respond specifically and independently to the environment and the behaviours of the users. For No. 00, each of the three architects worked autonomously on a different aspect (plan, study models, and details) while welcoming active participation from the clients, contractors, and community. The finished design combined these separate projects without attempting to smooth over the resulting divisions and contradictions. This is an example of the firm's 'super-parallel' design process, an experiment in non-hierarchical, socially-oriented architectural practice.

Location: Nishinomiya, Hyogo
Total floor area: 187.33 m^2

1　Exterior

Chie Konno
Sunny Loggia House, 2011

1

Sunny Loggia House is a house for the architect's mother and sister. Resisting the tendency to maximize interior space by building houses that fill the limits of the site, Konno subdivided the plot into three distinct areas – house, garden, and a semi-exterior space that the architect refers to as a 'loggia'. This device is the fruit of Chie Konno's field research into windows (conducted when she was a student in Yoshiharu Tsukamoto's laboratory at the Tokyo Institute of Technology), loggias, and verandas in Japan, Southern Europe, India, the USA, and Australia. Mirroring the gabled form of the house itself, it forms a kind of negative space that inverts the relationship of inside and outside, opening the house to both the small garden and surrounding neighbourhood. A series of windows (each a different size and shape) allows all interior rooms to open in turn onto the loggia. The garden was a central element of the design, and the architect carefully selected different plants to create a small landscape that reflects the changing seasons. A gate that directly opens onto the street encourages neighbours to access the garden so that the architect's elderly mother, who is alone in the house during the day, is connected to the wider community.

Location: Sagamihara, Kanagawa
Total floor area: 99.17 m²

1   Exterior viewed from the garden
2   Garden and loggia viewed from first-floor bedroom

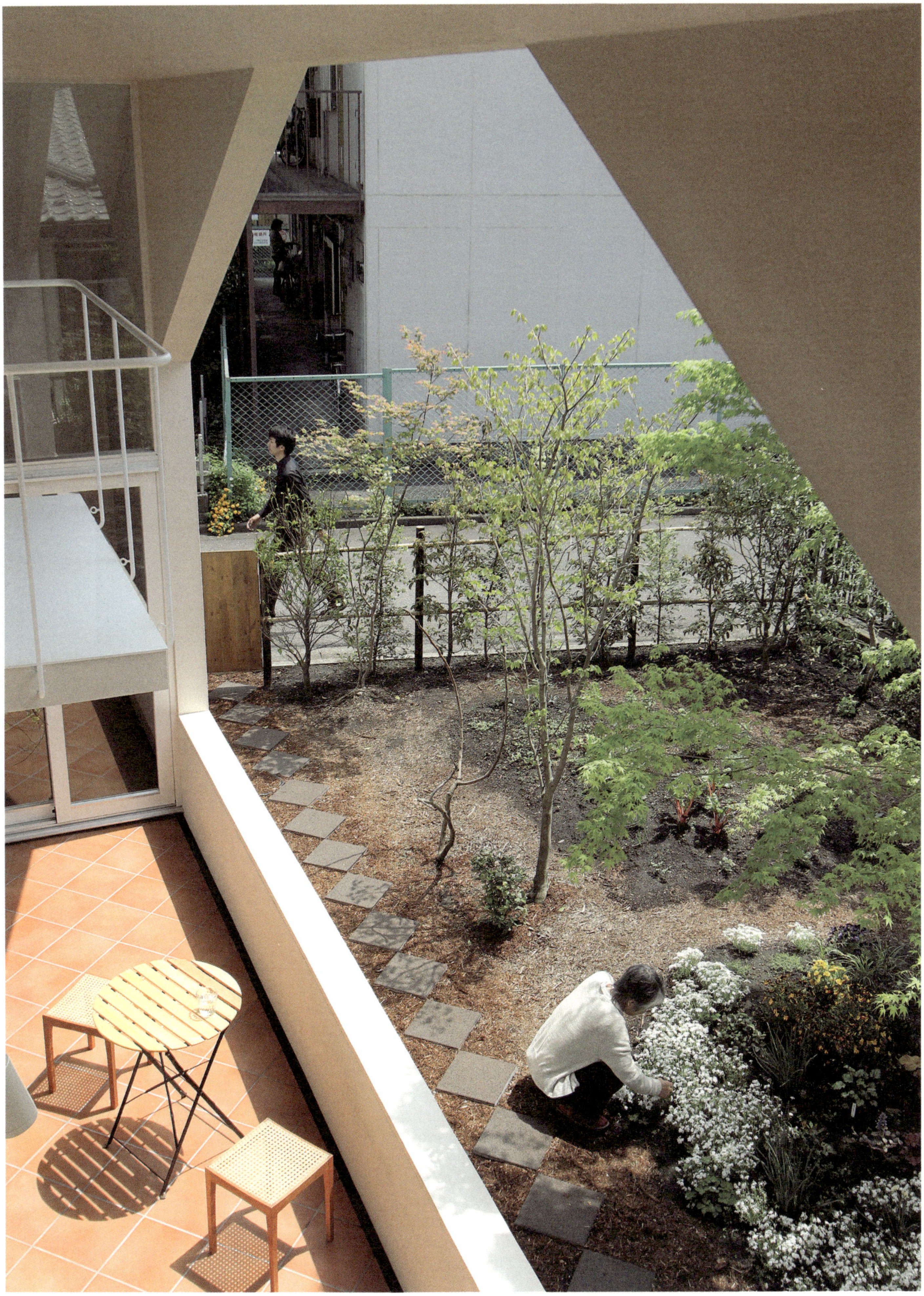

2

Kumiko Inui
House M, 2015

1

House M is characteristic of the way Kumiko Inui combines the practical attitudes of vernacular architecture with a strong sense of formal expression. A newly constructed, busy road runs along one side of the plot, making it unusually generous in length but shallow in depth. Each of the house's three storeys is placed at a different angle, creating a skewed composition that maximizes light flow while controlling views in and out of the building. The reinforced concrete structure cantilevers beyond the limits of the interior, and the spaces established between the eaves and floor form generous semi-exterior spaces that act as traditional *engawa* and facilitate a flexible programme of activities. The house, while appearing almost structurally precarious, is an intelligent and precise response to the complex spatial restrictions of the Tokyo urban context. This approach is influenced by anonymous, vernacular buildings and structures, which often solve specific problems of use and site in a way that can at first seem visually incoherent. Inui has travelled around Japan documenting and classifying many of these structures.

Location: Toshima, Tokyo
Total floor area: 84.86 m^2

1, 2　Exterior
3　　First-floor balcony and living room

2

3

Unmarketable

In 1966, amid the years of Japan's accelerated economic growth and emergence as one of the world's foremost technological and industrial powers – a period associated with the success of the Metabolist movement – self-taught engineer Kenji Kawai designed a house for himself, building it from a large section of corrugated piping of the kind ordinarily buried deep underground and used for drains. The material – light, cheap, and easy to transport and assemble – allowed Kawai to bypass the traditional bureaucracies, financial constraints, and middle men of construction, taking the process of building his house into his own hands. Almost every aspect of the house seems to question the normal procedures and definitions of house-building in the twentieth century. With no foundations and a continuous curved surface, it does not stand as a building is normally thought to do but merely lies on the floor like an object. To stop it shaking or even moving, mounds of gravel are piled up at its sides to hold it in place. This makeshift solution means the house evades property tax, which in Japan is defined in terms of whether or not a building is fixed to the ground – in the dry and literal eyes of the law, the house is not considered a building at all. In its lack of fixedness, therefore, it critiques the legal definition of architecture. The way it simply sits on the surface of the earth, minimally altering its immediate environment, forms an additional critique of the violent transformations and interventions wrought on the ecosystem in the name of architecture and development. In the very construction of the house, meanwhile, Kawai launched a potent critique of the house-building industry that was rapidly transforming the Japanese landscape at the time. Why should the house be transformed into one more commodity within the ever-expanding grasp of capitalist society? Why, Kawai asked, should we not build our own homes?

The critical, do-it-yourself approach of the Kawai residence spawned followers and admirers across Japanese architecture. First and foremost has been the maverick Osamu Ishiyama, who, since the early 1970s, has argued for a kind of architecture that wrests control from bureaucrats, developers, and local authorities and places it back in the hands of the individual. His practice restlessly incorporates technologies and materials from all kinds of fields outside of architecture and mainstream construction, attempting to reconfigure architecture as an open, democratic process. His houses are a continuously evolving project, which sees him test out experimental methods of construction and design that can later be communicated to a larger audience. His focus on the active participation of the client has been fruitful – both in his own work and in the work of those who have learned from him. Ishiyama is Professor of Architecture at Waseda University, an architecture school known for its emphasis on individual expression rather than engineering, and has become an influential figure for younger generations. Both his teaching and his practice, which push collaboration, improvisation, and independent thinking to the fore, have continued the legacy of the Kawai Residence into the twenty-first century. There is no better example than that of former dancer Keisuke Oka who, encouraged by Ishiyama, embarked on the ambitious project of constructing his own home in 2005, entirely by hand, in a quiet neighbourhood of central Tokyo. His fantastical concrete structure is still under construction after fifteen years, and has become a kind of living artwork.

   The average lifespan of the Japanese house is just twenty-five years, and this chronological structure has imprinted itself on the urban landscape, which is constantly put through the cycle of 'build, demolish, build, demolish'. The houses in this section posit other chronologies that counter this perpetual renewal. Ishiyama's Farmer's House (1986) and Oka's Arimaston Building involve a protracted, gradual labour that critiques the constant need for the new and the immediate, while Katsuhiro Miyamoto's polemic renovations of structures hit by earthquakes insist on the continued presence of history and memory in the amnesiac culture of a consumer society. Shigeru Ban, meanwhile, has utilized his innovatory structures and materials to provide cheap, temporary shelters for refugees and the victims of natural disasters, staking a claim for architecture's utility in spheres entirely removed from image, commodity, and property speculation. These buildings offer the potential for a type of house that exists outside of the conventions and constraints of capitalism, a house in which making, living, and working become defiant acts of independence and individuality.

Osamu Ishiyama
Kaitakusha-no-ie (The Farmer's House), 1986

1

The client of Farmer's House was a young farmer who lived with his family in the remote Sugadaira Highlands. They previously inhabited a log cabin they had built themselves, and wanted to live in another self-built home. He was put in contact with Osamu Ishiyama by the engineer Kenji Kawai, who had built his own house in a large piece of industrial corrugated piping. For Farmer's House, Ishiyama further honed this technique. Architect and client developed an unusual working relationship, in which Ishiyama sent drawings to the client, who built the house with his own hands – the process took thirteen years. The mundane, industrial material of the structure contrasts with the exuberant detailing and ornament. Similarly to that of contemporaries such as Tadao Ando, Toyo Ito, and Kazunari Sakamoto, Ishiyama's architecture of the 1970s attempted to resist the commodification of the house. While those architects pursued an architecture of retreat and enclosure, however, Ishiyama attempted to utilize the surplus materials of industrial society to reconfigure the process of production. Assessing his work at the time, the architect claimed that his 'ultimate goal is to lay siege to the destitute island of architecture with batteries of adapted industrial products, encircling this "island" as the farm villages surround our cities'.*

Location: Ueda, Nagano
Total floor area: 142.73 m²

1 Exterior
2–4 Interior, details of ornamental metalwork and stained glass window
5 Exterior
6 Projected section of Farmer's House

* Osamu Ishiyama, 'Sewer-Pipe Architecture', *New Wave of Japanese Architecture*, ed. Kenneth Frampton (New York: The Institute for Architecture and Urban Studies, 1978), 42.

2

3

4

5

6

Katsuhiro Miyamoto
ZENKAI House, 1997

1

In 1995, the Great Hanshin Earthquake devastated the Kobe Metropolitan area, where Katsuhiro Miyamoto lived and worked in a row house dating from 1900. The house was left standing but suffered structural damage after the neighbouring house collapsed, leading the local authorities to declare it *zenkai*, or completely collapsed. In response, Miyamoto performed 'house surgery', inserting a white steel frame into the fabric of the house to reinforce the damaged wooden structure and make the building inhabitable once again. The wooden framework, which was now no longer load-bearing, was left standing. Miyamoto's intervention was not only practical, but also a form of protest against official urban policy, which favours wasteful post-quake demolition and new construction rather than restoration. This policy has seen countless constructions replaced by new buildings after each major natural disaster, and Miyamoto credits it with the production of a kind of cultural amnesia. By not only retaining the wooden structure but exposing the way this new framework supports the old architecture, Miyamoto emphasizes his understanding of the house as a vessel for memory – preserving the memories of its previous inhabitants, the skills and techniques of the carpenters who built it, and the terrible consequences of the earthquake itself.

Location: Takarazuka, Hyogo
Total floor area: 88.78 m²

1 Exterior
2 Ground-floor *tatami* room
3 1:50 concept model, wood and steel

2

3

Shigeru Ban
Paper Emergency Shelters for UNHCR, 1994–

1

One of the biggest global problems architecture faces today is the rescuing of masses of people after both natural and manmade catastrophes such as wars, earthquakes, mass migrations, and climate change. Low-cost, easily shipped temporary housing is thus one of most urgent and growing demands society makes on architects. It is no big surprise that the most effective answers to such needs come from the Japanese housing culture, still strongly mindful of the legacy of the *minka* tradition and other nomadic dwellings and, at the same time, used to dealing with the aftermath of catastrophes. It is therefore by no means difficult to state that Shigeru Ban is, in Japan and globally, the architect who has made the biggest design contribution to this field, from Rwanda to Ecuador, India, and the 2011 earthquake and tsunami in Japan. The Paper Emergency Shelter was designed to house millions of refugees following the 1994 Rwandan Civil War. The cardboard structure proposed by Ban was an alternative to the usual UN tents made of plastic and valuable aluminium that was eventually sold by the refugees who replaced it with the wood obtained by cutting down trees. The cardboard unit has since been used for other emergencies and catastrophes around the world.

1   Assembly of shelter in Byumba Refugee Camp, Rwanda, 1999

Keisuke Oka
Arimaston Building, 2005–

1

In 2003, Keisuke Oka attended a summer workshop at Waseda University led by Osamu Ishiyama. At the end of the workshop, Oka presented a conceptual drawing of a fantastical self-build house in reinforced concrete and, on the advice of Ishiyama, decided to put his design into action. He began the Arimaston Building in 2005 and continues to build it today, eventually intending it to form a house and shop for him and his wife. Mixing his own concrete in the basement, Oka casts the house in individual 70 cm blocks, a size dictated by the amount of wet concrete he can carry by himself. From the street, the exposed structure and scaffolding form an imposing, alien presence among the embassies and generic apartment buildings of central Tokyo's Mito district. Inside, the architecture has an almost muscular quality, space expanding and contracting from room to room and indefinable architectural elements (somewhere between beams and pilasters) slicing through the void. The architect follows a basic structural framework, but he improvises the details as he builds upward, experimenting with sculptural moulds and casts of everyday objects to produce a wide range of textures and surfaces. Oka, a former Butoh dancer, has imbued the construction with a powerful performative, improvisatory aspect that testifies to the creative potential of self-build houses.

Location: Minato, Tokyo

1 Panel used to mould concrete surface, with carved wood, stencilled card, string, and plastic sheeting
2, 3 Concept drawings
4 Exterior under construction
5 Page from 'Sekai!! Oka Keisuke no Nihyakunen' ('The World!! Two hundred years of Keisuke Oka') by Hideki Arai, published in *Biggu Komikku Superioru* (Big Comic Superior), no. 686 (February, 2015)

何かの完成である。
と同時に次人の舞台である。

何かの完成である。
と同時に次人の舞台である。

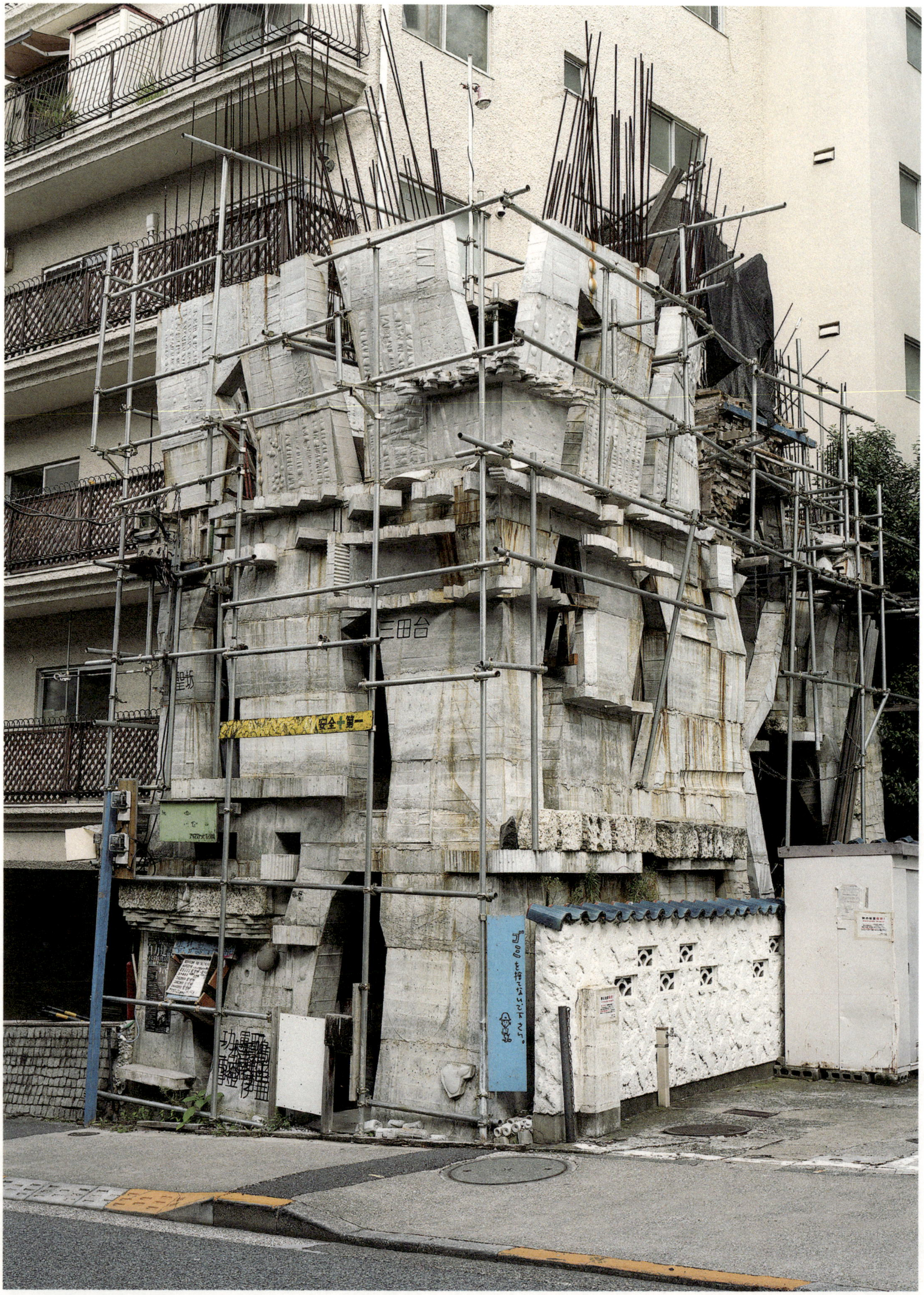

どこがどうなってんだ。

写真／中里和人 初出『コンフォルト』2014年2月号（建築資料研究社）

それは都心の住宅街のど真ん中に建っていた

!!

写真／中里和人 初出『コンフォルト』2014年2月号（建築資料研究社）

狂人の秘密基地か!? 反逆者の砦か!?
はたまた俺が嫌いな芸術家の暴走か!?

本物のアホがいる!!

わはは

Appendix

Architects' Biographies

Takefumi Aida (1937–)
pp. 177–179
Born in Tokyo. Graduated from Waseda University's 1st Department of Engineering, Department of Architecture, in 1960. Completed a master's degree and doctorate at the same university's graduate school in 1962 and 1966, respectively. Founded Takefumi Aida Urban Architectural Research Institute in 1967 (renamed the Takefumi Aida Design Research Institute in 1977, and reorganized as Aida Doi Architects in 2013). Associate professor at Shibaura Institute of Technology in 1973, which led to being nominated full professor at the same institute from 1977 to 2000. Guest professor at the University of California in 1986. Advising professor at Tongji University in China in 1992. Visiting professor at Dalian University of Technology in China in 1994. Emeritus professor at the Shibaura Institute of Technology in 2000, honorary member of the Japan Institute of Architects. Major works include the books *Architecture NOTE: Takefumi Aida, Block Houses* (Maruzen), and *Words from an Architect* (Shinkenchiku-sha). Major awards include the Saitama Scenery Award and the Japan Institute of Architects 25 Year Award.

Jun Aoki (1956–)
p. 200
After graduating from Tokyo University, worked at Arata Isozaki & Associates before establishing his own Tokyo-based practice in 1991 to do 'anything that seemed interesting'. Subsequent works have explored diverse directions such as a series of houses, public architecture, and fashion boutiques (including a current series of Louis Vuitton stores). Works also include a swimming pool at Yusuikan, which investigates some of the themes of his more recent projects; Fukushima Lagoon Museum (1997), which won the Architectural Institute of Japan Annual Award; and Aomori Museum of Art, which was given the Grand Award at an international competition. Recently completed Omiyamae Gymnasium in Tokyo, and Miyoshi City Hall in Hiroshima. Awarded the Minister of Education's Art Encouragement Prize in 2005 for architectural achievement.

Tadao Ando (1941–)
pp. 233–235
Born in Osaka. Self-taught in architecture, founded Tadao Ando Architect & Associates in 1969. Held positions as guest professor at Yale University, Columbia University, and Harvard University. Professor at Tokyo University from 1997, and emeritus professor at the same university from 2003. Established the Setouchi Olive Foundation in 2000 to support reconstruction following the Great Hanshin earthquake, and the Momo-Kaki Orphans Fund in 2011. Has received countless awards, including the Architectural Institute of Japan Award, the Japan Art Academy Award, the Pritzker Architecture Prize, the Royal Institute of British Architects (RIBA) Gold Medal, the AIA Gold Medal, the Kyoto Prize, the UIA (International Union of Architects) Gold Medal, and the Order of Culture. Major publications include *Discussing Architecture* and *Succession of Defeats* (both University of Tokyo Press).

Atelier Bow-Wow
(Yoshiharu Tsukamoto + Momoyo Kaijima)
pp. 222–223, 239–241, 246, 286
Founded in 1992 by Yoshiharu Tsukamoto and Momoyo Kaijima. Yoichi Tamai joined as a partner in 2015. Yoshiharu Tsukamoto was born in Kanagawa in 1965. Awarded an MA from the Tokyo Institute of Technology in 1989. From 1987 to 1988, was guest student at L'École d'Architecture de Belleville (University of Paris 8) and in 1996 received doctorate in engineering from Tokyo Institute of Technology. Became associate professor in 2000 and full professor at the Tokyo Institute of Technology in 2015. Momoyo Kaijima was born in Tokyo in 1969. Received her MA from Japan Women's University in 1991 and both graduate (M.Eng., 1994) and post-graduate degrees (1999) are from the Tokyo Institute of Technology. From 1996 to 1997, was guest student at Eidgenössische Technische Hochschule Zürich (ETH). In 2000 became assistant professor and in 2009 associate professor at the Art and Design School of the University of Tsukuba. Major publications including *Made in Tokyo* (Kajima Institute Publishing, 2001), *Pet Architecture* (World Photo Press, 2001), and *Behaviorology* (Rizzoli International Publications, 2010).

Takamitsu Azuma (1933–2015)
pp. 112–117
Born in Osaka. Graduated from Osaka University Faculty of Engineering in 1957, and then worked in the Ministry of Post and Telocommunications Department. Joined Junzo Sakakura Architectural Office in 1960. Worked as independent architect in 1967 and established Azuma Architects & Associates (later Takamitsu Azuma + Azuma Architects & Associates) in 1968. Formed counter-Metabolist group ArchiteXt with Aida Takefumi, Miyawaki Mayumi, Suzuki Makoto, and Takeyama Minoru in 1971. Professor at Osaka University from 1985 to 1997, and at Chiba Institute of Technology from 1997 to 2003.

Shigeru Ban (1957–)
p. 300
Born in Tokyo. Having studied at Southern California Institute of Architecture and Cooper Union School of Architecture in the United States, worked for Arata Isozaki in Tokyo in 1982–1983. Established private practice in Tokyo in 1985. Taught at various universities both in Japan and abroad. Has completed numerous buildings projects including houses, public and commercial institutions, and industrial and exhibition designs, and is also renowned for his social involvement, especially the disaster relief projects started following the 1995 earthquake. Since then, has provided many places affected by disasters in the world with emergency shelters and paper partitions systems. Has received numerous awards including the prestigious Pritzker Architecture Prize, L'Ordre des Arts et des Lettres, France (Grade de Commandeur), and the JIA Grand Prix 2015.

dot architects
p. 287
dot architects was founded in 2004 by Toshikatsu Ienari and Takeshi Shakushiro. Toshikatsu Ienari was born in Hyogo Prefecture in 1974. Graduated from the Faculty of Law at Kansai University in 1998 and the Osaka College of Technology in 2000. In 2014, he established dot architects. Currently works as associate professor at Kyoto University of Art and Design, and a part-time lecturer at Osaka College of Technology. Takeshi Shakushiro was born in Hyogo Prefecture in 1974 and graduated from the Department of Environmental Design at Kobe Design University in 1997. Worked at Rikuo Kitamura + Zoom Atelier & Design, and Katsuhiro Miyamoto & Associates before establishing dot architects in 2004. Currently works as a specially appointed lecturer at Osaka College of Technology and part-time lecturer at Kobe Design University.

Hiromi Fujii (1933–)
pp. 167, 168
Born in Tokyo and graduated from Waseda University Department of Architecture in 1958. Worked for the Waseda University Department of Architecture Moto Take Laboratory from 1958 to 1964. Studied abroad in Italy and Great Britain from 1964 to 1968. Founded the Hiromi Fujii Architects Studio in 1968. Worked as a part-time lecturer for the Waseda University Department of Architecture from 1977 to 1980. Professor with the Shibaura Institute of Technology Department of Engineering from 1981 to 2003. Associate member of Harvard University in 1987. Awarded an honorary doctorate from the Moscow Architectural Institute in 2003. Became an emeritus professor of Shibaura Institute of Technology in 2004. Major publications include *The Architecture of Hiromi Fujii* (Rizzoli International, 1987, and Suiseisha, 1998), and *Seven Architecture Essays by or related to Hiromi Fujii* (Suiseisha, 1999).

Terunobu Fujimori (1946–)
pp. 279–281
Born in Nagano. After graduating from the Department of Architecture at Tohoku University, completed doctorate at the University of Tokyo. Following positions as professor at the Institute of Industrial Science, the University of Tokyo, and Kogakuin University, assumed current position as emeritus professor at the University of Tokyo. Specially appointed professor, Kogakuin University, and director of the Edo Tokyo Museum. Specializing in history of architecture, began working in design at age forty-five. In 1986, formed Roadway Observation Society with Genpei Akasegawa *et al*. Recent works include museums, exhibit halls, residential spaces, and tearooms, including the Mosaic Tile Museum (Tajimi), Kusayane, and Doyane (Omi Hachiman, Taneya General Store). Recent publications include *Tearoom Theory: Arata Isozaki and Terunobu Fujimori* (Rikuyosha), *Fujimori Tea Studies* (Shokokusha), and other works on architectural history, architectural exploration, and design.

Sou Fujimoto (1971–)
pp. 180, 181, 201, 252–253
After graduating from the Department of Architecture, Faculty of Engineering, at the University of Tokyo, established Sou Fujimoto Architects in 2000. In 2016 won first prize for Pershing, one of the sites in the French Réinventer Paris competition, following victories in the Invitational International Competition for the New Learning Centre at Paris-Saclay's École Polytechnique and the International Competition for the Second Folly of Montpellier in 2014. In 2013 became the youngest architect to design the Serpentine Gallery Pavilion in London. Key publications include *Sou Fujimoto* (Phaidon, 2016), *Sou Fujimoto Architecture Works 1995–2015* (TOTO Publishing, 2015), *Sou Fujimoto – Recent project* (A. D. A. Edita, 2013), *Sou Fujimoto: Musashino Art University Museum & Library* (INAX, 2010).

Takashi Fujino (1975–)
(Ikimono Architects)
pp. 226–229
Born in Gunma. Graduated from Tohoku University with an MA in Architecture in 2000. Worked at Shimizu Corporation and Haryu Wood Studio. Established Ikimono Architects in 2006. Has taught at Maebashi Institute of Technology from 2012. Won Selected Architectural Designs Young Architects Award for Atelier Tenjinyama in 2013. Static Quarry and House of Seven Gardens, and Kamezawa Family Onsen were selected in 2014 and 2015 for the Architectural Institute of Japan Work Selection. Co-author of *Chihou de kenchiku wo shigoto ni suru* (Making a living with architecture in the local area) (Gakugei Syuppansha).

Go Hasegawa (1977–)
pp. 266–267
Born in Saitama. After obtaining a master's degree from the Graduate School of Science and Engineering, Tokyo Institute of Technology, in 2002, joined Taira Nishizawa Architects until 2004. In 2005, established Go Hasegawa and Associates. Taught at Tokyo Institute of Technology, Tokyo University of Science, Hosei University from 2009 to 2011. Has been invited as visiting professor by the Academy of Architecture of Mendrisio, Switzerland, the Oslo School of Architecture and Design, Norway, University of California, Los Angeles, USA, and MIAW2016 at the Politecnico di Milano, Italy. Awards include the Kajima Prize for *SD Review*, Tokyo Gas House Design Competition (Grand Prix), Gold Prize in Residential Architecture Award, Tokyo Society of Architects & Building Engineers, Gold Prize in the 28th INAX Design Contest, the 24th Shinkenchiku Prize, and AR Design Vanguard.

Itsuko Hasegawa (1941–)
pp. 189–191, 262–263
Born in Shizuoka prefecture. Graduated from Kanto Gakuin University Department of Architecture in 1964. Worked at Kiyonori Kikutake Architects. In 1969 became a research student at Shinohara Laboratory at the Tokyo Institute of Technology. Started working for the Tokyo Institute of Technology Department of Architecture in 1971. Established the Itsuko Hasegawa Atelier in 1979. Worked as a part-time lecturer for various places including Waseda University and the Tokyo Institute of Technology, and as a guest lecturer for Harvard University. Received an honorary membership from the Royal Institute of British Architects (RIBA) in 1997, and the American Institute of Architects (AIA) in 2006. Major awards include the Architectural Institute of Japan Award, the Japan Cultural Design Award, the Japan Art Academy Award, and the Public Building Award. Major works include *Houses & Housing 1972–2014* (Itsuko Hasegawa Atelier, 2014), and *Itsuko Hasegawa Section 1–3* (Kajima Institute Publishing, 2015).

Kenji Hirose (1922–2012)
p. 257
Born in Kanagawa prefecture. Graduated from the Musashi Engineering School in 1942, and joined Inoue Kogyo. Conscripted in 1944, joined the Akabane Engineers Corps, and after his discharge, enlisted in the Naval Facilities Engineering Division. Worked for Tokyo Mokko from 1946 to 1951. Worked for Murata Masachika Architects from 1949 to 1951. Founded Kenji Hirose Architect & Associates in 1952. From 1966 worked as a full-time professor at the Musashi Technical College Department of Architecture (now Tokyo City University). Became emeritus professor of Musashi Technical College in 1993, and founded the Hirose Laboratory.

Jun Igarashi (1970–)
pp. 284–285
Born in Hokkaido. Founded Jun Igarashi Architects in 1997. Major publications include *Jun Igarashi: Display of State* (Shokokusha, 2010), and *Architecture of State* (TOTO Publishing, 2011). Major exhibitions include *Architecture of State* (TOTO Gallery, Tokyo, 2011). Major awards include the 19th Yoshioka Prize, the Biennial International Prize for Architecture Barbara Cappochin Grand Prize, AR Awards 2006, and the Japan Institute of Architects New Face Prize. Teaches at Nagoya Institute of Technology.

Kiyoshi Ikebe (1920–1979)
pp. 90–91
Born in Pusan, South Korea. Graduated from the Tokyo Imperial University Department of Architecture in 1942, and entered the Tokyo Imperial University Graduate School in the same year. Joined Sakakura Associates in 1944. Became a lecturer at the Tokyo University 2nd Department of Engineering in 1946. Took part in founding the New Architect's Union of Japan (NAU) in 1947. Took part in founding the SHINSEISAKU Architectural Department (now the Space Design Department) in 1948. Became associate professor at the Tokyo University 2nd Department of Engineering in 1949. Became professor at the Tokyo University Institute of Industrial Science in 1965. Major awards include the Minister of Economy, Trade, and Industry Award.

Tsutomu Ikuta (1912–1980)
pp. 78–79
Born in Hokkaido. Graduated from the architecture department, Tokyo Imperial University. After working for the Ministry of Communication became professor at the First Higher School, Japan. In 1950 became associate professor at the College of Arts and Science of the University of Tokyo and taught there until retirement in 1972. Along with his academic career he established his own architectural office in 1967. Translated many books, including works by American literary critic and philosopher of technology, Lewis Mumford.

Kumiko Inui (1969–)
pp. 290–291
Born in Osaka. Graduated from Tokyo University of the Arts, Faculty of Fine Arts, Department of Architecture in 1992. Completed master's program at Yale School of Architecture in 1996. Worked at Jun Aoki & Associates from 1996 to 2000. Established Office of Kumiko Inui in 2000. Associate professor at Tokyo University of the Arts from 2011 to 2016. Professor at Yokohama Graduate School of Architecture from 2016. Awards include Shinkenchiku Award, Tokyo Society of Architects & Building Engineers Housing prize, Japan Federation of Architects & Building Engineers Association Prize, 2010 Good Design Gold Award, Japan Institute of Architects Young Architect Award, and BCS Award. Also awarded the Golden Lion for the *Architecture, Possible Here? 'Home-for-All'* exhibition (co-produced with Toyo Ito, Sou Fujimoto, Akihisa Hirata, and Naoya Hatakeyama) for the Japan Pavilion at the 13th International Architecture Exhibition of the Venice Biennale in 2012. Publications include *Episodes* (INAX), *Home of Asakusa* (Heibonsya), *Little Spaces* (TOTO Publishing).

Junya Ishigami (1974–)
pp. 184–185
Born in Kanagawa. Studied architecture at Tokyo University of the Arts, receiving an MFA in 2000. Worked at Kazuyo Sejima & Associates from 2000 to 2004. Established junya.ishigami+associates in 20a04. Associate professor at Tohoku University in Sendai, and has taught at Princeton University School of Architecture and Harvard Graduate School of Design. Major awards include the Architectural Institute of Japan Prize for Kanagawa Institute of Technology (2009) and the Golden Lion at the Venice Biennale (2010). Publications include Junya Ishigami: *How Small? How Vast? How Architecture Grows* (Hatje Cantz, 2014) and *Junya Ishigami: Another Scale of Architecture* (Seigensha, 2011).

Osamu Ishiyama (1944–)
pp. 215–217, 218–221, 295–297
Born in Okayama. Graduated from Waseda University Department of Architecture. In 1968, after completing University Graduate School Master's course, launched dam-dan (name later changed to dam-dan corporation). Professor at Waseda University from 1988 to 2014, and has hosted workshops in Japan and overseas since 1998. Nominated emeritus professor, Waseda University, in 2012. Founded Studio Gaya in 2014. Recipient of numerous awards, including Isoya Yoshida Award, Architectural Institute of Japan Award, Venice Biennale Golden Lion, Japan Inter-Design Award, Oribe Award, and Award from the Ministry of Education in the Arts Encouragement Prizes. Major works include *Architecture for Survival* (NTT, 2010) and *Dreams of Architecture* (Kodansha, 2008).

Toyo Ito (1941–)
pp. 146–149, 152–153, 156–157, 158–161, 192–195, 210–213
Born in Nagano prefecture. Graduated from Tokyo University Department of Architecture in 1965. Worked at Kiyonori Kikutake & Associates from 1965 to 1971. Established his own office, Urban Robot, in 1971, subsequently renamed Toyo Ito & Associates, Architects in 1979. Has received countless awards, including JIA Newcomer Award, Architectural Institute of Japan Award, Murano Togo Prize, Mainichi Art Award, Ministry of Education Award for Fine Arts, Japan Art Academy Award, Brunner Memorial Prize, Royal Institute of British Architects Gold Medal, and Pritzker Architecture Prize. In 2002 was awarded the Golden Lion at the Venice Biennale of Architecture. Has been guest professor at numerous international universities, including the University of Tokyo, Columbia University, the University of California Los Angeles, Kyoto University, and Tama University. In 2012 hosted an overseas studio for Harvard's Graduate School of Design.

Yuusuke Karasawa (1976–)
pp. 182–183
Born in Tokyo. Graduated with an MA in Architecture and Urban Design at Keio University Graduate School of Media and Governance in 2001. Worked at MVRDV as a trainee for the Japanese Government Overseas Study Program for Artists from 2002 to 2003 and worked at Shigeru Ban Architects from 2004 to 2005. Established Yuusuke Karasawa Architects in 2006. Key publications include *Aakitekucha to kura udo ouhou niyoru kuukan no henyou* (Architecture and cloud) (Millegraph) and *Sekkei no sekkei kenchiku kuukan jouhou seisaku no houhou* (Design by design) (INAX).

Kiyonori Kikutake (1928–2011)
pp. 258–261
Born in Fukuoka prefecture. Graduated from Waseda University Department of Architecture in 1950, and joined Takenaka Corporation. Joined Murano & Mori Architects in 1953. Founded Kiyonori Kikutake Architects in 1953. Formed the Metabolism Group with Kisho Kurokawa, Noboru Kawazoe, and others in 1960. Took part in the Team X Convention in 1962. Announced his 'Ka / Kata / Katachi' design theory in 1963 (*Metabolism Architectural Theory: Ka / Kata / Katachi*, Shohokusha Publishing, 1969). Major awards include Ministry of Education Award for Fine Arts, Architectural Institute of Japan Award, International Union of Architects August Perret Prize, and Mainichi Art Award. Worked as a member of the Tsukuba Expo master-plan production committee, and as supervisor for the Nagano Winter Olympics spatial organization.

Waro Kishi (1950–)
p. 238
Born in Kanagawa. Graduated from the Department of Architecture, Kyoto University, in 1975. Completed post-graduate course of Architecture, Kyoto University, in 1978. Taught architectural design in Kyoto Institute of Technology from 1993 to 2010. Professor at Kyoto University from 2010 to 2016. Professor at Kyoto University of Art and Design from 2016 to the present. Also taught at the University of California Berkeley and MIT as visiting professor. Awards include Gold Award, 16th Asia Pacific Interior Design Awards, The Prize of Architectural Institute of Japan for Design, JIA Award for best young architect of the year. Major published works include *Journey Through Architecture* (Kyoritsu Shuppan, 2003), *Waro Kishi* (Electa, 2005), *CA Waro Kishi* (CA Press, 2013), *Waro Kishi + K. Associates* (Equal Books, 2014), *Waro Kishi* (TOTO Publishing, 2016).

Chie Konno (1981–)
pp. 288–289
Born in Kanagawa Prefecture. After graduating from the Department of Architecture at Tokyo Institute of Technology in 2005, attended the Swiss Federal Institute of Technology as a scholarship student from 2005 to 2006. In 2011, earned a doctorate in engineering from Tokyo Institute of Technology and started working at Kobe Design University as a graduate assistant. Also established KONNO in the same year. Became an assistant professor at Nippon Institute of Technology in 2013, and established teco with Rie Allison in 2015.

Kengo Kuma (1954–)
pp. 264–265
Born in Kanagawa. Completed MA at the University of Tokyo in 1979. Attended Columbia University as visiting researcher from 1985 to 1986. Launched Kengo Kuma and Associates in 1990. Has received numerous awards, including the AIA Benedictus Award, Architectural Institute of Japan Prize, International Stone Architecture Award, Murano Togo Award, and Spirit of Nature Wood Architecture Award, and was made an Officier de l'Ordre des Arts et des Lettres in France. Professor at the Graduate School of Architecture, University of Tokyo, and has been visiting professor at the University of Illinois and Columbia University. A prolific writer, major publications include *Anti-Object: The Dissolution and Disintegration of Architecture* (AA Publications, 2008).

Kisho Kurokawa (1934–2007)
pp. 98–99
Born in Nagoya. Graduated from Kyoto University Department of Architecture in 1957 before joining Kenzo Tange Laboratory at the Tokyo University Graduate School of Engineering, obtaining an MA in architecture. Formed the Metabolism Group with Noboru Kawazoe and others in 1960. Founded Kisho Kurokawa Architect & Associates in 1962. Completed the course requirements for a doctorate at the Tokyo University Graduate School in 1964. The *Kisho Kurokawa* Exhibition was held in 1997 (Centre Pompidou, Paris). Received countless awards both in Japan and abroad, including French Academy of Architecture Gold Medal, Dedalo Minosse International Prize (Grand Prix) Gold Medal, Architectural Institute of Japan Award, and Japan Art Academy Award. Major designs include *Urban Design* (Books Kinokuniya, 1965), *Action Architecture* (1967), *The Philosophy of Symbiosis* (Tokuma Shoten, 1987), and *Revolution of City* (Shinsha, 2006).

Takashi Kurosawa (1941–2014)
p. 209
Born in Tokyo. Graduated from Nihon University Department of Engineering in 1965. Research student at Tsutomu Ikuta Laboratory at University of Tokyo's College of Arts and Sciences until 1967. Enrolled in a doctorate course at the university's graduate school in 1971. Established the Takashi Kurosawa Laboratory in 1973. Taught at various locations, including Shibaura Institute of Technology, Nihon University Arts Department, and Nihon University College of Industrial Technology, and held seminars as part-time lecturer at the Nihon University College of Science and Technology Oumi Laboratory. Major works include *Experiments in Housing Complex Theory* (Kajima Institute Publishing), *Private Room Group Dwellings: Crumbling Modern Families and Architectural Challenges* (Sumai Library Publishing Group), and *Conceptual Japanese Architecture* (Kajima Institute Publishing, 2016).

Kunio Maekawa (1905–1986)
p. 87
Born in Niigata. Graduated from the architecture department of the University of Tokyo. Studied architecture at Le Corbusier's atelier in Paris from 1928 to 1930. After returning to Japan in 1930 worked for Antonin Raymond Design Office until he established his own office, Mayekawa Kunio Associate Architects & Engineers in 1935. Received countless prestigious awards, including six AIJ Awards, Grand Prix of the Architectural Institute of Japan, Mainichi Art Award, and Japan Art Academy Award.

Makoto Masuzawa (1925–1990)
pp. 92–95
Born in Tokyo. After graduating from the Tokyo University Department of Architecture in 1947, studied under architect Antonin Raymond. Founded Masuzawa Architect & Associates in 1956. Director of the Japan Institute of Architects from 1963 to 1965. Lecturer at the University of Tokyo Faculty of Engineering from 1964 to 1965. Guest professor at the University of Hawaii in 1970. Director of the Japan Institute of Architects from 1976 to 1978. Major works include *Housing Complexes* (Inoueshoin, 1980), and *Housing Feature – Minor Thoughts on Architecture* (1987). Major awards include BCS Award, Chubu Architecture Award, and Library Association Award.

Katsuhiro Miyamoto (1961–)
pp. 298–299
Born in Hyogo. Bachelor of Architecture, University of Tokyo in 1984. Master of Architecture, University of Tokyo in 1987. Established Atelier Cinquième Architects in 1988. In 2002 reorganized as Katsuhiro Miyamoto & Associates. Professor, Graduate School of Engineering, Osaka City University, from 2008. In 1996 awarded the Golden Lion for Best Pavilion, 6th Venice Biennale International Architecture Exhibition; in 1998 Jean Nouvel Award, Japan Commercial Environment Designers Association Design Awards, Young Japanese Architect of the Year, Japan Institute of Architects for House Surgery; in 2007 Japan Institute of Architects Award for Clover House; in 2008 Grand Prize, Japan Commercial Environment Designers Association Design Award, for Hankai House; in 2012 Annual Architectural Design Commendation by Architectural Institute of Japan, for Chushin-ji Temple Priest's Quarters. Major publications include *Grown* (flick studio, 2010), *Katsuhiro Miyamoto* (Libria, 2010), *Katsuhiro Miyamoto & Associates* (NemoFactory, 2016).

Kiko Mozuna (1941–2001)
pp. 172–175
Born in Kushiro, Hokkaido. Graduated from Kobe University's Department of Architecture in 1965, and then worked as a tutor at the same university until 1967. Started working in design under the name of Monta Mozuna. Established Kiko Mozuna Architects & Associates in 1978. Formed Basara in 1978 with Kijo Rokkaku, Osamu Ishiyama, and others. Professor at Tama Art University Department of Architecture from 1995 onwards. Major awards include Architectural Institute of Japan Award. Major works include *Urban Genetics* (Seidosha, 1987), *Architecture That Brought About the Seven Gods of Fortune* (Kobunsha, 1988), and *Anonymous Design* (TOTO Publishing, 1993).

Hideyuki Nakayama (1972–)
pp. 202–203
Born in Fukuoka. Awarded an MA in Architecture and Planning, Faculty of Fine Arts, Tokyo National University of Fine Arts and Music in 2000. In 2000–2007 worked at Toyo Ito & Associates, Architects, and in 2007 established Hideyuki Nakayama Architecture. In 2014 was made associate professor, Architecture and Planning Course, Faculty of Fine Arts, Tokyo National University of Fine Arts and Music. Main awards include *SD* review 2004 Kajima prize, 23rd Yoshioka Award, Tea House Competition winner, D&AD Award, Red Dot Design Award, winning proposal for Frans Masereel Centrum. Major publications include *Create a library to create – An experiment by Toyo Ito and Tama Art University* (Kajima Institute Publishing, 2007, as a contributor), and *Hideyuki Nakayama / Sketching* (2010, Shinjuku-Shobo).

Kazuhiko Namba (1947–)
pp. 100, 101
Born in Osaka. Graduated from the Department of Architecture, University of Tokyo in 1969. Completed doctorate course, University of Tokyo in 1974. Established Kai Workshop in 1977, subsequently renaming it Kazuhiko Namba + Kai Workshop. Part-time instructor at Department of Architecture, University of Tokyo, Department of Architecture, Waseda University, and Department of Architecture, Tokyo Institute of Technology. Professor at Department of Architecture, Osaka City University from 2000, and professor in Department of Architecture, Graduate School of Engineering, the University of Tokyo, from 2003 to 2010. Major awards include Yoshioka Prize, Residential Architecture Prize, JIA Environmental Architecture Prize, and Architectural Institute of Japan Prize. Major published works include *The Evolving Box: 20 Years in a Box House* (TOTO Publishing, 2015), *House Box: Towards an Eco-House* (NTT, 2006), and *The Extremes of Postwar Modernist Architecture: Essays on Kiyoshi Ikebe* (Shokokusha, 1999).

Osamu Nishida + Erika Nakagawa
pp. 224–225
Osamu Nishida was born in Kanagawa Prefecture in 1976. Graduated from Yokohama National University in 1999. In 2002 established architecture firm Speed Studio. From 2002 to 2007 worked as graduate assistant at Tokyo Metropolitan University Graduate School, and established ON Design in 2004. Worked as assistant at Yokohama Graduate School of Architecture (Y-GSA) from 2005 to 2009 and part-time lecturer at the University of Tokyo and Tokyo University of Science from 2013 to 2016. Erika Nakagawa was born in 1983 in Tokyo. Graduated from Yokohama National University in 2005 and obtained an MA from Graduate School of Fine Arts, Tokyo University of the Arts, in 2007. Worked at ON Design from 2007 to 2014. In 2014, established erika nakagawa office. Worked as part-time lecturer at Yokohama National University in 2012, and worked as design assistant at Y-GSA from 2014 to 2016. Started teaching at Tokyo University of the Arts as part-time lecturer in 2016.

Ryue Nishizawa (1966–)
pp. 247–251, 270–275
Born in Kanagawa. After completing graduate program at Yokohama National University and working in Toyo Ito & Associates, joined Kazuyo Sejima & Associates in 1990. Established SANAA with Sejima in 1997, and established the Office of Ryue Nishizawa in the same year. Currently associate professor at Yokohama National University Graduate School. Awards include Architectural Institute of Japan Prize, Yoshioka Prize, Tokyo Society of Architects and Building Engineers Residential Architecture Prize, Arnold W Brunner Memorial Prize, Pritzker Architecture Prize, and Golden Lion at the 9th International Architecture Biennale, Venice. Major publications include *Kazuyo Sejima + Ryue Nishizawa / SANAA: Works 1995–2003* (TOTO Publishing, 2003), *Talk about Architecture* (Okokusha, 2007), and *Dialogues around the Museum* (Shueisha, 2010).

Taira Nishizawa (1964–)
p. 245
Born in Tokyo. Graduated from Tokyo Institute of Technology in 1987. After working for Keiichi Irie Architectural Office, established own office in 1992. Has taught at various universities in Japan. Professor at Shibaura Institute of Technology since 2011. Publications include *Taira Nishizawa 1994–2004* (TOTO Publishing, 2004) and *Taira Nishizawa Wooden Works 2004–2010* (INAX, 2011). Major awards include Residential Architecture Prize, AR Awards Grand Prix, BARBARA CAPPOCHIN International Award, Faith&Form Awards International Awards.

Katsuhiko Ohno (1944–2012)
pp. 96–97
Born in Fukushima. Graduated from the Department of Architecture, Graduate School of Engineering, University of Tokyo in 1967. Developed the Sekisui Heim M1 with Sekisui Chemical Corporation in 1970. Established Ohno Atelier in 1971. Awarded doctorate in Component Architecture Theory (Yoshichika Uchida Lab) at University of Tokyo Graduate School in 1972. Engaged in city and urban planning for a range of locations around Japan, including Kitakata in Fukushima, Ohno in Fukui, Yuki in Ibaraki, and the HOPE Project. Major works include *Contemporary Residences and the Residential Climate* (Kajima Publishing), *Local Residential Studio Networks* (Shokokusha), *Contemporary Tsukumo: 7 Town Plan Designs*.

Keisuke Oka (1965–)
pp. 301–305
Born in Yanagawa City. Raised at the Funagoya Onsen in the south of Chikugo city. After graduating from the Department of Architecture at Ariake National College of Technology, became a company employee and then worked as a labourer on construction sites, steeplejack, formwork carpenter, and carpenter for prefabricated houses, and spent a few months each year cycling throughout Japan for architectural sightseeing. At the age of twenty-two, enrolled in the Takayama Architecture School (a training camp established by Yasuo Kurata) to study architecture. Has continued to attend this school since then. Later studied dance and ran a space called Oka Gallery, organizing parties and events in places such as Kabukicho and Yoyogi Park, but ended most of these activities in 2005 and launched the self-build Arimasutonbiru project.

onishimaki + hyakudayuki architects / o + h
pp. 204–205
onishimaki + hyakudayuki / o + h was established in 2008 by Maki Onishi and Yuki Hyakuda in 2008. Maki Onishi was born in Aichi in 1983. Graduated from Kyoto University in 2006. Completed Master's course at University of Tokyo graduate school in 2008. GSA design assistant, Yokohama National University Graduate School from 2011 to 2013. Yuki Hyakuda was born in Hyogo in 1982. Graduated from Kyoto University in 2006. Completed Master's course at Kyoto University Graduate School in 2008. Toyo Ito & Associates from 2009 to 2014. Major awards include SD Review 2007 Kajima Prize and 2012 New Architecture Prize. Major published works include *onishimaki + hyakudayuki Works* (Garden City Publishers, 2012) and *8 Stories* (LIXIL, 2014).

Antonin Raymond (1888–1976)
pp. 69–71
Born in Bohemia (then in Austria, now Czech Republic). After graduating from the Czech Technical University in Prague, went to the United States in 1910 and worked at Cass Gilbert's office in New York. In 1916 became an American citizen. In 1919 came to Japan with Frank Lloyd Wright to supervise the construction of the Imperial Hotel. In 1921 established design office in Japan and worked there until he left Japan and returned to the US in 1973. Both before and after World War II, built some of Japan's most important modernist buildings, including the concrete Reinanzaka House (1924), Reader's Digest Building (1951), St Anselm's Catholic Church and Priory, and the Gunma Music Centre (1955–1961). Received many awards, including AIJ Awards, a medal of honour from UIJ, and Third Order of Merit from the Japanese Government.

Junzo Sakakura (1901–1969)
pp. 88–89
Born in Gifu. Graduated from the Art History Department of Tokyo Imperial University, where he became interested in architecture. In 1929 went to France and worked for Le Corbusier's atelier from 1931 to 1936. After returning to Japan in 1936, designed the Japanese Pavilion at the 1937 Paris Exposition of Art and Technology, which received the architectural Grand Prix in 1937. In 1940 established his own office, Junzo Sakakura Architectural Office, and completed more than 300 built works before his death at the age of 68. Alongside his architectural achievements, was also engaged in design in post-war Japan through activities such as curating the Contact avec L'Art japonais: tradition, selection, creation exhibition (Tokyo and Osaka, Takashimaya) with Charlotte Perriand in 1941 and the Japanese exhibitions at the 1957 and 1960 Milan Triennale, as well as serving as the first chairman of the jury for the Good Design Selection System established in 1957.

Kazunari Sakamoto (1943–)
pp. 141–145, 150–151, 154–155, 162–163, 236–237
Born in Tokyo. Studied under Kazuo Shinohara in the Department of Architecture and Building Engineering at the Tokyo Institute of Technology, graduating in 1966. Completed doctorate at the Tokyo Institute of Technology in 1971 and became full-time lecturer at Department of Architecture, Musashino Art University. Associate professor, Musashino Art University in 1977. Associate professor, Tokyo Institute of Technology in 1983. Professor, Tokyo Institute of Technology in 1999. Emeritus professor, Tokyo Institute of Technology Head of Kazunari Sakamoto Atelier in 2009. Major awards include Architectural Institute of Japan Prize and Murano Togo Prize. Major works include *HOUSE: Poetics in the ordinary* (TOTO Publishing, 2001), *Words in Architecture* (TOTO Publishing, 2011), and *Anti-Climax Poetry: Sakamoto's Architecture* (Power Station of Art, 2015).

Kiyoshi Seike (1918–2005)
pp. 72–73
Born in Kyoto. Graduated from the Tokyo School of Fine Arts (now Tokyo National University of Fine Arts and Music) Department of Architecture in 1941. Graduated from the Tokyo Institute of Technology Department of Architecture in 1943, and enlisted in the navy. Worked as tutor, lecturer, and associate professor at the Tokyo Institute of Technology from 1945 onwards, and in 1962 became professor in the Tokyo Institute of Technology Department of Architecture. In 1968 founded Design System. In 1977 was also appointed professor in the Tokyo National University of Fine Arts and Music Department of Architecture. In 1979 retired from the Tokyo Institute of Technology, and became an emeritus professor at the same university. Held successive positions, including chairman of the Architectural Institute of Japan, and chairman of the Tokyo Society of Architects & Building Engineers. Headmaster of the Sapporo School of The Arts from 1991 to 1997.

Kazuyo Sejima (1956–)
pp. 196–199
Born in Ibaraki. Completed an MA at Japan Women's University in 1981. Worked for Toyo Ito & Associates, Architects, from 1981 to 1987. Established Kazuyo Sejima & Associates in 1987, and established SANAA with Ryue Nishizawa in 1995. Currently Professor at Keio University. Has taught at Princeton University, the Polytechnique de Lausanne, and Tama Art University. Has received numerous awards for both her independent work and collaborations with Nishizawa, including the Yoshioka Prize (1989), Japan Institute of Architects New Face Award (1998), Architectural Institute of Japan Award (2000), Erich Schelling Architecture Prize (2000), Arnold W Brunner Memorial Prize (2002), the Golden Lion at the Architecture Biennale, Venice (2004), and the Pritzker Architecture Prize (2010). Appointed director of the 2010 Venice Biennale, which she curated with the theme 'People Meet in Architecture'.

Yo Shimada (1972–)
pp. 268–269
Born in Kobe. Yo Shimada founded Tato Architects in 1997, after graduating from Kyoto City University of Art. The name Tato (タト) is derived from the decomposition of the kanji character 外 (outside), which can be read in multiple ways. Has received numerous awards and honours including Yoshioka Prize in 2013 and AIA Brisbane Regional Awards, House of the Year Award in 2016. Major publications include *7iP #04 YO SHIMADA* (7inch project, 2012) and *Everyday Design Everyday: Yo Shimada* (Contemporary Architect's Concept Series 22, 2016). Has been visiting professor at Kyoto University of Art and Design since 2016.

Kazuo Shinohara (1925–2006)
pp. 121–125, 126–129, 130–133, 134–137
Born in Shizuoka prefecture. Graduated from the Tokyo Academy of Physics in 1947, and enrolled in the Tokyo Institute of Technology Department of Architecture in 1949 via the Tohoku University Mathematical Institute, studying under Kiyoshi Seike. After graduating in 1953, became a graphics tutor at the same university, then associate professor from 1962, and full professor from 1970 to 1986. After retiring from the Tokyo Institute of Technology in 1986, became an emeritus professor of the same institute. Held the positions of guest lecturer at Yale University and guest lecturer at the Vienna University of Technology. Founded the Shinohara Atelier in 1986. Major awards include Architectural Institute of Japan Award, Minister of Education Award for Fine Arts, Medal with Purple Ribbon, Mainichi Art Award Special Award, and the Order of the Rising Sun, Gold Rays with Neck Ribbon. Major works include *Residential Architecture* (Books Kinokuniya, 1964), *Residential Theory* (Kajima Institute Publishing, 1970), *Towards Very Large Scale Urban Sprawls* (A. D. A Edita Tokyo, 2001), and *By Kazuo Shinohara: Leaving Tokyo, Tokyo Theory* (Kajima Institute Publishing, 2001).

Satoko Shinohara (1958–)
pp. 264–265
Born in Chiba. Graduated from Japan Women's University in 1981 and completed an MA at the same institution in 1983. Worked at Hisao Kohyama Atelier from 1983 to 1985. Established Spatial Design Studio in 1986. Has been professor at Japan Women's University since 2010. Main awards include AIJ Award, Residential Architecture Prize, and Good Design Award.

Seiichi Shirai (1905–1983)
pp. 80–83
Born in Kyoto. Graduated from Kyoto College of Technology (present-day Kyoto Institute of Technology) in 1928. From 1927 to 1933 studied at Heidelberg University and Berlin University, studying modern German philosophy as well as Gothic architecture. On returning to Japan started architectural design. Major awards include Kotaro Takamura Prize in the visual arts category, Award of the Annual of Architecture in Japan, AIJ Awards, Mainichi Art Awards, and the Japan Art Academy Prize. Designed many books, including his own.

Kenzo Tange (1913–2005)
pp. 74–77
Born in Osaka prefecture. Graduated from the Tokyo Imperial University Department of Architecture in 1938, and then worked for Maekawa Kunio Associates. After leaving the company, enrolled in the Tokyo Imperial University Graduate School in 1942. In 1961 founded Kenzo Tange Associates. After working as associate professor at the Tokyo University Department of Architecture from 1946 to 1963, served as professor in the Urban Engineering Department from 1963 to 1974 before being nominated emeritus professor. Major exhibitions include *Kenzo Tange: From One Pencil* (Nihon Tosho Centre, 1997). Major awards include Royal Institute of British Architects (RIBA) Gold Medal, American Institute of Architecture Gold Medal, Order of Culture, French Ordre des Arts et des Lettres Commandeur, Pritzker Architecture Prize, and Prince Takamatsu Memorial World Culture Prize in the building sector category.

Tezuka Architects
(Takaharu Tezuka + Yui Tezuka)
pp. 282–283
Takaharu Tezuka and Yui Tezuka founded Tezuka Architects in 1994. Takaharu Tezuka was born in Tokyo in 1964. Graduated from Musashi Institute of Technology in 1987, and was awarded an MA from the University of Pennsylvania in 1990. Associate Professor, Musashi Institute of Technology from 1996 to 2008. Professor, Tokyo City University in 2009. Yui Tezuka was born in Kanagawa in 1969. Graduated from Musashi Institute of Technology in 1992. Studied at the Bartlett School of Architecture, University College of London, from 1992 to 1993. Awards include Good Design Gold Award and Prize of Architectural Institute of Japan for Design, Japan Institute of Architects Award. Main publications include *Takaharu + Yui Tezuka Architecture Catalogue 13* (TOTO Publishing).

Riken Yamamoto (1945–)
p. 214
Born in Beijing, China. Graduated from the School of Architecture, Nihon University. MA degree, Tokyo University of the Arts. Major awards include Architectural Institute of Japan Award, BCS Award, Mainichi Arts Prize, and Japan Academy of Art Prize. Major works include Hotakubo Housing Project #1 in Kumamoto, Iwadeyama Municipal Middle School, Saitama Prefectural University, and Future University Hakodate. Major published works include *Cellular Cities* (INAX), *Theory of Residence* (SUMAI Library Publishing Company), *Thinking while Building, Building while Using* (TOTO Publishing), *Local Society-ism* (INAX, joint authorship).

Kazumasa Yamashita (1937–)
p. 176
Born in Aichi prefecture. Studied at the Tokyo Institute of Technology Department of Architecture in the Kiyoshi Seike Laboratory, and graduated in 1959. After working for Nikken Sekkei and London City Hall, founded Kazumasa Yamashita Architects in 1969. Retired from his position as professor at the Department of Architecture, Tokyo Institute of Technology in 1993. Major awards include Architectural Institute of Japan Best Work Award, Tokyo Association of Architectural Firms Award of Excellence, and Ministry of Construction Award. Also responsible for many industrial designs, including Alessi coffee set (displayed at the Kyoto National Museum of Modern Art). Worked as Japanese representative of the International Map Collectors' Society (IMCoS) for more than thirty years, collecting antique maps. Works include *On Antique Maps from the Edo Period*.

Junzo Yoshimura (1908–1997)
pp. 108–111
Born in Tokyo. After graduating from the Tokyo Fine Arts College (present-day Tokyo National University of Fine Arts and Music) in 1931, joined Antonin Raymond Architectural Design Office. In 1941 established his own office. In 1962 began teaching architecture at Tokyo National University of Fine Arts and Music, becoming professor emeritus in 1970. Awards include AIJ Award, Person Prize, First Prize for Design of Institute of Architects in New York, Prize of the Japan Art Academy, Third Class Order of Cultural Merit from the Japanese Government, and Mainichi Art Prize.

Takamasa Yoshizaka (1917–1980)
pp. 105–107
Born in Tokyo. Graduated from the International School of Geneva in 1933 and Waseda University Department of Architecture in 1941. Studied under Wajiro Kon researching private housing and dwellings. Worked at Le Corbusier's workshop in Paris from 1950 to 1952. In 1954 founded Atelier Yoshizaka (reorganized as Atelier U in 1964). Professor at Waseda University from 1959. Head of the Waseda University Department of Science and Engineering from 1969. Chairman of the Architectural Institute of Japan in 1973. Left many literary works as an educator, alpinist, and a cultural critic. Also translated Le Corbusier, including *Towards an Architecture*.

**The Japanese House:
Architecture and Life after 1945**

First published in 2016 by Marsilio Editori in association with Barbican Art Gallery, London and MAXXI, National Museum of the 21st Century Arts, Rome

on the occasion of the exhibition *The Japanese House: Architecture and Life after 1945*

Edited by Pippo Ciorra and Florence Ostende

Designed by Kellenberger–White

Thematic introductions to sections by Pippo Ciorra, Kenjiro Hosaka, Luke Naessens, Florence Ostende, Yoshiharu Tsukamoto

House captions by
Luke Naessens
Pippo Ciorra and Kenjiro Hosaka (pp. 80, 183, 202, 211, 226, 240, 247, 266, 302)

Front cover
Kazuo Shinohara, Tanikawa Villa, 1974, interior

Translations by Nathan Elchert, Gen Machida, Ruth S McCreery, Pamela Miki, Valentina Moriconi, Christopher Stevens, Adelaide Cioni, Huw Evans

Copy-editing by Lemuel Caution; Alessandra Rossi and Andrea Moras, Oltrepagina

All Rights Reserved. No part of this publication may be reproduced or transmitted in any form or by any means, electronic or mechanical, including photocopy, recording or any other information storage and retrieval system, without prior permission in writing from the publishers.

British Library Cataloguing-in-Publication Data
A catalogue record for this book is available from the British Library

ISBN: 978-88-317-2576-7

Reproduction
Opero s.r.l., Verona

Print
Cortella Poligrafica s.r.l., Verona
for Marsilio Editori® s.p.a., in Venice

Marsilio Editori
Marittima Fabbricato 205,
30135 Venice, Italy
www.marsilioeditori.it

MAXXI
Via Guido Reni, 4/A
00196 Rome, Italy
www.fondazionemaxxi.it

Barbican Art Gallery
Barbican Centre
Silk Street
London EC2Y 8DS, United Kingdom
www.barbican.org.uk

Official copyright © 2016 by Barbican Centre, City of London. The Authors and Artists.
Images © see page 319

The exhibitions in Rome and London are co-organized by Japan Foundation, MAXXI and Barbican Art Gallery. They are co-produced by Japan Foundation, MAXXI, Barbican Art Gallery and National Museum of Modern Art, Tokyo. The project was initially conceived in Tokyo by Kenjiro Hosaka and Yoshiharu Tsukamoto.

Chief Architectural Advisor: Yoshiharu Tsukamoto (Atelier Bow-Wow)
Academic Advisor: Hiroyasu Fujioka (Dr. Eng., Professor Emeritus, Tokyo Institute of Technology)

MAXXI – National Museum of the 21st Century Arts

9 November 2016 – 26 February 2017

Curated by Pippo Ciorra (MAXXI, Rome) and Kenjiro Hosaka (The National Museum of Modern Art, Tokyo) in collaboration with Florence Ostende (Barbican Art Gallery, London)

President: Giovanna Melandri
Artistic Director: Hou Hanru
Executive Director: Pietro Barrera
DIPARTIMENTO MAXXI ARCHITETTURA
Director: Margherita Guccione
DIPARTIMENTO MAXXI ARTE
Director: Bartolomeo Pietromarchi
Exhibition Manager: Elena Motisi
Curatorial Assistance: Alessandra Spagnoli
Exhibition Design Manager: Silvia La Pergola
Exhibition Design: Atelier Bow-Wow, Yoshiharu Tsukamoto with Simona Ferrari
Publishing Office: Flavia De Sanctis Mangelli
Registrar: Monica Pignatti Morano
Graphic Design: Etaoin Shrdlu Studio

Barbican Centre

23 March – 25 June 2017

Curated by Florence Ostende (Barbican Art Gallery, London) in collaboration with Pippo Ciorra (MAXXI, Rome)

Managing Director: Sir Nicholas Kenyon
Director of Arts: Louise Jeffreys
Head of Visual Arts: Jane Alison
Exhibition Assistants: Luke Naessens, Sonoko Nakanishi
Exhibition Design: Lucy Styles
Production team: Claire Feeley, Ulrika Danielsson, Peter Sutton, Margaret Liley, Bruce Stracy
Exhibition Graphic Design: Kellenberger–White

The Japan Foundation

Masanobu Ito
Atsuko Sato
Keiko Tasaki
Ayako Nagata
Akiko Tokuyama

ACKNOWLEDGEMENTS

Architects' Offices
Aida-Doi-Architects
Atelier and I Kazunari Sakamoto Architectural Laboratory
Atelier Bow-Wow
Azuma Architect & Associates
Design System
dot architects
Erika Nakagawa Office
Fujii Architects Studio
Terunobu Fujimori
Go Hasegawa and Associates
Hideyuki Nakayama Architecture
Ikimono Architects
Itsuko Hasegawa Atelier
Jun Aoki & Associates
Jun Igarashi Architects
junya.ishigami + associates
K.Associates / Architects
Katsuhiro Miyamoto & Associates
Kazuhiko Namba + Kai-Workshop
Kazuyo Sejima + Ryue Nishizawa / SANAA
Kengo Kuma & Associates
Kisho Kurokawa Architect & Associates
Kiyonori Kikutake Architectural Office
Masuzawa Architect & Associates
Mayekawa Associates, Architects & Engineers
Office of Kumiko Inui
Keisuke Oka
onishimaki + hyakudayuki architects / o + h
Raymond Architectural Design Office
Riken Yamamoto & Fieldshop
Sakakura Associates
Shigeru Ban Architects
Sirai architectural institute
Sou Fujimoto Architects
Studio Gaya
Tadao Ando Architect & Associates
Taira Nishizawa Architects
Tato Architects / Yo Shimada
teco
Tezuka Architects
Toyo Ito & Associates, Architects
Kazumasa Yamashita
Yoshimura Architectural Office
Yuusuke Karasawa Architects

Other Lenders
Hideki Arai
Rie Azuma
Bêka & Lemoine
Chino City Art Museum
Department of Architecture, Tokyo Institute of Technology
EnviroLife Research Institute Co., Ltd.
FRAC Centre
Naoya Hatakeyama
Hisako Sugiura Lab., Showa Women's University
Hyogo Prefectural Art Museum
Konomi Ikebe
Taka Ishii Gallery
Japan Cultural Heritage Consultancy
Toshiko Kato
Mitsunori Kikutake
Yuki Kikutake
Kogakuin University Library
Kogonada
Tomoharu Makabe
MUJI HOUSE Co., Ltd.
Norihito Nakanishi
National Archives of Modern Architecture, Agency for Cultural Affairs, Government of Japan
Nihon University, Department of Architecture, College of Science and Technology
Mie Prefectural Art Museum
Eizo Okada
Research Institute for Architectural Archives, Kanazawa Institute of Technology
Ryohin Keikaku Co., Ltd
Sekisui Chemical Co., Ltd.
Mutsuko Smith
Tokyo Tech Museum and Archives
Michiko Uchida
Waseda Architecture Archives
Takako Yoshimura
Taisei Corporation
NHK International, Inc.

Film Directors
Daisuke Yamashiro
ARTIST'S GUILD
Tomomi Ishiyama
Hidenori Noda
Tsubame Architects
Michiko Tsuda
Haruka Furuya

We would also like to thank:
Noura Al-Maashouq, Architectural Institute of Japan, Art Translators Collective, Mathieu Capel, Cristiana Colli, Abdelkader Damani, Thomas Daniell, Inge Daniels, Eleonora Devreux, Koichi Endo, Mitsumasa Fujitsuka, Satoshi Furuya, Maria Cristina Gasperini (Istituto Giapponese di Cultura in Rome), Seiko Harumi, Itaru Hirano, Jiro Hirayama, Hiroyuki Hoshi, Taro Igarashi, Yu Iseki, Shuichi Izui, Michiko Kowatari, Makoto Kubota, Shunsuke Kurakata, Izumi Kuroishi, Barbara Lehmann (Cassina), Emmanuele Marcotullio, Mori Arts Museum, Koichi Masahashi, Yasuo Moriyama, Jin Motohashi, Chieko Mozuna, Takashi Muto, Atsuko Nishimaki, Eleanor Nairne, Eri Nakamura, Yuko Nakamura, Flavio Nughes, Shigeru Ohno, Shin'ichi Okuyama, Masaki Onishi, Mari Ota, Yoko Oyamada, Reiji Saito, Yohei Sasakura, Mitsuhiko Sato, Atsushi Seike, Naomi Shibata, Genta Shirai, Tomoki Shoda, "SUPERIOR" Editorial Department (Shogakukan), Ryuhei Suzuki, Shinnosuke Tadokoro, Kazuya Takagawa, Motoko Tanaka, Jilly Traganou, Warehouse Terrada, Università degli Studi di Camerino (Scuola di Ateneo di Architettura e Design), Izumi Yamashita, Kazuhiro Yasufuku, Yuki Yoshikawa, Yutaka Suzuki Photo Atelier

We would like to express our deepest sadness at the recent loss of photographer Osamu Murai (1928–2016).

Photo Credits

© Digital Image, The Museum of Modern Art, New York / Scala, Florence, 2016: p. 41 (top)
© AIDA DOI ARCHITECTS: pp. 178, 179
© Daici Ano: p. 200
© Hideki Arai / Big Comic Superior, SHOGAKUKAN Inc.: p. 305
Courtesy of Asahi Shimbun Company and Michiko Uchida: p. 76
© Atelier and I: pp. 22 (top), 151, 155 (bottom), 237
© Atelier Bow-Wow: pp. 26 (top), 223, 239, 240 (top), 286
An Autumn Afternoon directed by Yasujiro Ozu and produced by Shizuo Yamauchi: pp. 43 (top), 44 (bottom)
© Iwan Baan: pp. 181, 252, 253, 266, 267, 270–273
© Bêka & Lemoine: p. 51
The Crazy Family directed by Sogo Ishii and produced by Kazuhiko Hasegawa, Toyoji Yamane, and Shiro Sasaki: p. 49 (top)
Equinox Flower directed by Yasujiro Ozu and produced by Shizuo Yamauchi: p. 43 (bottom)
© Takashi Fujino: p. 49 (bottom left)
© Takashi Fujino / Ikimono Architects: pp. 226, 229
Harvard Art Museums / Arthur M. Sackler Museum, Bequest of the Hofer Collection of the Arts of Asia, 1985.352.52.A Photo: Imaging Department © President and Fellows of Harvard College: p. 53
© Itsuko Hasegawa: p. 190
HIROYUKI HIRAI © HIRAI PHOTO OFFICE: pp. 100, 238
© Chuji Hirayama: pp. 72–74, 75 (top), 78, 79 (bottom), 90, 257
© Chuji Hirayama, Courtesy of Masuzawa Architect & Associates: pp. 92, 93
© Takashi Homma: pp. 247, 248
© Yasuhiro Ishimoto: p. 28
© Osamu Ishiyama: pp. 215–221, 295–297
© JIA-KIT Architectural Archives (Japan Institute of Architects – Kanazawa Institute of Technology Architectural Archives): p. 79 (top)
© junya.ishigami+associates: pp. 184, 185
© Katsuhiro Miyamoto & Associates: pp. 298, 299 (top)
Photos by Akio Kawasumi © Kawasumi – Kobayashi Kenji Photograph Office: pp. 258, 259, 261 (top)
© Kazuyo Sejima and Associates: pp. 21 (bottom), 197–199
Photos by Keizo Kioku: pp. 49 (bottom right), 302, 303
Photo by Keizo Kioku, Collection of Atelier Bow-Wow: p. 240 (bottom)
Photo by Keizo Kioku, Collection of AZUMA ARCHITECT & ASSOCIATES: p. 116
Photo by Keizo Kioku, Collection of Terunobu Fujimori: p. 281
Photos by Keizo Kioku, © Takashi Fujino: pp. 227, 228
Photos by Keizo Kioku, Collection of Itsuko Hasegawa: pp. 191, 263 (bottom)
Photo by Keizo Kioku, Collection of Katsuhiro Miyamoto & Associates: p. 299 (bottom)
Photo by Keizo Kioku, Collection of KENGO KUMA & ASSOCIATES: p. 264
Photo by Keizo Kioku, Collection of Masuzawa Architect & Associates: p. 95
Photo by Keizo Kioku, Collection of Norihito Nakatani: p. 172
Photo by Keizo Kioku, Collection of Keisuke Oka: p. 301
Photo by Keizo Kioku, Collection of Kazunari Sakamoto: p. 145
Photo by Keizo Kioku, Collection of Housuke Shirai: p. 82
Photos by Keizo Kioku, Collection of Toyo Ito and Associates, Architects: pp. 157 (bottom), 194 (bottom)
Photo by Keizo Kioku, Collection of Michiko Uchida: p. 75 (bottom)
© Katsuhisa Kida / FOTOTECA: pp. 282, 283
© Eiji Kitada: p. 106
Photo by Eiji Kitada, Collection of WASEDA ARCHITECTURE ARCHIVES: p. 105
Photo by Armin Linke: p. 34
© Mitsutaka Kitamura: p. 202
Courtesy of Koichi Kitazawa: pp. 69, 71
Collection of Kogakuin University Library: p. 38
© Chie Konno: pp. 288, 289

© Susumu Koshimizu: p. 209
Late Autumn directed by Yasujiro Ozu and produced by Shizuo Yamauchi: p. 44 (top)
Photos by Françoise Lauginie: pp. 146, 148, 167, 180
© Akihisa Masuda: pp. 279, 280
Courtesy of Masuzawa Architect & Associates: pp. 18 (bottom), 94
MAXXI Museo nazionale delle arti del XXI secolo, Collezione MAXXI Architettura, Archivio Carlo Scarpa: pp. 31, 32
Courtesy of MAYEKAWA ASSOCIATES, ARCHITECTS & ENGINEERS: p. 87
© Ryuji Miyamoto, Courtesy of Kazumasa Yamashita, Architect and Associations: p. 176
© MUJI HOUSE, CO., LTD.: p. 101
© Osamu Murai: pp. 80, 81, 83, 112–115
© Osamu Murai, Courtesy of Kumi Murai: pp. 82, 83, 85, 114–117
© Osamu Murai, Courtesy of Koichi Kitazawa: p. 70 (bottom)
Photos by Osamu Murai, Courtesy of Shin'ichi Okuyama Lab.: pp. 121–123, 125
Photo Musacchio & Ianniello, Courtesy Fondazione MAXXI: p. 26 (bottom)
© The Museum of Fine Arts, Houston: p. 41 (bottom)
© Erika Nakagawa: p. 224
Photo by Kai Nakamura: p. 205
© Hideyuki Nakayama: p. 203
Courtesy of National Archives of Modern Architecture, Agency for Cultural Affairs, Government of Japan: pp. 88, 89, 107
© National Archives of Modern Architecture, Agency for Cultural Affairs, Government of Japan, Collection of Kikutake Architects: pp. 260, 261 (bottom)
© Office of Ryue Nishizawa: pp. 249–251, 274, 275
© Tomio Ohashi: pp. 91, 98, 99, 152, 153, 156, 157 (top), 158, 160, 192, 193, 195 (bottom), 210–212, 214, 262, 263 (top)
© onishimaki + hyakudayuki architects / o + h: p. 204
Photo by Takumi Ota: p. 287
© Manuel Oka: p. 117
© Manuel Oka, Courtesy of Atelier Bow-Wow: p. 241
Courtesy of RAYMOND ARCHITECTURAL DESIGN OFFICE, INC.: p. 71 (top)
Photo by Hiroyasu Sakaguchi: p. 222
© Tomohiro Sakashita, Courtesy of akihisa hirata architecture office: p. 22 (bottom)
© Tsuneo Sato, Courtesy of Yoshimura Architectural Office: pp. 108, 111
© SEKISUI CHEMICAL CO., LTD.: pp. 96, 97
© Shigeru Ban Architects: p. 300
Courtesy of Shin'ichi Okuyama Lab.: pp. 18 (top), 124
Photos by Shinkenchiku-sha: pp. 21 (top), 109, 130–137, 141, 147, 149, 150, 154, 155 (top), 162, 163, 168–171, 177, 182, 183, 189, 233–235, 245, 246, 265, 284, 285, 290, 291
Photos by Shokokusha Photographers: pp. 173–175.
© Sou Fujimoto Architects: p. 201
Tokyo, September 2 2010 – House in a Plum Grove by Kazuyo Sejima (from the *Tokyo no ie* series) © Jérémie Souteyrat: p. 196.
Photos by Ken'ichi Suzuki: pp. 268, 269
© Ryudai Takano, Courtesy of Yumiko Chiba Associates, Zeit-Foto Salon: p. 304
Photos by Koji Taki: pp. 46 (bottom), 128 (bottom), 129 (bottom), 194 (top), 195 (top), 236
Photo by Koji Taki, RIBA Collections: cover, p. 127
Photos by Koji Taki, Courtesy of Shin'ichi Okuyama Lab.: pp. 126, 128 (top), 129 (top)
© Koichi Torimura: p. 225
© Toyo Ito and Associates: p. 213
Courtesy of Toyo Ito and Associates, Architects: p. 161 (top)
Courtesy of Michiko Uchida: p. 77
Woman in the Dunes directed by Hiroshi Teshigahara and produced by Kiichi Ichikawa and Tadashi Ohno: p. 46 (top)
© Shuji Yamada: pp. 142–144
Courtesy of Takako Yoshimura: p. 110
Courtesy of Yoshio Taniguchi: p. 15 (top left)